NEW HAMPSHIRE
FISHING MAPS

by Charlton J. Swasey
and Donald A. Wilson

ISBN 0-89933-040-1
© 1986 DeLorme Mapping Company
Freeport, Maine 04032
All rights reserved.

The information in this book does not imply landowner permission;
private property or landowner restrictions must be respected.

cover painting by Ed Murdock

ISBN 0-89933-040-1

9 780899 330402

TABLE OF CONTENTS

INTRODUCTION

Fishermen and vacationers alike have long been attracted to New Hampshire's scenic waters. The state offers a wide variety of fishing conditions - lakes and ponds, rivers and streams, freshwater and saltwater - as well as an extensive variety of fish - salmon, several species of trout, bass, pickerel, pike, perch and more.

This volume describes and maps almost 100 lakes, ponds, and rivers in New Hampshire - from remote mountain streams to large resort lakes. While most of these waters are the better-known fishing sites in the state, you'll find a directory in the back of this book suggesting hundreds of additional spots and detailing the species available at each.

We believe you will find this book to be the most ambitious, up-to-date and comprehensive source of information about fishing in New Hampshire. There is nothing else like it.

We wish to express our sincere appreciation to those who helped us by providing information included in the descriptions and maps:

Ron Alie, Philip D. Bell, Gerard Bernier, David Beyerle, Bob Bryant, Carl T. Carlson, Ed Cournoyer, Ronald Evans, Bob Harris, George Hilton Jr., Brian Howe, Bill Ingham Jr., Melvin Jenkins, Warren Jenkins, Doug Menzies, Don Merrill, Clayton B. Phillips, Forrest Perkins, William R. Phinney, Leonard S. Riel, John Sampson, Richard Schanda (Joe Dixx), David Sidmore, Jim Souter, Glen Taylor, Oliver Wallace and Kenneth Warren.

The reader is reminded that the words "lake" and "pond" are often used interchangeably. The names presented here are the ones most commonly used.

Also note that these maps are not intended for navigational purposes. The water level in some lakes and ponds is drawn down in late summer and fall. Then, and in extreme drought, there may be significant departures from the depths listed here.

With this book in hand, we wish you good luck in fishing the waters of New Hampshire.

Charlton J. Swasey

Donald A. Wilson

NEW HAMPSHIRE'S RECORD FISH

SMALLMOUTH BASS: 23¼", 7 pounds, 14½ ounces.
Francis H. Lord, Goose Pond, Canaan, 1970.
LARGEMOUTH BASS: 10 pounds, 8 ounces
G. Bullpitt, Lake Potanipo, Brookline, 1967.
BLUEGILL: 10½", 1 pound, 4½ ounces.
Ed Massucco, Connecticut River, Charlestown, 1980.
BROWN BULLHEAD: 16 5/8", 2 pounds, 2 ounces.

Merrimack River, 1974.
YELLOW BULLHEAD: 16", 2 pounds, 8 ounces.
Gerald Menard, Pecknolds Pond, Chester, 1980.
CARP: 34", 27 pounds.
M. Katryez, Merrimack River, 1968.
CUSK: 34¾", 10 pounds, 8 ounces.
Karl Strong, Big Diamond Pond, Stewartstown, 1972.
AMERICAN EEL: 44½", 8 pounds.
Michael Honsharak, Crystal Lake, Eaton, 1975.
WHITE PERCH: 19", 3 pounds, 6 ounces.
Barry A. Laraway, Goose Pond, Canaan, 1975.
YELLOW PERCH: 15½", 2 pounds, 6 ounces.
R. Hebert, Head's Pond, Hookset, 1969.
CHAIN PICKEREL: 26", 8 pounds.
Carroll R. Akeley, Plummer Lake, Sanbornton, 1966.
NORTHERN PIKE: 43½", 20 pounds, 9 ounces.
Richard Ryder, Spofford Lake, Chesterfield, 1978.
CHINOOK SALMON: 34", 12 pounds.
Roger J. MacDowall, Lamprey River, Durham. 1976.
COHO SALMON: 32¼", 16.06 pounds.
Michael Walsh, Lamprey River, Newmarket, 1979.
LANDLOCKED SALMON: 34½", 18 pounds, 8 ounces.
Mrs. Letty M. Clark, Pleasant Lake, New London, 1942.
BROOK TROUT: 25½", 9 pounds.
A. Val Woodruff, Pleasant Lake, New London, 1911.
BROWN TROUT: 32½", 16 pounds, 6 ounces.
Ken Reed Jr., Connecticut River, Pittsburg, 1975.
LAKE TROUT: 39½", 28 pounds, 8 ounces.
Albert C. Staples, Newfound Lake, Bristol, 1958.
RAINBOW TROUT: 29½", 14 pounds, 3/10 ounce.
Loxley Ness. Connecticut River, Monroe, 1978.
SPLAKE TROUT: 26 7/8", 9 pounds.
Thomas Barbour, Crystal Lake, Eaton, 1980.
SUNAPEE TROUT: 33", 11 pounds, 8 ounces.
Ernest Theoharris, Sunapee Lake, Sunapee, 1954.
WALLEYE: 30½", 11 pounds, 8 ounces.
James Bennett Sr., Connecticut River, Lebanon, 1979.
LAKE WHITEFISH: 21¾", 5 pounds, 1 ounce.
Paul E. Littlefield, Lake Winnipesaukee, Alton, 1974.

TROPHY FISH PROGRAM

The New Hampshire Fish and Game Department initiated the Trophy Fish Program to recognize anglers who take exceptionally large fish in New Hampshire waters.

A framed certificate is awarded annually to the angler who enters the *heaviest* fish in each of the eligible categories. Other anglers who submit eligible applications receive embroidered arm patches. Before an entry is accepted, it must be verified by a notary public, justice of the peace, town clerk, postmaster, member of the state or local law enforcement agency or a N.H. Fish and Game Department official.

All entries must be submitted on the official form provided by the N.H. Fish and Game Department (available from any department official). Entrants must have a valid N.H. fishing license, and fish must have been taken on sporting tackle in keeping with state regulations.

You must submit your entry within 30 days of the catch. The program runs from Jan. 1 to Dec. 31; the deadline for entries is Jan. 15.

Species eligible and minimum qualifying weights are:

Smallmouth Bass	4 lbs.	Brook Trout	2 lbs.
Largemouth Bass	5 lbs.	Brown Trout	5 lbs.
Chain Pickerel	4 lbs.	Lake Trout	10 lbs.
Coho Salmon	10 lbs.	Rainbow Trout	4 lbs.
Landlocked Salmon	7 lbs.	Walleye	6 lbs.

FISH OF NEW HAMPSHIRE

ALEWIFE
(Alosa pseudoharengus)
Also known as river herring or sawbelly, little is known about the habits of this fish in salt water. During its spawning migration in the spring it ascends most of the suitable streams. It ascends the Merrimack River in abundance as far as Amoskeag Falls, Manchester. Landlocked populations occur in Cobbetts Pond and Rock Pond, both in Windham. Sea-run alewives occasionally attain a length of 15 inches, but average 10 to 12 inches and about ½ pound. Landlocked alewives become dwarfed, usually reaching only 4 to 6 inches. This fish is an important commercial species along the Atlantic Coast. It is marketed in a variety of ways, including smoked, salted, and pickled, for human consumption and as pet food, fish meal and bait. The alewife is an important food source for many ocean fish including striped bass and salmon.

AMERICAN EEL
(Anguilla rostrata)
Found nearly everywhere in the state, this fish species lives in fresh water but spawns in salt water, in the Sargasso Sea of the Atlantic Ocean. After hatching, young eels migrate back to fresh water, even 400 miles of Connecticut River to the Connecticut Lakes, the females returning to fresh waters while the males remain in coastal brackish and salt water. Eels are very tolerant of adverse water conditions and can live out of water for an extended period of time. During the winter, they are generally inactive, buried in the mud. In fresh water, eels live in lakes and large slow-moving streams, preferring deep water and mud bottom. They feed on small fish, insects, crustaceans and shrimp and almost any other animal matter. Feeding takes place mainly at night, when this fish sometimes even leaves the water to search for frogs and small mammals in wet grassy meadows and fields. Eels have a delicious flavor and may be taken easily when descending rivers to spawn, in spring, in tidewater using worms or during the open water season by bottom fishing at night with almost any kind of bait. Full-grown females may reach a length of 6 feet, but usually range from 2 to 3½ feet. The New Hampshire record is an 8-pound fish taken in Crystal Lake, Eaton in 1975.

AMERICAN SHAD
(Alosa sapidissima)
This species formerly abounded in both the Merrimack and Connecticut Rivers, but now exists only in the latter as far as Turner's Falls, Massachusetts. Efforts are being made to restore this fish to its former spawning grounds in both watersheds.

LARGEMOUTH BASS (LB)
(Micropterus salmoides)
The largemouth bass, also called black bass, is a highly valued game fish. It thrives best in warm, shallow, weedy, mud-bottomed lakes, ponds and sluggish streams. It is a solitary fish and spends most of its time lurking among aquatic vegetation or under overhanging banks and structures such as logs, ledges and wharves, waiting for its prey to swim by. Largemouth bass seldom moves into open water, but seeks deeper water during winter where it seeks shelter near the bottom. It remains more active than the smallmouth and is occasionally taken through the ice. While a good eating fish, it sometimes has a "weedy" flavor. The largemouth will eat almost anything it can catch including insects, fish, crayfish, frogs, snails and mice. Therefore it may best be taken with "poppers" and plastic worms, although streamer flies and trolled lures will also catch fish. Fishing open spaces among lily pads, around stumps and sunken logs or along overhangs is the most effective. Most feeding occurs in early morning and evening. A 6-pound fish would be considered large in New Hampshire although 7 to 8-pound fish are occasionally taken. A 10½-pounder taken in Potanipo Pond, Brookline, in 1967, is the New Hampshire record.

ROCK BASS
(Ambloplites rupestris)
The rock bass contributes little to sport fishing in New Hampshire. The flavor of its flesh is considered inferior and it never grows very large so it is not as popular as other panfish. Rock bass is, however, found in schools and is relatively easy to catch so it is sometimes popular with children. This fish is abundant in the Connecticut River as far north as the southern border of Coos County. As far as is known, it only occurs in a few waters; a thriving population exists in Granite Lake, Stoddard. Rock bass is found along the rocky shores and in rocky flowing water, usually where there is a heavy growth of aquatic vegetation.

Rock bass eats primarily crayfish, small fish and insects and may be caught on nearly any kind of bait, living or dead. Small flies and plugs on ultra-light tackle are popular with fishermen. A 12-inch rock bass is considered large as is anything over a pound in weight. The usual size is 6 to 8 inches and ½ pound.

SMALLMOUTH BASS (SB)
(Micropterus dolomieui)
The smallmouth bass is one of the most valuable game fish anywhere. Pound for pound, it is one of the gamest there is, giving an untiring fight right to the end. It can be readily separated from the largemouth by examining the upper lip — the lip of the largemouth extends beyond the middle of the eye, while that of the smallmouth does not. Unlike the largemouth, this fish prefers cool, clear water of lakes and streams with a gravelly or rocky bottom. It, too, is solitary and will be found around ledges and reefs where the water is from 3 to 20 feet deep. In streams it usually lies in the protective backwaters of large boulders or stumps or at the heads of pools with an upstream riffle. It retreats to deeper water in winter and remains semi-dormant under rocks and logs until spring. Smallmouth bass are fine eating and feed mainly on crayfish, but also on insects and fish. Feeding takes place mostly in early morning and evening. It may be taken by fly casting, trolling or casting with plug or spinner. Another common and successful method is still-fishing with worms, minnows or crayfish. Smallmouth generally run about 2 to 3 pounds but occasionally may reach 4 to 6 pounds. The largest recorded from New Hampshire was caught in Goose Pond, Canaan, in 1970. It weighed 7 pounds 14½ ounces, and was 23¼ inches in length.

BLACK CRAPPIE
(Pomoxis nigromaculatus)
Also known as calico bass, the crappie has been introduced into several New Hampshire waters. As far as is known, it is limited to Balch Pond, Wakefield; Horseshoe Pond, Merrimack; Scobie Pond, Londonderry; Pennichuck Reservoir, Hollis; and the Merrimack River below Nashua. Its habits are very similar to those of the largemouth bass — it lives in quiet, weedy waters of lakes, ponds and streams and feeds largely on small crustaceans, insects and small fish. Crappie may be taken on nearly any fly pattern, small minnows, small bass bugs or small lures and spoons. The flesh is firm and sweet and the fish is classed as "delicious." The usual size is 5 to 12 inches, weighing less than a pound. A 15-inch two-pound crappie would be considered large. No record has been established for New Hampshire.

BULLHEAD or HORNED POUT (HP)
(Ictalurus nebulosus, Ictalurus natalis and *Noturus insignis)*
New Hampshire has three species of horned pout; the brown bullhead, yellow bullhead and margined madtom. Of the three, only the brown bullhead is native to the state. It is the most widespread and occurs throughout the state, although it may not be native to the Androscoggin watershed. The yellow bullhead is found in the Merrimack River and several other waters. The madtom has been taken from only a few places in the Merrimack watershed: the Cockermouth, Pemigewasset, Suncook and Merrimack Rivers.

Horned pout are bottom feeders, and usually feed at night. They eat nearly anything, alive or dead, and may easily be taken at night or on cloudy days, by fishing at or near the bottom with worms, minnows, corn kernels, crayfish, hellgrammites or dough balls. The brown bullhead is a favorite among fishermen. Its flesh is firm and sweet tasting. Many fishermen will claim it is the best eating fish there is. Brown bullhead ranges from 6 to 14 inches in length and usually weighs less than a pound. It is, however, capable of reaching 18 inches and 4 pounds. The yellow bullhead usually runs 6 to 10 inches and less than a pound but may attain 18 inches and 3 pounds. The madtom rarely exceeds 6 inches in length and usually ranges 4 to 5 inches. Its biggest value is as bait, or as food fish for other game fishes, particularly brook trout. The New Hampshire record for brown bullhead is 2 pounds, 2 ounces, caught in the Merrimack River in 1974; for yellow bullhead, 2 pounds, 8 ounces from Pecknolds Pond, Chester, in 1980.

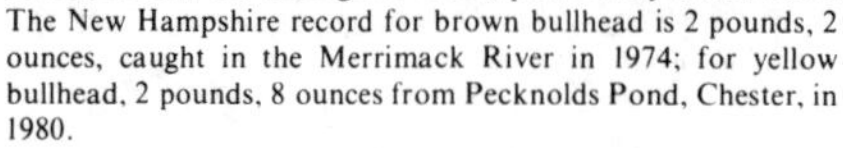

BURBOT or CUSK (C)
(Lota lota)
The burbot is the only freshwater member of the codfish family. Like the bullhead, it is a bottom feeder and will eat nearly anything. It is a cold water fish and is chiefly found in larger, cool, deep lakes. It is not very active during the summer months and therefore is usually taken through the ice. It is chiefly a nighttime feeder, but may also be taken on dark, cloudy days. Since its flesh is firm and very tasty, this fish is often sought by local fishermen. It is easily taken by bottom fishing, at night, with cut bait or live minnows. The burbot can attain a length of 4 feet and a weight of 75 pounds. In New Hampshire a 5-pound fish is large and the largest recorded is 10½ pounds and 34½ inches, taken in Big Diamond Pond in 1972. Reports occur, however, of fish that were substantially larger.

CARP
(Cyprinus carpio)
This native of Asia was introduced into North America about the 1830's and into New Hampshire in 1880, and flourishes in the Connecticut River, lower Merrimack River and a few lakes and ponds, including Mascoma Lake. It thrives best in warm, quiet or slow-moving water where there is an abundance of aquatic vegetation. It is extremely hardy and is able to tolerate low oxygen conditions and high levels of pollution. Carp feed on most everything, including algae, plant roots, insects, snails, worms and fish eggs. They compete heavily with game fishes and waterfowl since they uproot plants, destroying great quantities of vegetation. These fish may be taken with hook and line and are exciting to catch as they put up a strong fight. In the Connecticut River and Mascoma Lake, it is lawful to take them with bow and arrow, which is a highly prized activity by archers. When properly prepared, carp is a good table fish. The carp is one of the largest members of the minnow family. Three to five pounds is a common weight and a 10 to 15-pound fish is not uncommon. The New Hampshire record is 27 pounds, taken in the Merrimack River in 1968.

LAMPREYS
(Petromyzon marinus, Lampetra lamottei)
Referred to as lamprey eels, these fish are not eels at all, but do have a similar appearance. Spawning runs take place in the spring when the sea lamprey ascends all suitable coastal streams in large numbers, while the American brook lamprey ascends only a few streams in the coastal watershed, including the Oyster River and its tributaries. The sea lamprey is the larger of the two, averaging 2 to 2½ feet in length, but sometimes attaining 3 feet. The brook lamprey rarely exceeds 6 inches. Sea lamprey have been known to be detrimental to certain fish species by attaching themselves to a host and sucking its blood to the extent where the host often dies. The fish was at one time considered a great delicacy and was taken in great numbers for food.

MINNOWS
There are 15 species of minnows occurring in New Hampshire. The popular aquarium fish, the goldfish, thrives in Cobbetts Pond, Windham; Horseshoe Pond, Merrimack; and the lower Merrimack River. Through unauthorized stocking, it probably occurs in other waters as well. This species has the capability of growing to 3 pounds, but usually does not exceed 1 pound in New Hampshire. Other species of minnows are: lake chub, golden shiner, common shiner, bridle shiner, blacknose shiner, spottail shiner, northern redbelly dace, finescale dace, blacknose dace, longnose dace, fallfish, creek chub, silvery minnow and fathead minnow. Most average 2 to 6 inches in length and some are excellent forage fish, especially for trout. The fallfish is the largest native minnow, reaching 14 to 16 inches and weighing as much as 2 to 3 pounds. Many of the species of minnow are useful as bait fish and are regularly caught and sold as such.

MUMMICHOG
(Fundulus heteroclitus)
Usually called tommy cod, this fish occurs in salt and brackish waters, frequently moving into the freshwater lower reaches of coastal streams. It may establish permanent freshwater populations such as those in several ponds in Windham, where it has been introduced. The usual adult size is 2 to 4 inches, though it sometimes attains a length of 6 inches. This species is probably the second most important bait fish in New Hampshire, surpassed only by the common shiner. It is extremely hardy on the hook and in the bait pail.

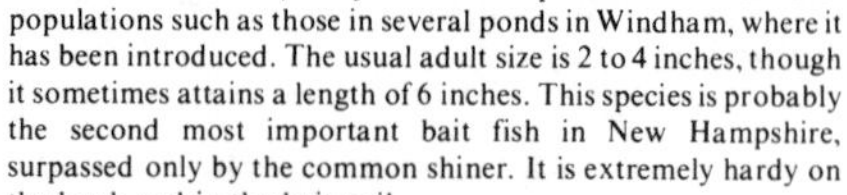

CHAIN PICKEREL (PK)
(Esox niger)
Pickerel occur throughout New Hampshire wherever suitable habitat exists. They prefer quiet, shallow water with mud bottom, an abundance of aquatic vegetation and food fishes. They will, however, be found in the deeper waters of lakes where there is little or no vegetation and the bottom is rocky. Pickerel feed on insects and crustaceans but prefer larger food like shiners, bullheads, perch and sunfish whenever available. It will also eat its own kind and add frogs, ducklings, snakes and young muskrats to its diet. They may be taken with minnows or frogs, or by trolling or spincasting with plugs or spoons. Considerable numbers are easily taken while ice-fishing either with handline or by using tip-ups with live bait. Food value of pickerel is considered fair as it contains many tiny bones. When fish are not taken in cold, clear water they may taste somewhat "weedy." They will put up a good fight. The largest recorded pickerel from New Hampshire was from Plummer Pond, Sanbornton in 1966, weighing 8 pounds and measuring 26 inches.

REDFIN PICKEREL (PK)
(Esox americanus americanus)
Also known as the bulldog pickerel, this smaller species is found in the southernmost part of the Merrimack drainage and the coastal watershed. Its habits are similar to the chain pickerel and its diet consists almost entirely of small fishes. It is the smallest member of the pike family, attaining a maximum length of 12 inches. It is usually mistaken for a small chain pickerel, but can be separated from the latter by its barred coloration rather than the chain-like pattern and also by its red or orange-spotted fins.

NORTHERN PIKE (P)
(Esox lucius)
This species may be separated from other members of the pike family in that it is greenish-gray with numerous yellowish-white bean-shaped spots on the sides and has dorsal, caudal and anal fins blotched with brownish or black. It is an introduced species in New Hampshire and is found in the Connecticut River and Spofford Lake, Chesterfield. They prefer cooler waters than pickerel; otherwise their habitat is similar. Pike feed mostly on fish, but also eat insects, leeches, frogs, ducklings and small muskrats. The northern pike is highly sought by fishermen for its game qualities. It is a tremendous fighter and may be taken on almost any kind of lure, as well as flies and large bass bugs. The pike is not highly valued as a food fish, is rather bony and, because of a heavy mucous secretion on the skin, should be skinned before cooking, otherwise a disagreeable flavor may result. The pike is one of the fastest-growing freshwater fishes. The New Hampshire record is 20 pounds 9 ounces and 43½ inches in length, taken in Spofford Lake in 1978.

ATLANTIC SALMON
(Salmo salar)
Atlantic salmon spend part of their lives at sea, ascending freshwater rivers in the fall to spawn. Once very abundant in several New Hampshire rivers, this sea-run salmon is now the subject of tremendous restoration projects in the Northeast. Successful attempts are being made in the Connecticut and Merrimack rivers where it previously occurred in great numbers. Atlantic salmon, through recent efforts, are now able to ascend the Connecticut River as far as Bellows Falls. Attempts are also being made in tributaries to Great Bay with a fish which is actually a cross between the Atlantic and landlocked varieties. A few of these are now beginning to return to fresh water.

CHINOOK SALMON
(Oncorhynchus tshawytscha)
This species has been introduced into Great Bay tributaries for several years and, if successful, should result in a run of large salmon, possibly in excess of 25 pounds. A few of these fish show up now and then.

COHO SALMON
(Oncorhynchus kisutch)
As in a number of other states, introduction of this species of salmon has been quite successful. Each year this fish returns to fresh water in significant numbers, ascending several of the Great Bay freshwater tributaries. The majority of the fish ascend the Exeter and Lamprey rivers, at the latter to be collected at the fishway in Newmarket. Some are retained as breeding stock for the next year's stocking, the remainder placed above the dam into the fresh water of the Lamprey River where they are able to ascend another 3½ miles of river. The salmon do not feed after entering fresh water and therefore are difficult to catch. They are, however, taken on a variety of artificial lures and plugs, as well as flies. Coho salmon turn red upon entering fresh water and, due to not eating as well as from physiological changes, they begin to deteriorate and lose flavor. They are edible for some time however, and are tasty if taken early after leaving salt water.

See section on Great Bay for further information.

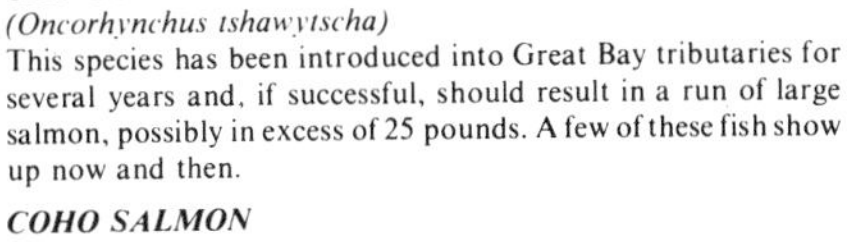

LANDLOCKED SALMON (S)
(Salmo salar sebago)
This salmon is the only one which does not spend part of its life in the sea and is considered to be one of the most prized freshwater game fishes. It was first introduced into New Hampshire when fish were planted in Newfound Lake in 1866. The landlocked salmon is restricted to the larger, deep, cold lakes and are found in a number of lakes in the northern part of the state. They are also found in the cool, swift-flowing rivers and streams running into these lakes. Salmon feed primarily on smelt, but also eat other fish as well as insects. During the spring months, salmon may be taken at the surface with streamer flies, lures and natural baits but as the water becomes warmer, fishing must be done at progressively greater depths. Trolling with artificial spoons and natural baits proves successful in deep water. Salmon is one of the most valued game and food fish in the world. It is a terrific fighter, usually leaping clear of the water several times, and its table quality rates among the highest. The average weight is from 2 to 3 pounds, with fish from 10 to 12 pounds occasionally caught. The New Hampshire record is 18 pounds 8 ounces, measuring 34½ inches long from Pleasant Lake, New London in 1942.

RAINBOW SMELT (SM)
(Osmerus mordax)
This fish species is both landlocked and sea-run. It provides an excellent food source for many species of fish. Smelt inhabit deep, cold lakes and seek cool depths during the summer. Their diet consists mainly of shrimp and other small crustaceans, small fishes and occasionally insects. They are cannibalistic and larger smelt may subsist almost entirely on smaller smelt. They may be taken through the ice using small tackle and cut bait. During the spawning runs in the spring, smelt may be dipped in quantity with nets in streams and along lake shores. Most of these runs occur at night. Smelt are highly valued for eating. The average size is about 8 inches, but fish occasionally attain 12 to 13 inches in length. In a few lakes, they have been known to grow larger.

Smelt ascend several of the fresh water streams and rivers during the winter and are readily taken there, as well as in Great Bay, by fishing through the ice. The Exeter and Lamprey rivers are popular sites for groups of "bob houses" and fishermen take sizeable fish in good numbers.

SPLAKE (SP)
(Salvelinus fontinalis × Salvelinus namaycush)
The splake is the result of crossing brook trout with lake trout, the goal being to breed a fish which has the desirable characteristics of both species. Many such hybrids are sterile but splake is one of the exceptions. In appearance, it maintains the square tail of the brook trout but the red speckles are less pronounced and the markings on the back more closely resemble the lake trout. The fish has similar requirements to its parents and food habits are also similar. It will strike viciously at spinners, plugs or live bait and is a more sporting fish than either parent, often making spectacular leaps. The flesh is deep orange-red and has an excellent taste. Splake grow fast and are capable of reaching at least 7 or 8 pounds in many waters. This fish is known to occur in Crystal Lake, Eaton, and Long Pond, Lempster. The New Hampshire record is a 9-pound, 26⅞-inch fish taken in Crystal Lake in 1980.

SUCKERS
(Catostomus commersoni, Catostomus catostomus, Erimyzon oblongus)
There are three species of sucker found in New Hampshire, the white sucker, the longnose sucker and the creek chubsucker. The white sucker is the state's most common fish species, and it may be found in nearly every lake and stream. It is adaptable to practically every habitat and is found therefore in small streams, rivers, lakes and ponds; over muddy or rocky bottoms; in swift, sluggish or quiet waters; in both warm and rather cold waters; and where there is an abundance of aquatic weeds or none at all. It spends most of its time near bottom. Suckers are of great value as a food source for other fishes and very valuable as a bait fish. Larger fish are used as cut bait, especially for ice fishing. Fish caught in the spring have firm flesh and are sweet tasting, but during the summer months the flesh is soft and of poor flavor. Suckers are easily caught by fishing near the bottom with worms, or dead minnows. Fish will average between 10 and 13 inches and weigh from ½ to 3 pounds. In larger lakes, suckers 2 feet long and weighing 4 to 5 pounds are not uncommon.

The longnose sucker is more of a coldwater species, living in cold, rapid-flowing, gravel-bottomed trout streams and colder lakes. In lakes, it generally lives at greater depths than the white sucker. There are two forms in New Hampshire. The dwarf form is found in the Connecticut and Merrimack drainages and is usually about 10 inches in length except in lakes where it may grow to 15 inches. The other form, the eastern longnose, inhabits the Androscoggin drainage and will reach a length of 18 inches and a weight of about 2 pounds.

The creek chubsucker is restricted mainly to the southern half of the state, occurring in the lower Connecticut River drainage, Saco and Merrimack River drainages, and coastal drainage. It is a bottom feeder and serves as a forage fish for large and smallmouth bass and pickerel. In lakes it may grow to a length of 14 inches and weight of about 2 pounds, but in streams it is smaller.

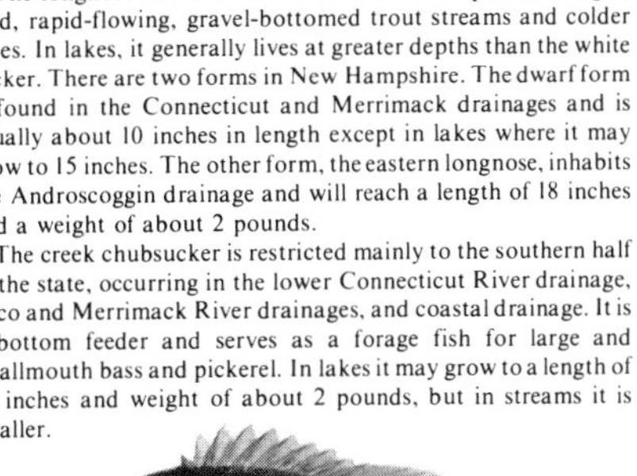

SUNFISH
(Lepomis gibbosus, Lepomis auritus, Lepomis macrochirus, Enneacanthus obesus)
There are four species of sunfish in New Hampshire: the pumpkinseed, the redbreast sunfish, the bluegill and the banded sunfish. The pumpkinseed is one of the most numerous fish in the state and is found in most of the streams, ponds and lakes. It prefers quiet or slow-moving water and is particularly abundant where there is good growth of aquatic vegetation. The redbreast sunfish inhabits lakes and ponds, but prefers clear, moderately-flowing streams and does not require heavily vegetated waters. Both species feed on insects, snails, small crustaceans and small fishes. The bluegill is not native to New Hampshire and is only known from Sip Pond, Fitzwilliam; Deer Meadow Pond, Chichester; Baboosic Lake, Amherst; Horseshoe Pond, Merrimack; and the Merrimack River downstream from Nashua. In addition to insects, crustaceans and small fishes, it also consumes fish eggs and aquatic vegetation. The banded sunfish is the smallest of the sunfishes and feeds primarily on small crustaceans. It is found in the southern portions of both the Connecticut and Merrimack drainages and in the coastal watershed. It inhabits lowland weedy lakes and quiet weedy backwaters of lowland brown water streams.

The larger sunfishes are considered to be tasty panfishes and are a favorite among children. They may be easily taken with worms and other baits and will also rise readily to fly and provide good sport on light tackle. The pumpkinseed averages between 5 and 7 inches and seldom exceeds 8 or 9 inches or ½ pound; redbreast sunfish may run 10 inches and about a pound; the bluegill averages 5 to 9 inches and may attain 12 inches and a weight of slightly over a pound; and the banded sunfish rarely exceeds 3 to 3½ inches. The New Hampshire record for the bluegill is 10½ inches and 1 pound 4½ ounces, taken in the Connecticut River, Charlestown in 1980.

BROOK TROUT (BK)
(Salvelinus fontinalis)
The brook trout inhabits virtually every coldwater, unpolluted stream in New Hampshire. Many ponds now contain suitable numbers of brook trout as a result of reclamation and regular stocking. This fish survives in many kinds of habitat, swift mountain streams or sluggish brown-water meadow brooks; over mud, gravel or bedrock bottoms; in heavy weed growths or in open waters; in tiny brooks, rivers or large lakes; and in shallow to rather deep water. Brook trout feed heavily on insects, adult forms in summer and larvae during the winter months. It also feeds on other fish, but does not heavily rely on them. It is more of a daytime feeder than either the brown or rainbow trout. This species is, without question, New Hampshire's favorite game fish. Its beauty, gaminess, easy catchability and fine taste appeal to all anglers. It may be taken with flies, small spinners and bait. This trout averages 5 to 8 inches but often attains 12 inches. The state record is a 9-pound, 25½-inch fish taken in Pleasant Lake, New London in 1911.

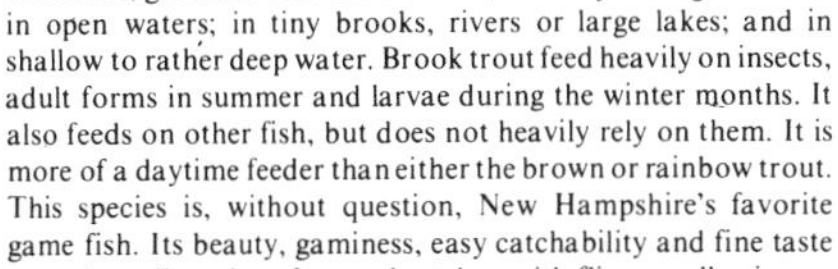

BROWN TROUT (BN)
(Salmo trutta)
This species of trout was introduced into New Hampshire in 1885 and is now widely distributed. It has greater adaptability to warm water than the brook trout and therefore can inhabit water that the latter cannot do well in. It prefers larger waters than the brook trout, such as streams, rivers and lakes, where there are submerged obstructions and overhanging banks. The diet of this fish consists mainly of insects when young, but older fish rely more heavily on fish. Feeding takes place mainly during twilight and nighttime hours. Brown trout are difficult to catch, and since a large part of their diet is insects, they are a prime target of fly fishermen. This fish may also be taken, however, on live bait and lures, both in open water and through the ice. Brown trout are tasty, especially when caught from swift, hard-bottom streams, or from spring-fed lakes. The average size in New Hampshire streams is from 7 to 14 inches and usually less than a pound. Two to four-pound fish are not uncommon and 6 to 8-pound fish are occasionally hooked. The state record is a 16-pound, 6-ounce fish measuring 32½ inches taken in the Connecticut River at Pittsburg in 1975.

Refer to sea-run section for further information.

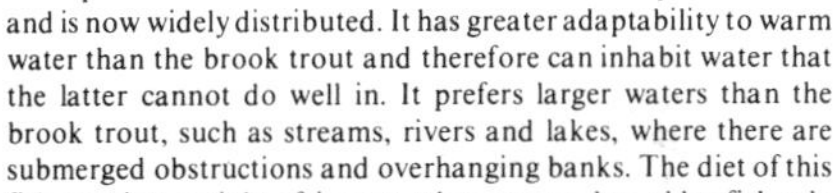

LAKE TROUT (LT)
(Salvelinus namaycush)
Also known as togue, lake trout originally occurred in seven New Hampshire lakes: First and Second Connecticut, Pittsburg; Crystal Lake, Enfield; Newfound, Squam, Winnipesaukee and Winnisquam. As a result of stocking it now occurs in many others. The lake trout is confined to lakes that are deep and have a large reservoir of cold, well-oxygenated water in their depths during the warm summer months. The food of adult lake trout consists mostly of fish. They frequently eat smelt but suckers, perch, whitefish and minnows are also important items in their diet. The lake trout is a prized game fish chiefly because of its size and power. It does not leap when hooked, but employs a depth-seeking, bulldog fighting tactic and makes strong runs. It may be

cont. pg. 112

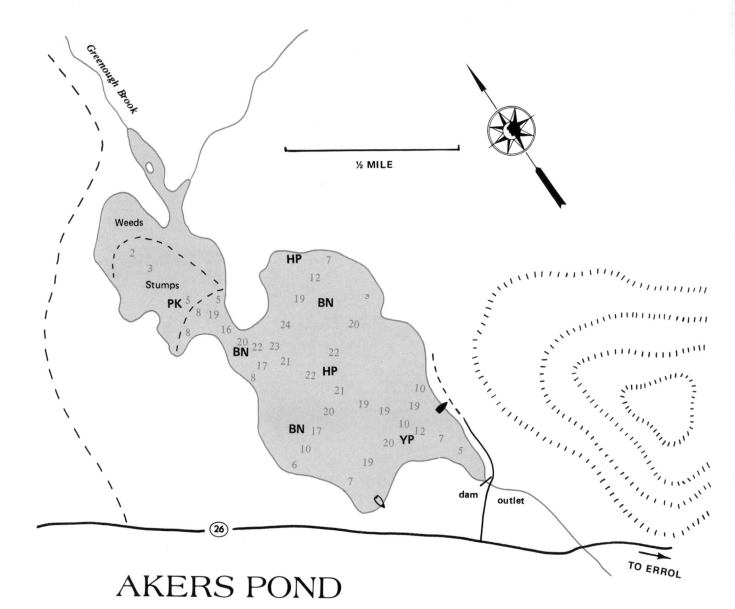

AKERS POND

ERROL
COOS COUNTY
NEW HAMPSHIRE ATLAS AND GAZETTEER MAP 57

Area: 309 acres. *Maximum depth:* 26 feet.
Fish: Brown trout, pickerel, yellow perch, hornpout.

Akers Pond offers the fine combination of excellent warm water fishing for pickerel and cold water fishing for brown trout, along with a healthy population of yellow perch and hornpout. The pond has been raised by damming and the shallow, northern end is full of weeds and stumps. Ice-out is mid-April/early May. The shoreline of the pond is mostly wooded and undeveloped. There are two launching sites - one is state-owned and free of charge, the other is privately-owned and includes gasoline and concessions.

LEGEND OF MAP SYMBOLS

⛺ **CAMPGROUND**   🛶 **LAUNCH SITE**

🪑 **PICNIC SITE**   ◗ **BOAT RAMP**

MAP 1

ARLINGTON MILLS RESERVOIR

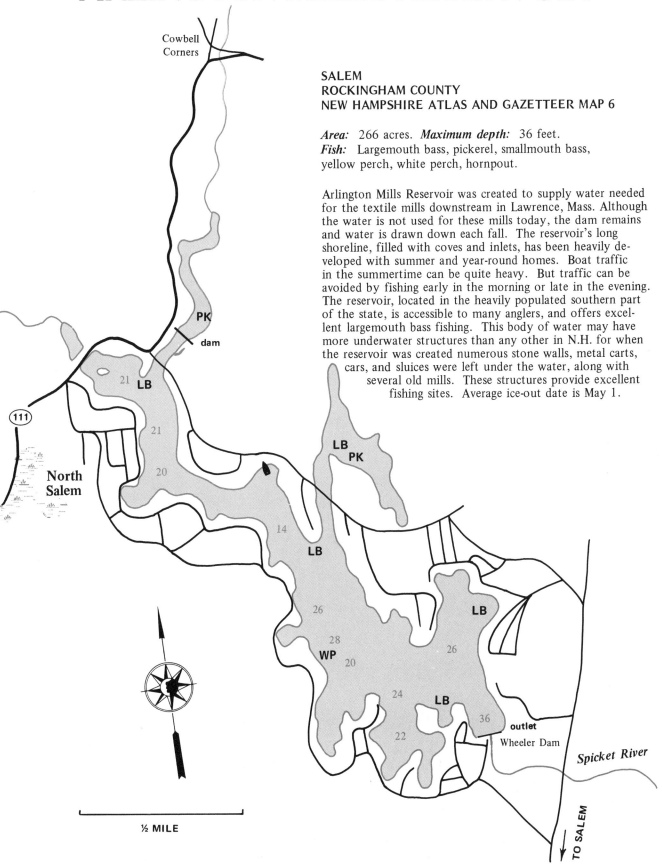

Cowbell Corners

**SALEM
ROCKINGHAM COUNTY
NEW HAMPSHIRE ATLAS AND GAZETTEER MAP 6**

Area: 266 acres. *Maximum depth:* 36 feet.
Fish: Largemouth bass, pickerel, smallmouth bass, yellow perch, white perch, hornpout.

Arlington Mills Reservoir was created to supply water needed for the textile mills downstream in Lawrence, Mass. Although the water is not used for these mills today, the dam remains and water is drawn down each fall. The reservoir's long shoreline, filled with coves and inlets, has been heavily developed with summer and year-round homes. Boat traffic in the summertime can be quite heavy. But traffic can be avoided by fishing early in the morning or late in the evening. The reservoir, located in the heavily populated southern part of the state, is accessible to many anglers, and offers excellent largemouth bass fishing. This body of water may have more underwater structures than any other in N.H. for when the reservoir was created numerous stone walls, metal carts, cars, and sluices were left under the water, along with several old mills. These structures provide excellent fishing sites. Average ice-out date is May 1.

PK
dam

21 LB

(111)

North Salem

21

20

LB
PK

14

LB

LB

26

28
WP 20

26

24

LB

22

36

outlet
Wheeler Dam

Spicket River

TO SALEM

½ MILE

MAP 2

ASHUELOT POND

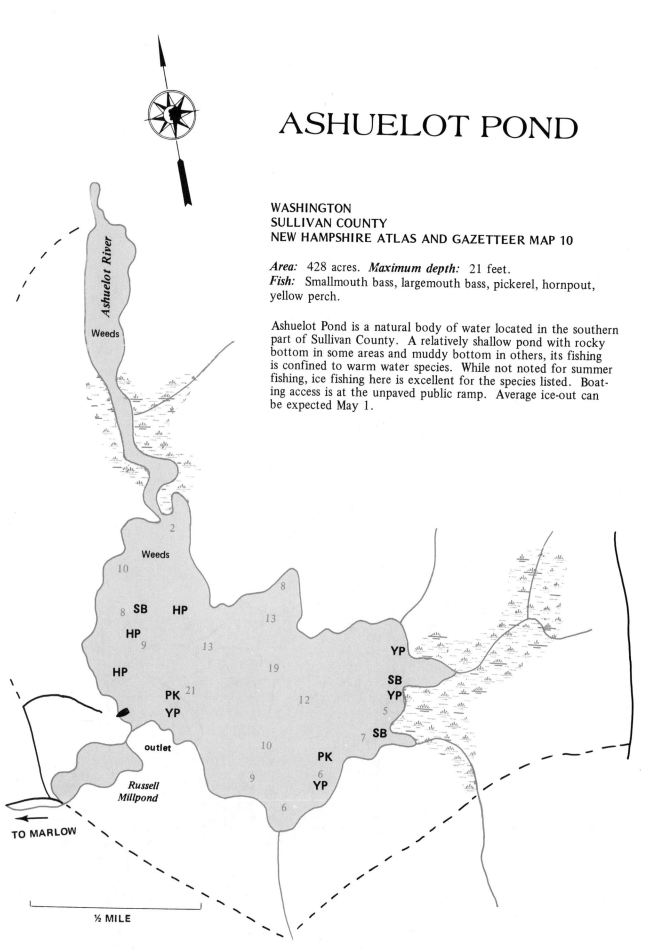

WASHINGTON
SULLIVAN COUNTY
NEW HAMPSHIRE ATLAS AND GAZETTEER MAP 10

Area: 428 acres. *Maximum depth:* 21 feet.
Fish: Smallmouth bass, largemouth bass, pickerel, hornpout, yellow perch.

Ashuelot Pond is a natural body of water located in the southern part of Sullivan County. A relatively shallow pond with rocky bottom in some areas and muddy bottom in others, its fishing is confined to warm water species. While not noted for summer fishing, ice fishing here is excellent for the species listed. Boating access is at the unpaved public ramp. Average ice-out can be expected May 1.

Ashuelot River

Weeds

2

Weeds

10

8 SB HP

HP

9

13

8

13

19

YP

SB
YP

HP

PK 21

YP

12

5

outlet

10

7 SB

PK

Russell
Millpond

9

6
YP

6

TO MARLOW

½ MILE

MAP 3

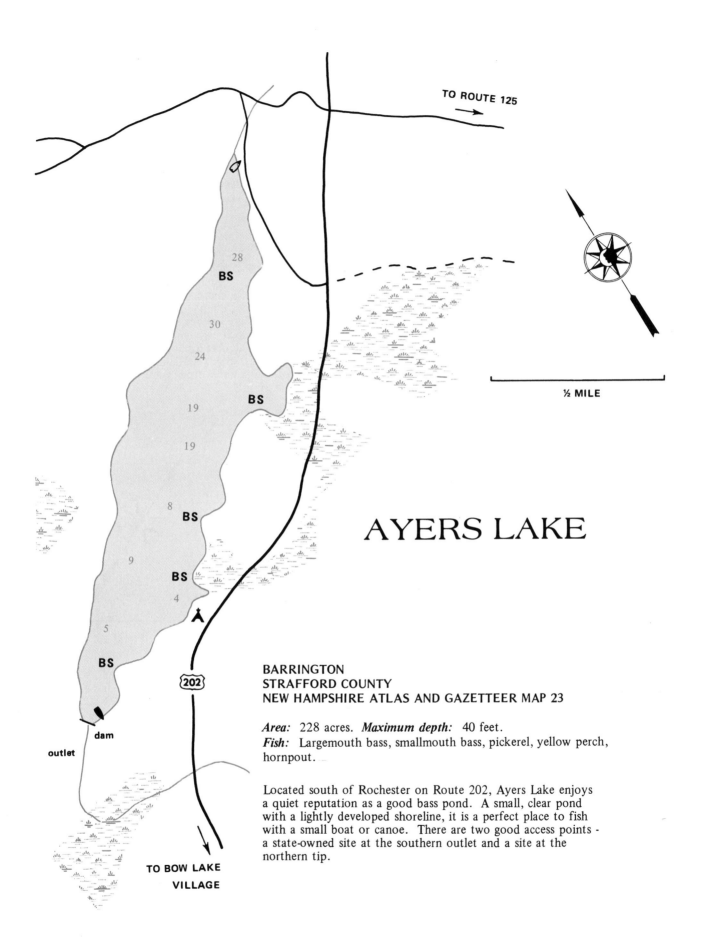

TO ROUTE 125

28

BS

30

24

19

19

8

BS

9

BS

4

5

BS

202

dam

outlet

½ MILE

AYERS LAKE

BARRINGTON
STRAFFORD COUNTY
NEW HAMPSHIRE ATLAS AND GAZETTEER MAP 23

Area: 228 acres. *Maximum depth:* 40 feet.
Fish: Largemouth bass, smallmouth bass, pickerel, yellow perch, hornpout.

Located south of Rochester on Route 202, Ayers Lake enjoys a quiet reputation as a good bass pond. A small, clear pond with a lightly developed shoreline, it is a perfect place to fish with a small boat or canoe. There are two good access points - a state-owned site at the southern outlet and a site at the northern tip.

TO BOW LAKE
VILLAGE

MAP 4

BABOOSIC LAKE

AMHERST
HILLSBOROUGH COUNTY
NEW HAMPSHIRE ATLAS AND GAZETTEER MAP 5

Area: 222 acres. *Maximum Depth:* 29 feet.
Fish: Largemouth bass, pickerel, yellow perch, hornpout.

Smallmouth bass were originally stocked in this pond in 1938. Numerous stockings during the next two decades failed to establish an adequate smallmouth bass fishery. In 1955 over-populations of competing undesirable species were reduced and the lake was restocked with largemouth bass, pickerel and hornpout. This lake is also one of the few which contains an excellent bluegill fishery. These panfish, although under utilized by anglers, provide fast ice fishing or open water fishing opportunities which are hard to match. The shoreline is varied, containing areas which are wooded, rocky and swampy. The bottom of the lake also is varied from gravel to mud with moderate amount of gravel shoals. Average ice-out date is May 1.

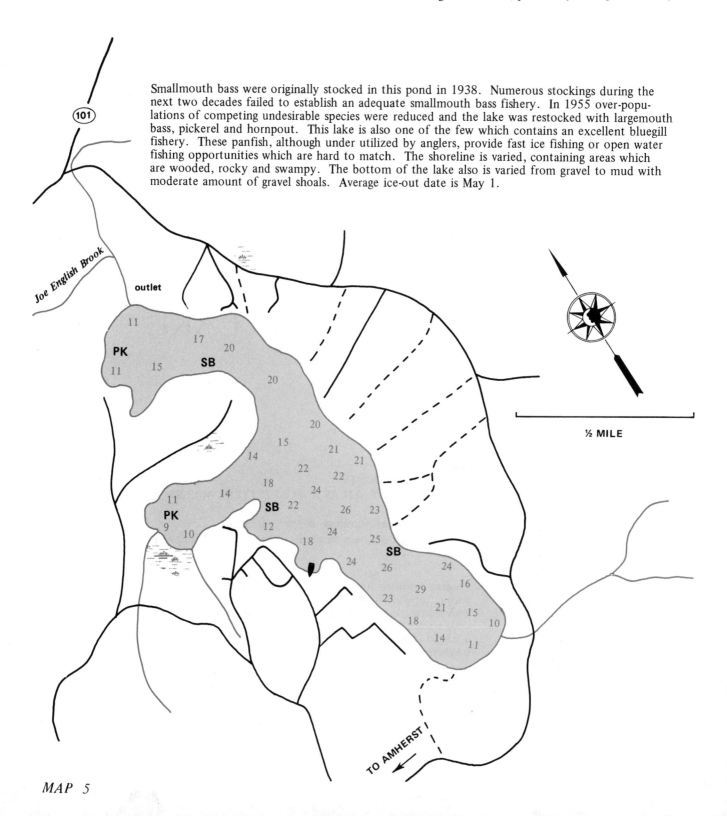

MAP 5

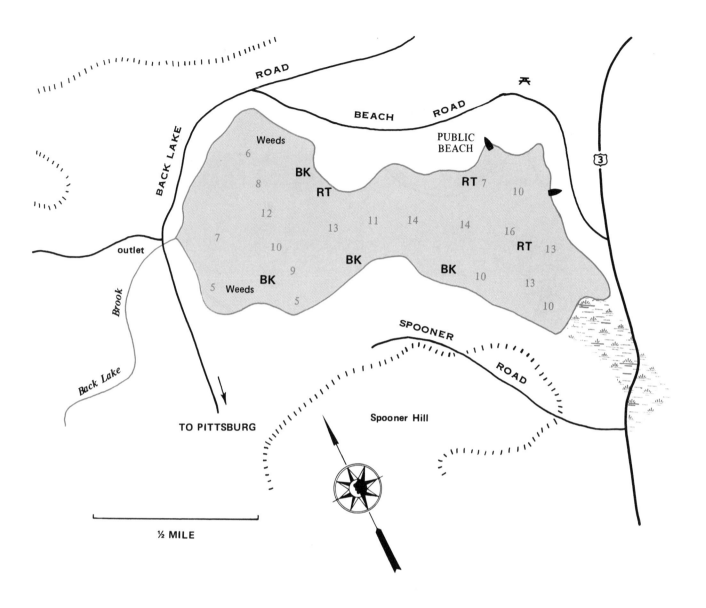

BACK LAKE

PITTSBURG
COOS COUNTY
NEW HAMPSHIRE ATLAS AND GAZETTEER MAP 59

Area: 358 acres. *Maximum depth:* 14 feet.
Fish: Brook trout, rainbow trout, brown trout.

Back Lake, located in Pittsburg, is one of the better known and more productive trout lakes in
New Hampshire. Its trout fishing can be exceptional at times and, as a general rule, consistently
good. Although it is shallow and tends to warm up earlier than other lakes in the north country,
it is still an excellent trout lake. It is easily accessible with at least two launch sites and a public
beach. The best fishing is from May to June and from September to October. Fly fishing is
excellent on this body of water with many large fish taken yearly. Fish may be taken with wet
or dry flies and it is not uncommon to have many surface fish feeding on this lake. Back Lake
is stocked periodically by the Fish and Game Department, and although the fish may not be
biting, there is never a lack of fish in the lake.

MAP 6

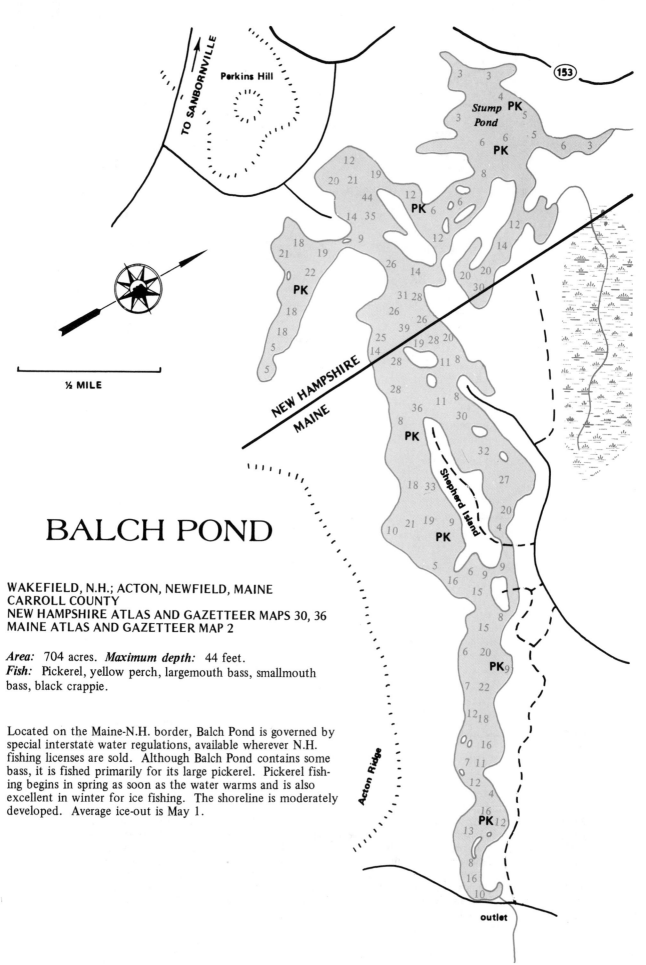

BALCH POND

WAKEFIELD, N.H.; ACTON, NEWFIELD, MAINE
CARROLL COUNTY
NEW HAMPSHIRE ATLAS AND GAZETTEER MAPS 30, 36
MAINE ATLAS AND GAZETTEER MAP 2

Area: 704 acres. *Maximum depth:* 44 feet.
Fish: Pickerel, yellow perch, largemouth bass, smallmouth
bass, black crappie.

Located on the Maine-N.H. border, Balch Pond is governed by
special interstate water regulations, available wherever N.H.
fishing licenses are sold. Although Balch Pond contains some
bass, it is fished primarily for its large pickerel. Pickerel fishing begins in spring as soon as the water warms and is also
excellent in winter for ice fishing. The shoreline is moderately
developed. Average ice-out is May 1.

MAP 7

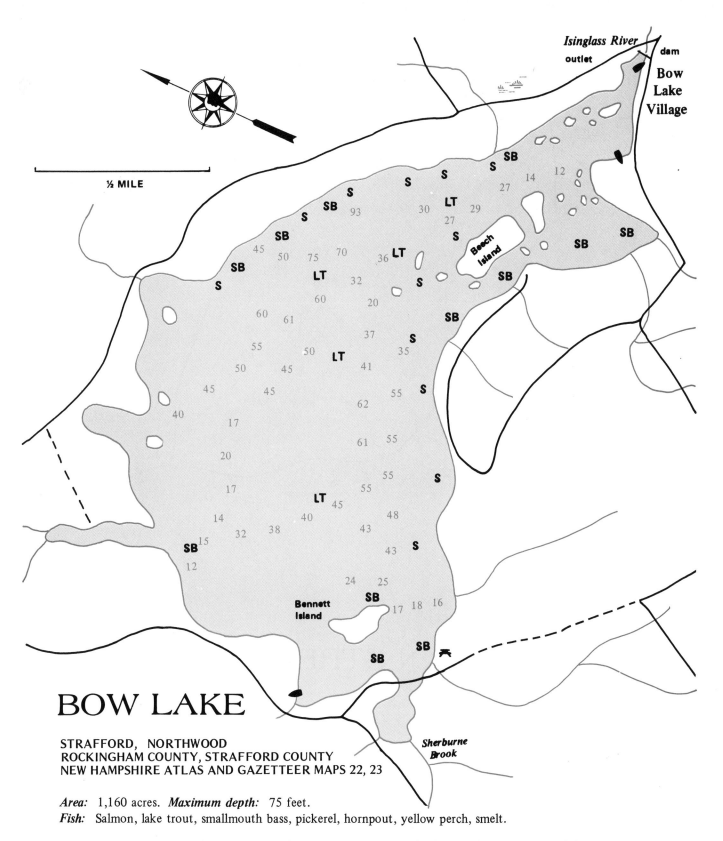

BOW LAKE

STRAFFORD, NORTHWOOD
ROCKINGHAM COUNTY, STRAFFORD COUNTY
NEW HAMPSHIRE ATLAS AND GAZETTEER MAPS 22, 23

Area: 1,160 acres. *Maximum depth:* 75 feet.
Fish: Salmon, lake trout, smallmouth bass, pickerel, hornpout, yellow perch, smelt.

The New Hampshire Fish and Game Department has worked very hard in recent years to establish salmon and lake trout fishing in Bow Lake and recent reports from anglers indicate the effort has been successful. Salmon and trout fishing is at its peak in early spring just after ice-out (mid April to early May). A large lake with many small islands and a varied and wooded shoreline with light development, Bow Lake is best known for its excellent smallmouth bass fishing. It is a convenient fishing site for those who live in southern New Hampshire and who prefer not to travel north to the Lake Regions for lake trout, salmon and smallmouth bass. The lake has three boat launching facilities, two commercial and one public.

MAP 8

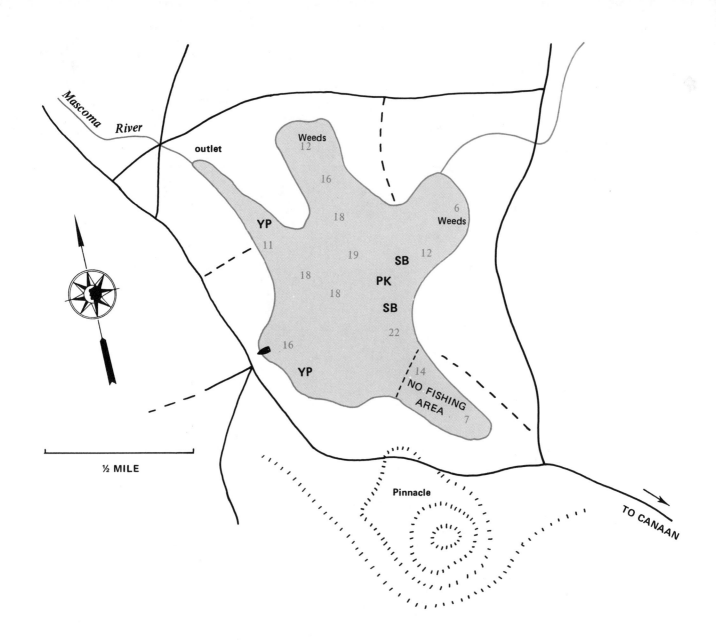

CANAAN STREET LAKE

CANAAN
GRAFTON COUNTY
NEW HAMPSHIRE ATLAS AND GAZETTEER MAP 32

Area: 303 acres. *Maximum depth:* 20 feet.
Fish: Largemouth bass, smallmouth bass, pickerel, yellow perch.

Canaan Street Lake is easily accessible from a free town-owned gravel launch site. The shoreline of this natural body of water is dotted with homes and summer camps, but it is mostly wooded. Ice-out occurs about the third week in April. Fishing for warm water species is good over the entire body of water, but it is restricted in one cove which supplies the town's drinking water. The angler should have no trouble catching any of the warm water species. The fish may not be large, but they are abundant. Ice fishing is also excellent here and the fishing pressure is very light.

MAP 9

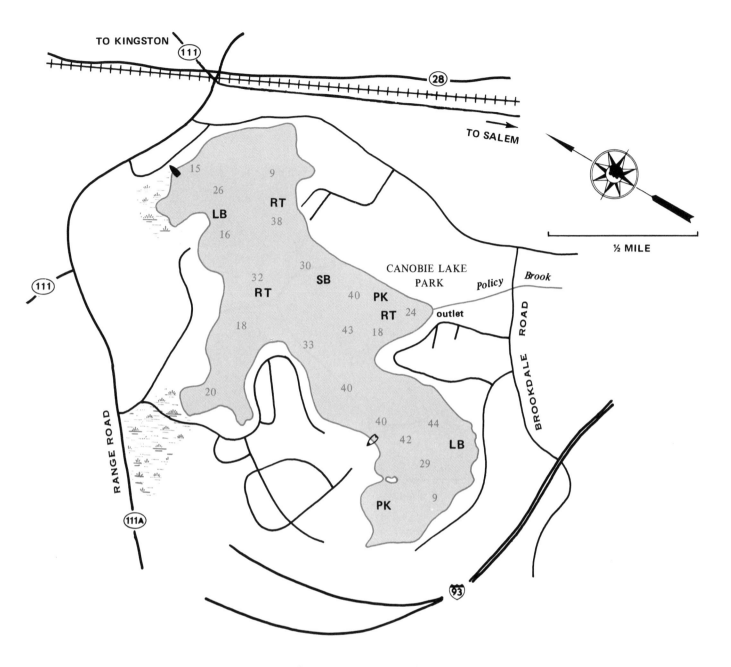

CANOBIE LAKE

SALEM, WINDHAM
ROCKINGHAM COUNTY
NEW HAMPSHIRE ATLAS AND GAZETTEER MAP 6

Area: 304 acres. *Maximum depth:* 44 feet.
Fish: Rainbow trout, largemouth bass, smallmouth bass, pickerel, yellow perch, hornpout.

Canobie Lake is well known for Canobie Lake Park, an amusement park on the lake's eastern shores. The rest of the shoreline is moderately developed. Canobie Lake contains both warm and cold water fish and is heavily stocked with rainbow trout. Because the area is heavily populated, the lake receives heavy fishing pressure for rainbow trout in the spring. But because the lake is well stocked, many limits are caught. Bait seems to be the best way to take the trout; local favorites are salmon eggs and marshmallows. Ice-out usually occurs during the latter part of April.

MAP 10

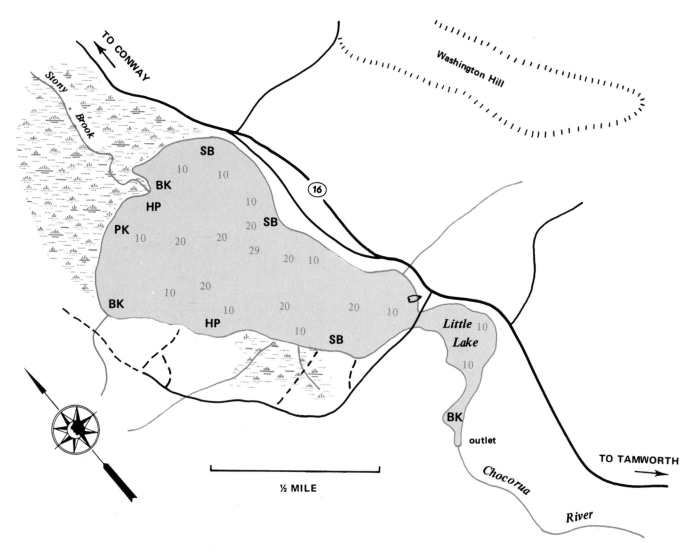

CHOCORUA LAKE

TAMWORTH
CARROLL COUNTY
NEW HAMPSHIRE ATLAS AND GAZETTEER MAP 41

Area: 222 acres. *Maximum depth:* 28 feet.
Fish: Brook trout, smallmouth bass, pickerel, hornpout.

Chocorua Lake, located at the base of one of New England's most famous and frequently photographed mountains, is a prime spot for fishing from mid-April to early June. The lake can be extremely rough during northwest gales which blow off Mount Chocorua. Keep an eye out for clouds forming at the mountain's peak, a sign of high winds to come. There is good brook trout fishing at the inlet and outlet on the lake. No outboard motors are allowed. Boats may be launched at the lower end of the lake where a bridge crosses the narrow neck of water. Average ice-out date is late April.

MAP 11

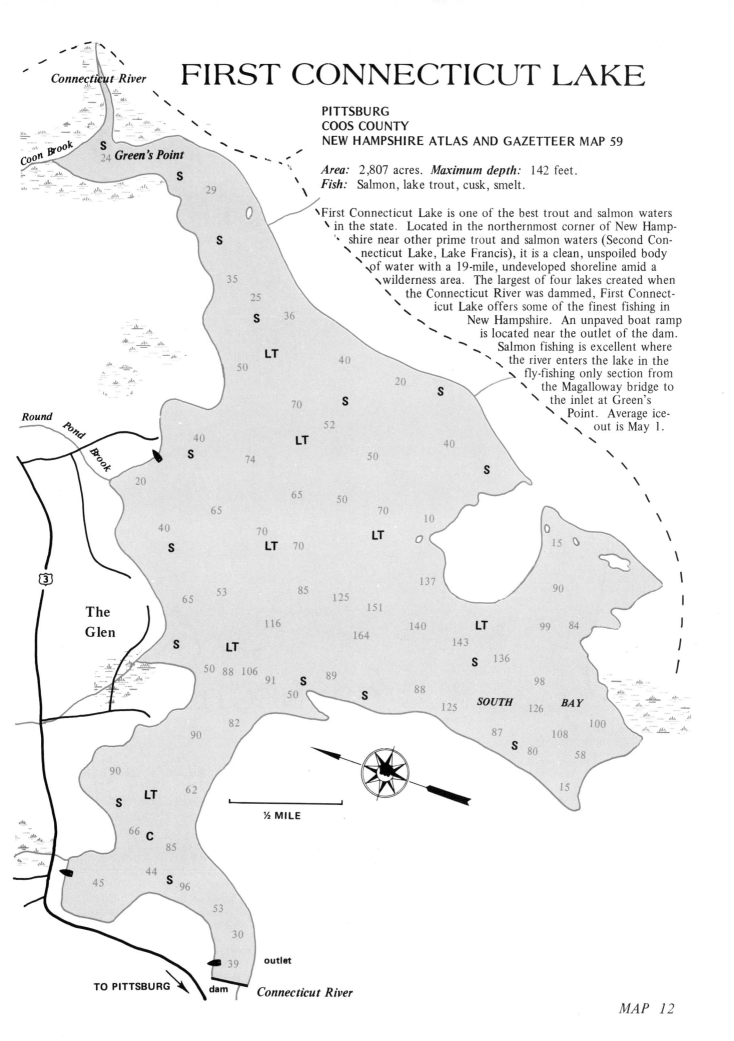

FIRST CONNECTICUT LAKE

PITTSBURG
COOS COUNTY
NEW HAMPSHIRE ATLAS AND GAZETTEER MAP 59

Area: 2,807 acres. *Maximum depth:* 142 feet.
Fish: Salmon, lake trout, cusk, smelt.

First Connecticut Lake is one of the best trout and salmon waters in the state. Located in the northernmost corner of New Hampshire near other prime trout and salmon waters (Second Connecticut Lake, Lake Francis), it is a clean, unspoiled body of water with a 19-mile, undeveloped shoreline amid a wilderness area. The largest of four lakes created when the Connecticut River was dammed, First Connecticut Lake offers some of the finest fishing in New Hampshire. An unpaved boat ramp is located near the outlet of the dam. Salmon fishing is excellent where the river enters the lake in the fly-fishing only section from the Magalloway bridge to the inlet at Green's Point. Average ice-out is May 1.

Connecticut River

Coon Brook

Green's Point

Round Pond Brook

The Glen

½ MILE

SOUTH BAY

outlet

dam

TO PITTSBURG

Connecticut River

MAP 12

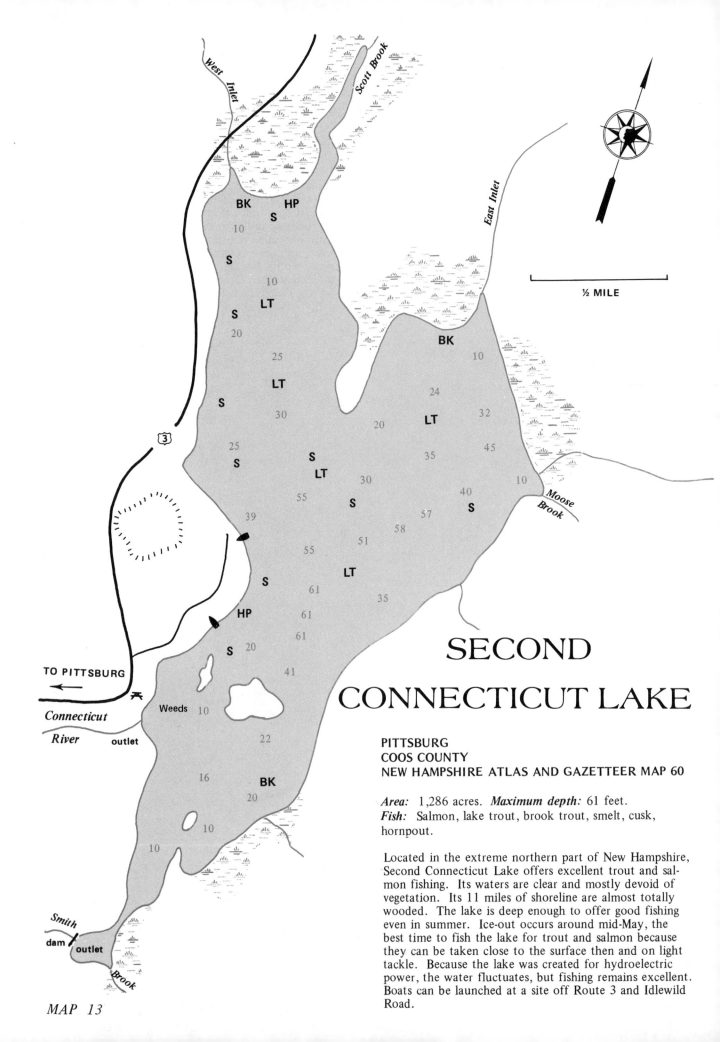

SECOND
CONNECTICUT LAKE

PITTSBURG
COOS COUNTY
NEW HAMPSHIRE ATLAS AND GAZETTEER MAP 60

Area: 1,286 acres. *Maximum depth:* 61 feet.
Fish: Salmon, lake trout, brook trout, smelt, cusk, hornpout.

Located in the extreme northern part of New Hampshire, Second Connecticut Lake offers excellent trout and salmon fishing. Its waters are clear and mostly devoid of vegetation. Its 11 miles of shoreline are almost totally wooded. The lake is deep enough to offer good fishing even in summer. Ice-out occurs around mid-May, the best time to fish the lake for trout and salmon because they can be taken close to the surface then and on light tackle. Because the lake was created for hydroelectric power, the water fluctuates, but fishing remains excellent. Boats can be launched at a site off Route 3 and Idlewild Road.

½ MILE

TO PITTSBURG

Connecticut
River   outlet

Weeds

Smith
dam outlet

Brook

MAP 13

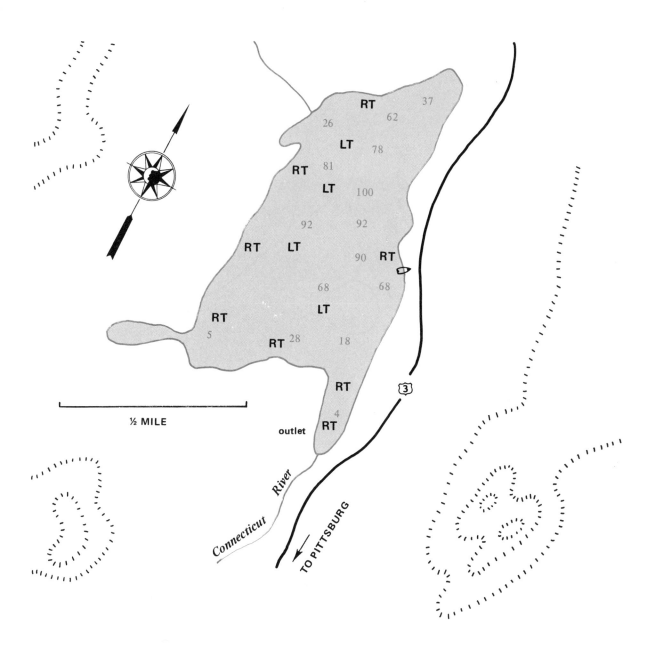

THIRD CONNECTICUT LAKE

PITTSBURG
COOS COUNTY
NEW HAMPSHIRE ATLAS AND
GAZETTEER MAP 59

Area: 278 acres. *Maximum depth:* 100 feet.
Fish: Brook trout, rainbow trout, lake trout, cusk, smelt.

Third Connecticut Lake is located just south of the Quebec border at the extreme northern tip of N.H. A natural body of water in a wilderness area, it offers fine trout fishing through the spring, summer, and fall. Ice-out is in mid-May. The shoreline is heavily wooded and the lake has a gravel bottom. Access to the lake is at a state-owned launch site on Route 3 (no ramp). Third Connecticut Lake is a good fishing spot for an angler with a small boat or for those who would rather not fish some of the larger lakes in the area.

MAP 14

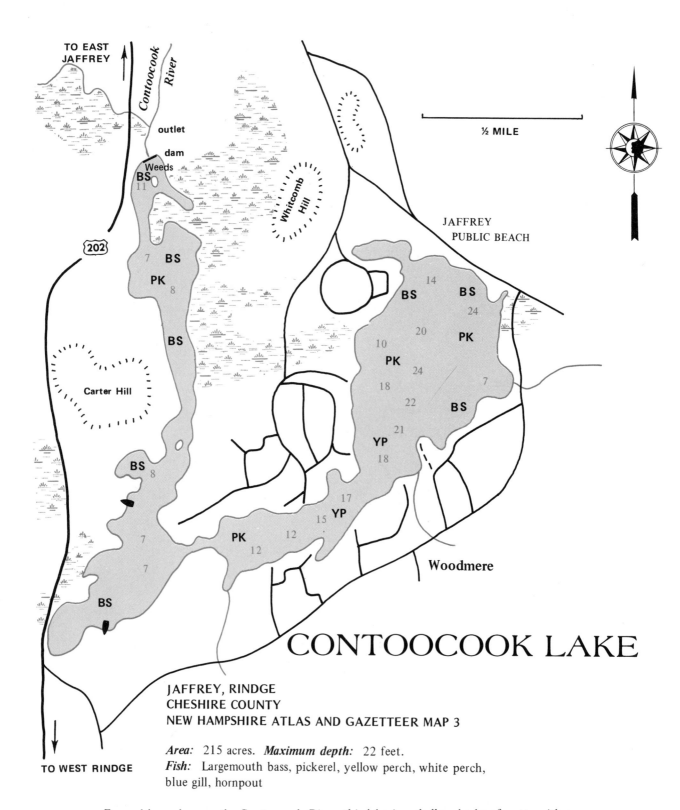

TO EAST JAFFREY

Contoocook River

outlet

dam

Weeds
BS
11

202

BS

PK
8

BS

Whitcomb Hill

Carter Hill

BS
8

7

7

PK
12

12

PK
12

15

17

YP

BS

½ MILE

JAFFREY PUBLIC BEACH

14

BS

BS
24

20

PK

10

PK
24

18

7

22

BS

21

YP
18

Woodmere

BS

CONTOOCOOK LAKE

JAFFREY, RINDGE
CHESHIRE COUNTY
NEW HAMPSHIRE ATLAS AND GAZETTEER MAP 3

Area: 215 acres. *Maximum depth:* 22 feet.
Fish: Largemouth bass, pickerel, yellow perch, white perch,
blue gill, hornpout

TO WEST RINDGE

Formed by a dam on the Contoocook River, this lake is a shallow body of water with a warm
water fishery. The lake is especially shallow at the long arm behind the dam which forms a
large marsh of more than 100 acres. The lake was originally stocked with smallmouth bass
in the early 40's, but today the main fishery is for largemouth bass although there is no record
of largemouth bass being stocked here. The lake also contains an excellent fishery for white
perch, bluegills and hornpout. Yellow perch are also well represented and provide good ice
fishing. Access to the lake is at the unpaved public boat ramp in Rindge. The shoreline is
moderately developed with the Jaffrey Public Beach and Woodmere Golf Course on the North-
eastern section of the lake. Average ice-out date is late April.

MAP 15

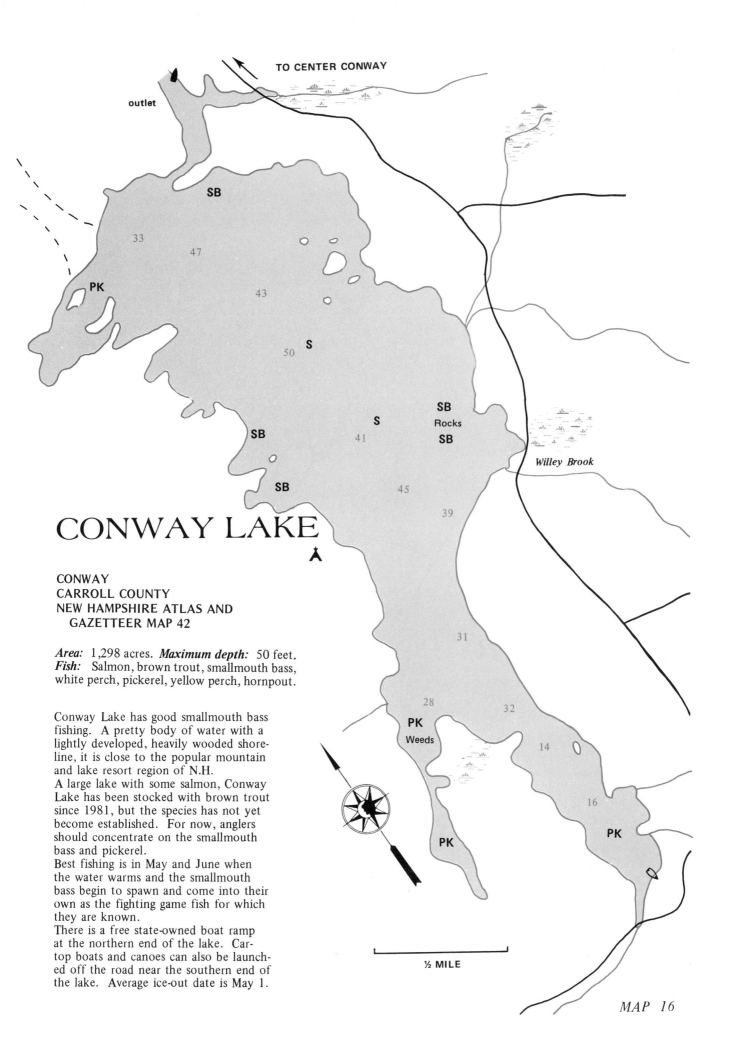

TO CENTER CONWAY

outlet

SB

33

47

PK

43

S

50

SB

S

SB
Rocks
SB

41

Willey Brook

SB

45

39

CONWAY LAKE

CONWAY
CARROLL COUNTY
NEW HAMPSHIRE ATLAS AND
GAZETTEER MAP 42

Area: 1,298 acres. *Maximum depth:* 50 feet.
Fish: Salmon, brown trout, smallmouth bass,
white perch, pickerel, yellow perch, hornpout.

Conway Lake has good smallmouth bass
fishing. A pretty body of water with a
lightly developed, heavily wooded shoreline, it is close to the popular mountain
and lake resort region of N.H.
A large lake with some salmon, Conway
Lake has been stocked with brown trout
since 1981, but the species has not yet
become established. For now, anglers
should concentrate on the smallmouth
bass and pickerel.
Best fishing is in May and June when
the water warms and the smallmouth
bass begin to spawn and come into their
own as the fighting game fish for which
they are known.
There is a free state-owned boat ramp
at the northern end of the lake. Car-
top boats and canoes can also be launched off the road near the southern end of
the lake. Average ice-out date is May 1.

31

28

32

PK
Weeds

14

16

PK

PK

½ MILE

MAP 16

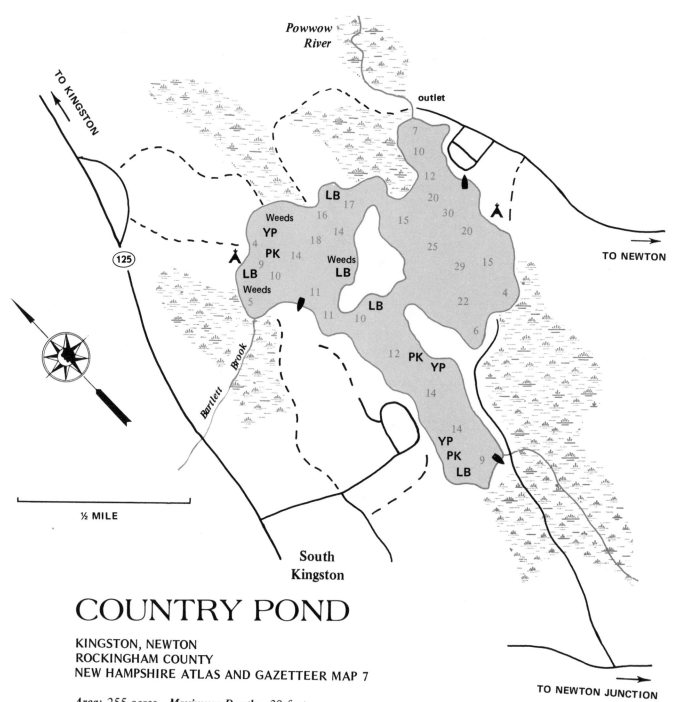

COUNTRY POND

KINGSTON, NEWTON
ROCKINGHAM COUNTY
NEW HAMPSHIRE ATLAS AND GAZETTEER MAP 7

Area: 255 acres. *Maximum Depth:* 30 feet.
Fish: Largemouth bass, smallmouth bass, pickerel, yellow perch, hornpout, white perch.

Country Pond, along with neighboring Powwow River Pond, Kingston Lake and Greenwood Lake, is one of the better-known, productive bass waters in southern N.H. Even though the area is fairly well-developed, this pond is not overfished. It is accessible from Route 125, a major highway in southeastern N.H. The shoreline is about 60 percent wooded and 40 percent swamp. The bottom is about 50 percent muck. Country Pond has good ice fishing and is the site of the Newton Fish and Game Club's annual ice-fishing derby. Ice-out can be expected around April 10. The best fishing here takes place from mid-May through June and again in September. Powwow River at the outlet has excellent bass and pickerel fishing. The pond has three unimproved trailer launching sites.

MAP 17

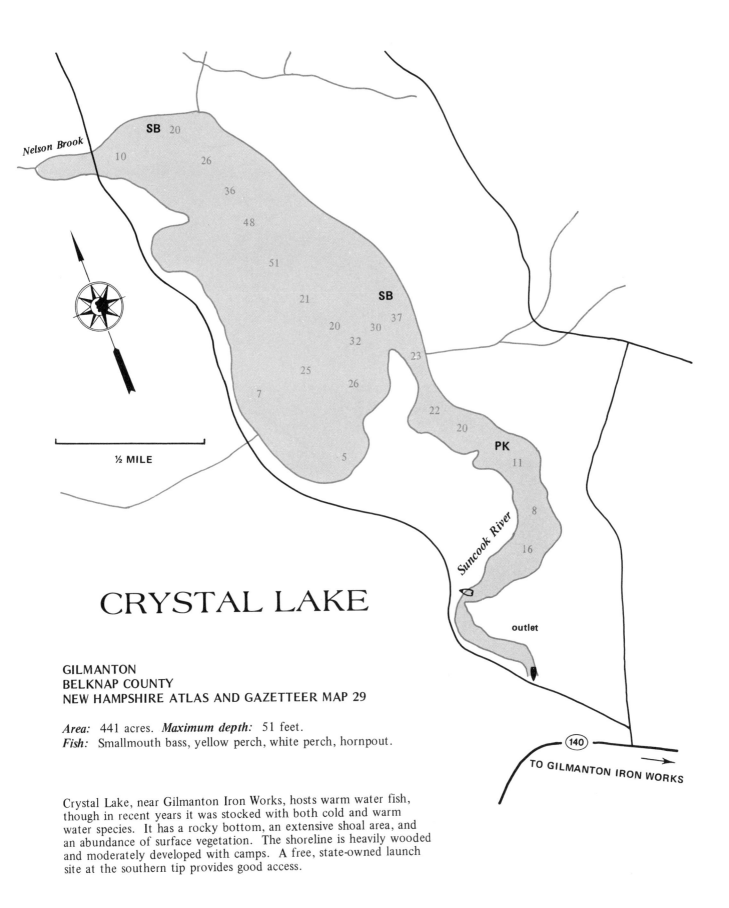

CRYSTAL LAKE

GILMANTON
BELKNAP COUNTY
NEW HAMPSHIRE ATLAS AND GAZETTEER MAP 29

Area: 441 acres. *Maximum depth:* 51 feet.
Fish: Smallmouth bass, yellow perch, white perch, hornpout.

Crystal Lake, near Gilmanton Iron Works, hosts warm water fish,
though in recent years it was stocked with both cold and warm
water species. It has a rocky bottom, an extensive shoal area, and
an abundance of surface vegetation. The shoreline is heavily wooded
and moderately developed with camps. A free, state-owned launch
site at the southern tip provides good access.

MAP 18

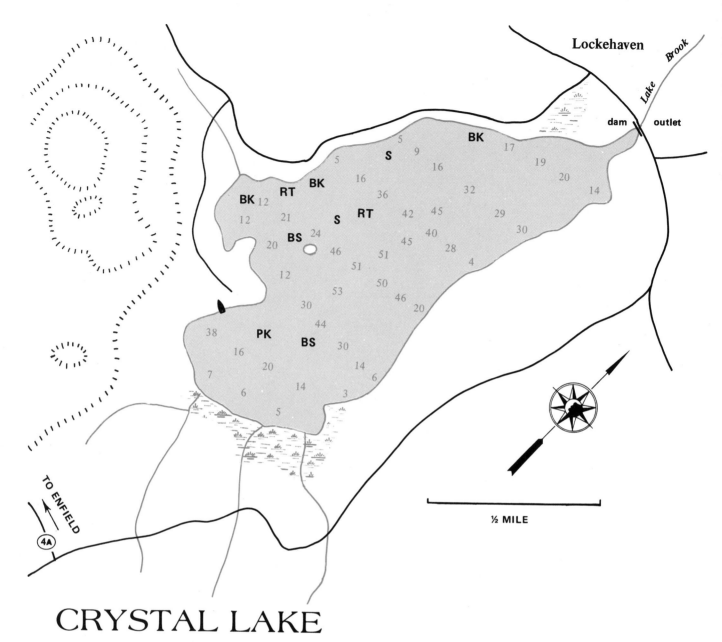

CRYSTAL LAKE

ENFIELD
GRAFTON COUNTY
NEW HAMPSHIRE ATLAS AND GAZETTEER MAP 25

Area: 354 acres. *Maximum depth:* 53 feet.
Fish: Salmon, brook trout, rainbow trout, smallmouth bass, rock bass,
lake trout, pickerel, smelt.

Anglers fish Crystal Lake for its exceptional rainbow and brook trout. The lake also contains some salmon and lake trout, but not in consistent numbers. Each spring and fall the N.H. Fish and Game Department heavily stocks the lake. The lake's deep waters coupled with a good supply of smelt offer a healthy rainbow trout population. Fishing here is best in the spring just after ice-out (around May 1) when many anglers troll the deep waters for rainbow trout. Along the shoreline, others troll and still fish for brook trout. Hit at the right time, fishing can be fast and limits taken easily. A state-owned launch offers easy access. The shoreline is moderately developed.

MAP 19

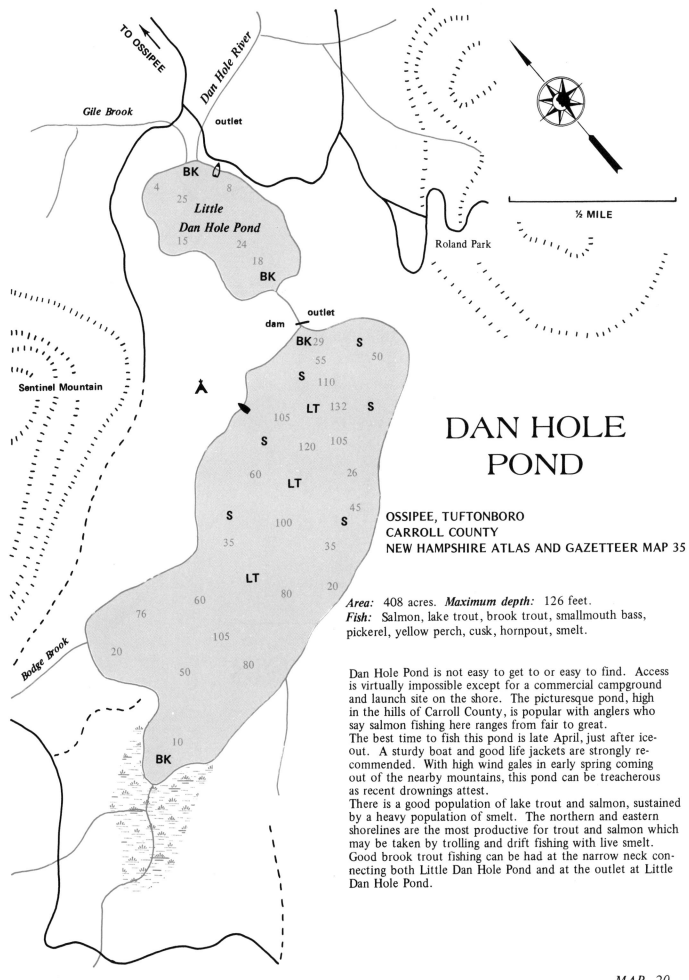

TO OSSIPEE

Dan Hole River

Gile Brook

outlet

BK

4
25
8

*Little
Dan Hole Pond*

15
24

18

BK

outlet

dam

BK 29   **S**

55   50

S   110

LT 132   **S**

105

S   105

120

60   26

LT

S   45

100   **S**

35   35

LT

80   20

60

76

20

50   80

10

BK

Sentinel Mountain

Roland Park

½ MILE

DAN HOLE
POND

**OSSIPEE, TUFTONBORO
CARROLL COUNTY
NEW HAMPSHIRE ATLAS AND GAZETTEER MAP 35**

Area: 408 acres. *Maximum depth:* 126 feet.
Fish: Salmon, lake trout, brook trout, smallmouth bass, pickerel, yellow perch, cusk, hornpout, smelt.

Dan Hole Pond is not easy to get to or easy to find. Access is virtually impossible except for a commercial campground and launch site on the shore. The picturesque pond, high in the hills of Carroll County, is popular with anglers who say salmon fishing here ranges from fair to great.
The best time to fish this pond is late April, just after ice-out. A sturdy boat and good life jackets are strongly recommended. With high wind gales in early spring coming out of the nearby mountains, this pond can be treacherous as recent drownings attest.
There is a good population of lake trout and salmon, sustained by a heavy population of smelt. The northern and eastern shorelines are the most productive for trout and salmon which may be taken by trolling and drift fishing with live smelt.
Good brook trout fishing can be had at the narrow neck connecting both Little Dan Hole Pond and at the outlet at Little Dan Hole Pond.

Bodge Brook

MAP 20

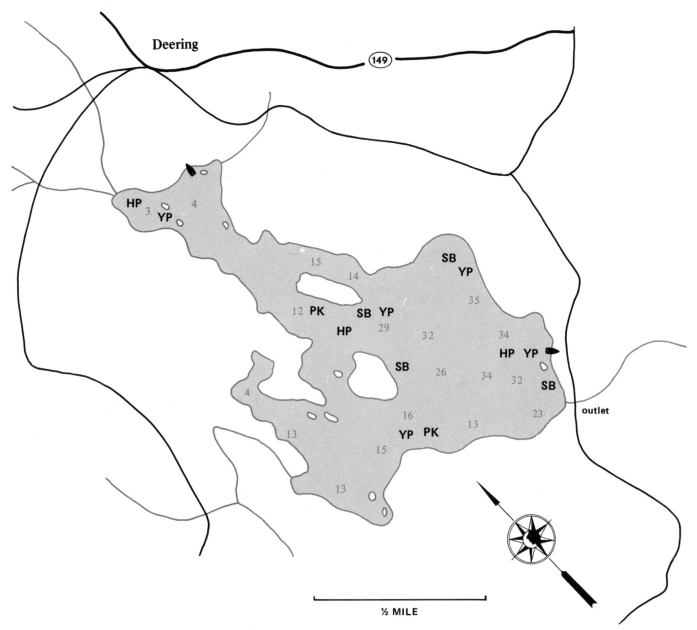

DEERING RESERVOIR

DEERING
HILLSBORO COUNTY
NEW HAMPSHIRE ATLAS AND GAZETTEER MAP 12

Area: 315 acres. *Maximum depth:* 35 feet.
Fish: Smallmouth bass, pickerel, yellow perch, hornpout.

Deering Reservoir, as the name implies, is an artificial body of water located between the towns of Hillsboro and South Weare, just off Route 149. The shoreline is wooded and undeveloped; the bottom is gravel and rock. The reservoir has an excellent reputation for ice fishing. There is also good smallmouth bass fishing in the warmer months. There are two launch sites here - one state-owned and one town-owned, but both are difficult to use because of their construction and location. Average ice-out can be expected the third week in April.

MAP 21

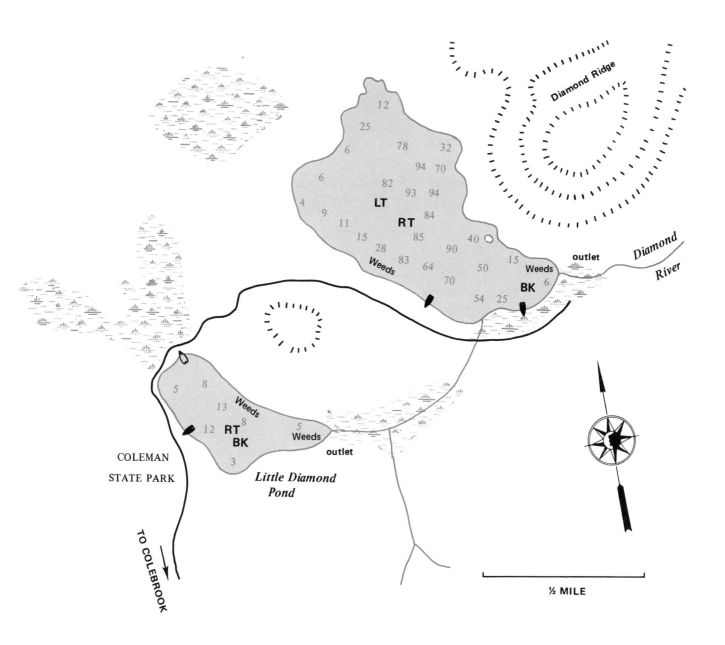

DIAMOND PONDS

STEWARTSTOWN
COOS COUNTY
NEW HAMPSHIRE ATLAS AND GAZETTEER MAP 56

Area: 179 acres/53 acres. *Maximum depth:* 117 feet/15 feet.

Fish: Lake trout, rainbow trout, brook trout, smelt, cusk.

The state's largest cusk was caught on Big Diamond Pond, one of two good trout fishing ponds adjacent to Coleman State Park in Stewartstown. Both ponds are readily accessible with two launch sites on each. Lake trout are found only in Big Diamond Pond. Big Diamond is also open for ice fishing for lake and rainbow trout. These ponds provide consistently good fishing during the year, especially in spring and fall. Ice-out is the second week in May.

MAP 22

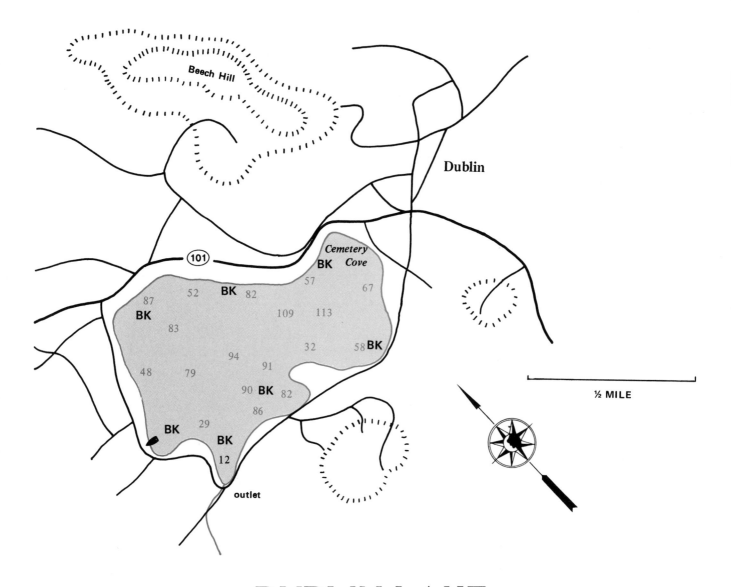

DUBLIN LAKE

(MONADNOCK POND)

DUBLIN
CHESHIRE COUNTY
NEW HAMPSHIRE ATLAS AND GAZETTEER MAPS 2, 3

Area: 239 acres. *Maximum depth:* 113 feet.
Fish: Brook trout, yellow perch, suckers, hornpout, smelt.

A productive and popular trout pond, Dublin Pond is easy to reach on busy Route 101 between the towns of Peterborough and Keene in southern N.H. Fish here can be wary at times; careful presentation or slow trolling may be necessary to take these trout. The public launch at the western edge of the pond is a good place to fly fish. Fishermen should know that the shore is privately owned and no trespassing is allowed. Wading anglers can enter at some areas close to the road, at the boat launch, or at Cemetery Cove. Average ice-out is mid April. The best fishing is from season opening to late June and again during the fly-fishing-only season in the fall.

MAP 23

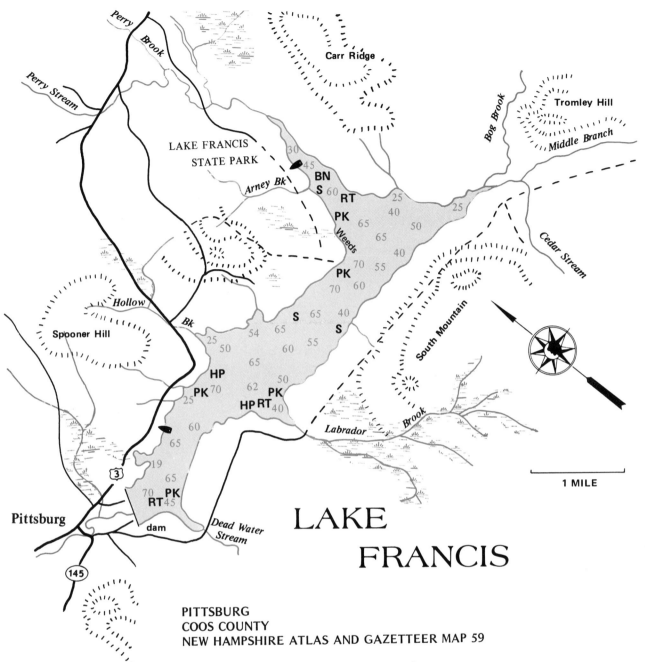

Perry Brook

Perry Stream

Carr Ridge

Bog Brook

Tromley Hill

Middle Branch

LAKE FRANCIS
STATE PARK

Arney Bk

BN
S 60 RT
PK 65
30
45

25
40
50
25

Weeds

70 55
PK
70 60

Cedar Stream

S 65 40
54 65 S
25 50 60 55
65

Hollow

Spooner Hill

Bk

HP
PK 70
25

50
62 PK
HP RT 40

South Mountain

60
65
19
65
70 PK
RT 45

Labrador Brook

1 MILE

Pittsburg

3

dam

Dead Water
Stream

145

LAKE
FRANCIS

PITTSBURG
COOS COUNTY
NEW HAMPSHIRE ATLAS AND GAZETTEER MAP 59

Area: 2,051 acres. *Maximum depth:* 85 feet.
Fish: Salmon, rainbow trout, smelt, pickerel, cusk, hornpout, brown trout.

Lake Francis is the first of four lakes created by the Connecticut River and its dams for the production of hydroelectric power in Pittsburg. Lake Francis, together with First, Second and Third Connecticut Lakes, offers the angler excellent opportunities and success for the fishing of cold water species. Located in the northern part of New Hampshire, Lake Francis, together with the Connecticut Lakes, offers truly exceptional trout and salmon fishing. The shoreline is not developed and is heavily wooded. Accessible off Route 3 with two launching sites and Lake Francis State Park, the angler will have no trouble finding a point of access or accommodations. Lake Francis offers exceptional brown trout fishing and in 1980 a record brown trout was taken here. It is open for ice fishing which should be excellent for brown trout. Although known for its cold water fisheries, Lake Francis also holds an excellent population of large pickerel which may be overlooked by the trout and salmon fisherman.

MAP 24

GOOSE POND

CANAAN
GRAFTON COUNTY
NEW HAMPSHIRE ATLAS AND GAZETTEER MAP 31

Area: 554 acres. *Maximum depth:* 30 feet.
Fish: Largemouth bass, smallmouth bass, rock bass, pickerel, yellow perch, white perch.

Both smallmouth bass and white perch records for the state come from Goose Pond, noted for its warm-water species. Average ice-out is in the latter part of April. The best time to fish here is in the spring after the water warms sufficiently. Fishing is excellent through the fall with exceptionally good ice fishing. Goose Pond offers ample opportunity to catch exceptionally large fish, particularly bass and pickerel. Ice fishing for yellow perch is excellent either with tip-ups or by jigging with fishing poles when a school of yellow perch is in the area. In summer, the lightly developed 6.3 miles of shoreline and the rocky bottom offer unlimited fishing opportunities. Free access is available at an unpaved public launching site.

½ MILE

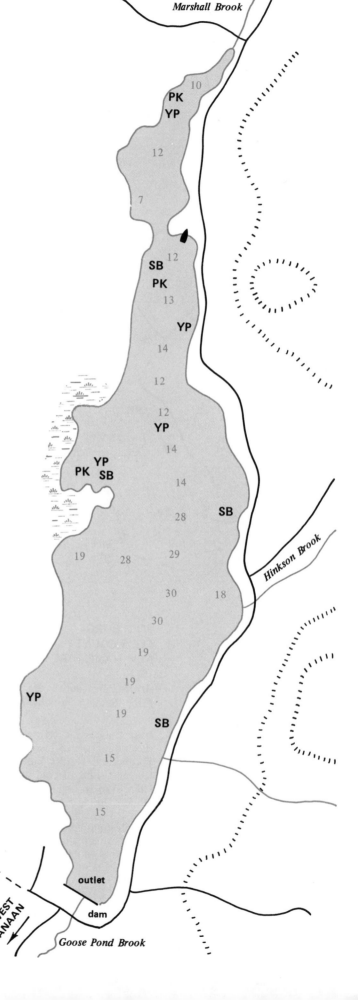

MAP 25

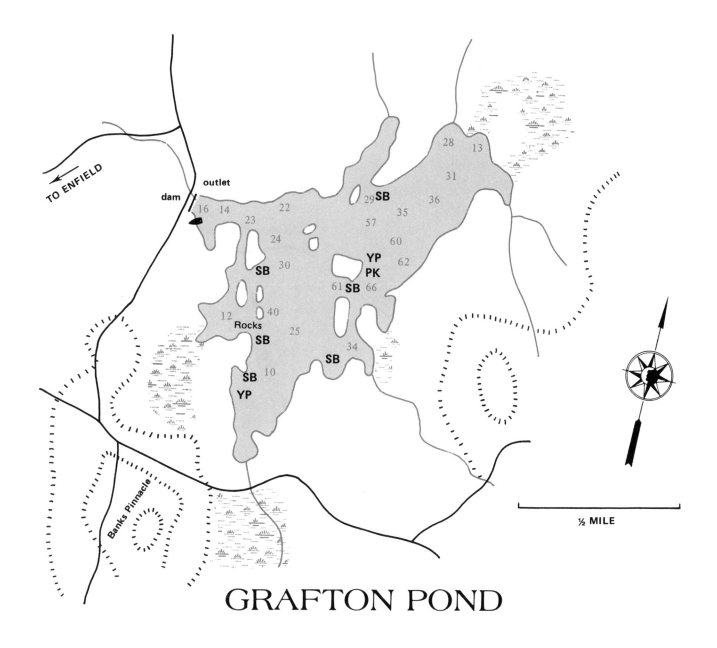

GRAFTON POND

GRAFTON
GRAFTON COUNTY
NEW HAMPSHIRE ATLAS AND GAZETTEER MAP 26

Area: 235 acres. *Maximum depth:* 66 feet.
Fish: Smallmouth bass, pickerel, hornpout, yellow perch.

Grafton Pond is a premier smallmouth bass pond. Dotted by many rocky islands and raised by damming, the shoreline and submerged coverings offer almost limitless fishing spots and cover for smallmouth bass. The pond is lightly fished and those who do fish it and become familiar with its waters are treated to exceptional fishing here at times. Many anglers use canoes and fish with flies for the smallmouth bass here. There is a six horsepower limit for motors on the pond and no camping is allowed on any of the islands or the shoreline. This is a loon nesting area and anyone fishing here will probably see several loons. The shoreline is undeveloped and unspoiled. There is no fee at the unimproved launch site at the dam, and small trailered boats and hand-launched boats will have no trouble gaining access to the pond.

MAP 26

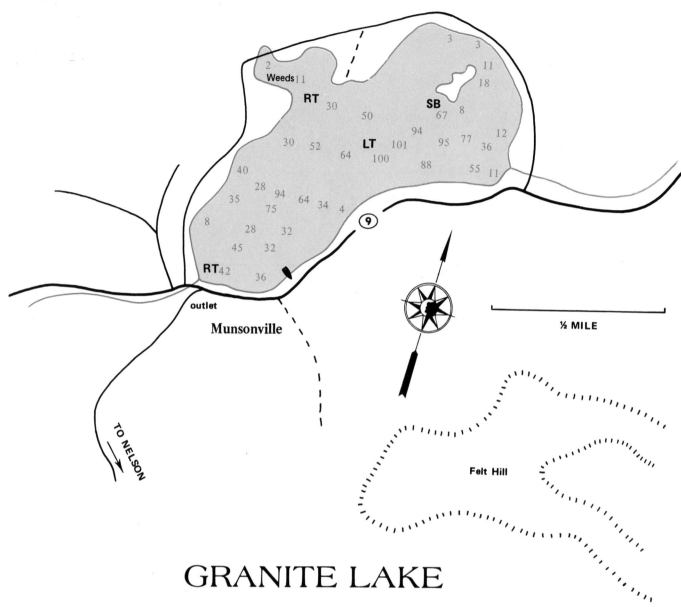

GRANITE LAKE

**NELSON, STODDARD
CHESHIRE COUNTY
NEW HAMPSHIRE ATLAS AND GAZETTEER MAP 10**

Area: 211 acres. *Maximum depth:* 101 feet.
Fish: Rainbow trout, lake trout, smallmouth bass, pickerel, hornpout,
yellow perch, smelt, rock bass.

Although small in size, Granite Lake is on the list of lake trout fishing sites
compiled by the N.H. Fish and Game Department. The lake is just off Route 9
and boats can easily be launched from a public launching ramp on the southern
shore. The shoreline is heavily wooded. The pond has a rock, gravel and sand
bottom. There is good smallmouth bass fishing near the island in the northern
end of the lake. Average ice-out is April 1.

MAP 27

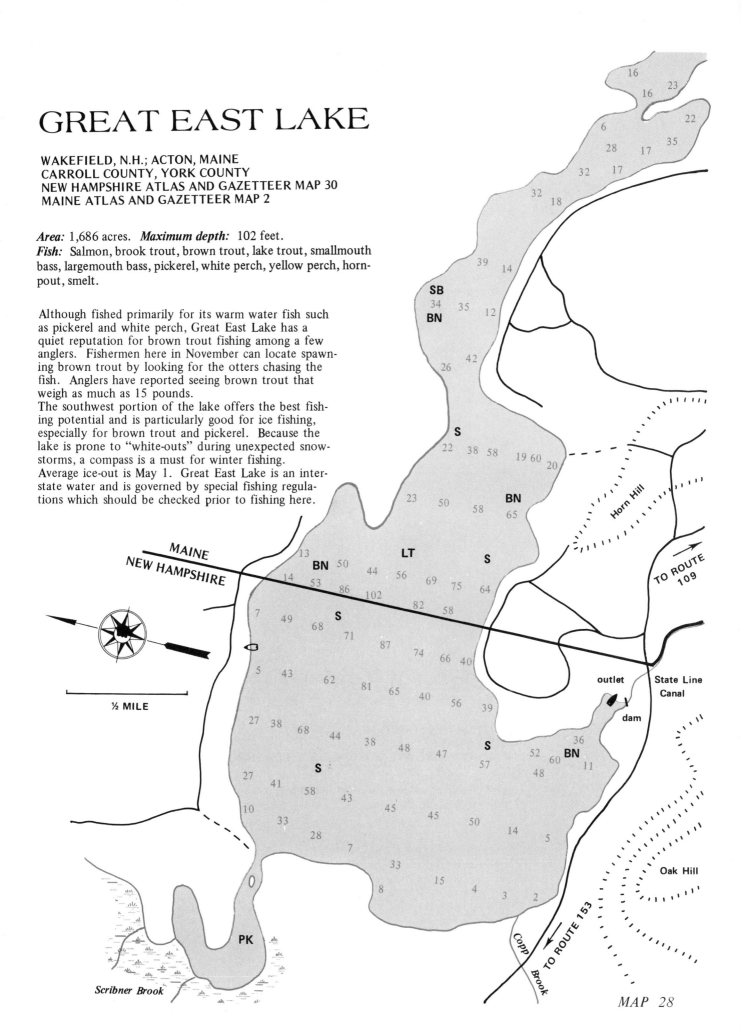

GREAT EAST LAKE

WAKEFIELD, N.H.; ACTON, MAINE
CARROLL COUNTY, YORK COUNTY
NEW HAMPSHIRE ATLAS AND GAZETTEER MAP 30
MAINE ATLAS AND GAZETTEER MAP 2

Area: 1,686 acres. *Maximum depth:* 102 feet.
Fish: Salmon, brook trout, brown trout, lake trout, smallmouth bass, largemouth bass, pickerel, white perch, yellow perch, hornpout, smelt.

Although fished primarily for its warm water fish such as pickerel and white perch, Great East Lake has a quiet reputation for brown trout fishing among a few anglers. Fishermen here in November can locate spawning brown trout by looking for the otters chasing the fish. Anglers have reported seeing brown trout that weigh as much as 15 pounds.

The southwest portion of the lake offers the best fishing potential and is particularly good for ice fishing, especially for brown trout and pickerel. Because the lake is prone to "white-outs" during unexpected snowstorms, a compass is a must for winter fishing. Average ice-out is May 1. Great East Lake is an interstate water and is governed by special fishing regulations which should be checked prior to fishing here.

½ MILE

MAINE
NEW HAMPSHIRE

MAP 28

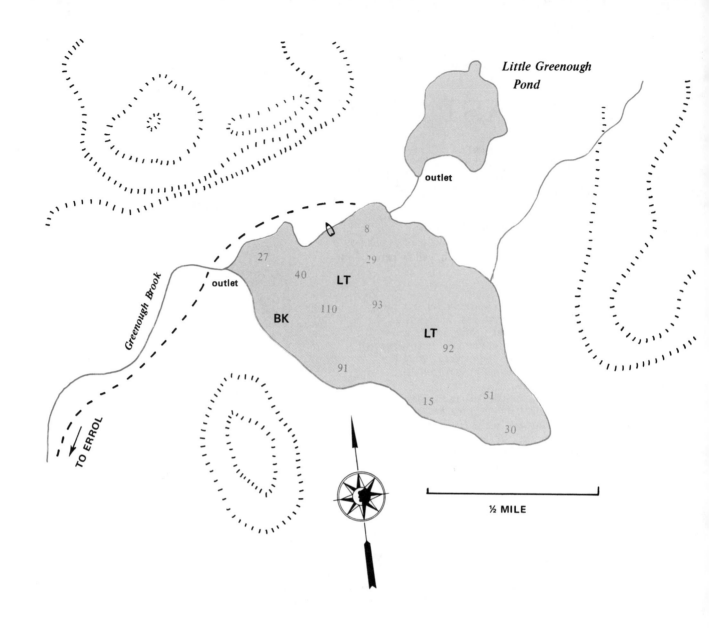

GREENOUGH PONDS

WENTWORTH'S LOCATION
COOS COUNTY
NEW HAMPSHIRE ATLAS AND GAZETTEER MAP 57

Area: 254 acres. *Maximum depth:* 110 feet.
Fish: Brook trout, lake trout.

Although a small pond, Big Greenough Pond is consistently very deep over a large area and, therefore, is a good place to fish for cold water species such as lake trout or brook trout. Big Greenough Pond is remote and accessible by foot only. The shoreline is totally wooded. Fishermen are advised to bring in their own boat or canoe. Ice-out is around May 1.

MAP 29

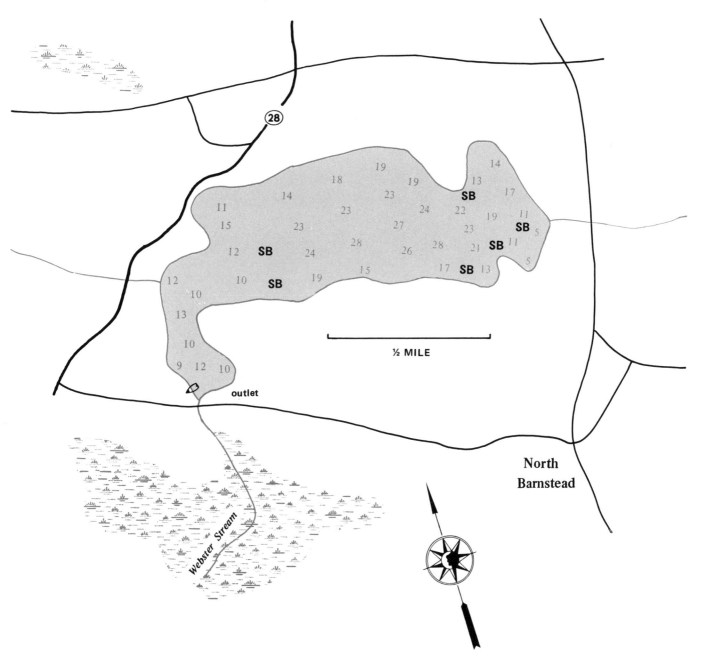

HALFMOON LAKE

BARNSTEAD, ALTON
BELKNAP COUNTY
NEW HAMPSHIRE ATLAS AND GAZETTEER MAPS 22, 29

Area: 280 acres. *Maximum depth:* 29 feet
Fish: Largemouth bass, smallmouth bass, pickerel, yellow perch, white perch, hornpout.

Halfmoon Lake is usually overlooked by fishermen heading for the big waters of Lake Winnipesaukee.
This lake, located just off Route 28, has excellent smallmouth bass fishing, particularly in May and June.
Ice-out can be expected in late April.

MAP 30

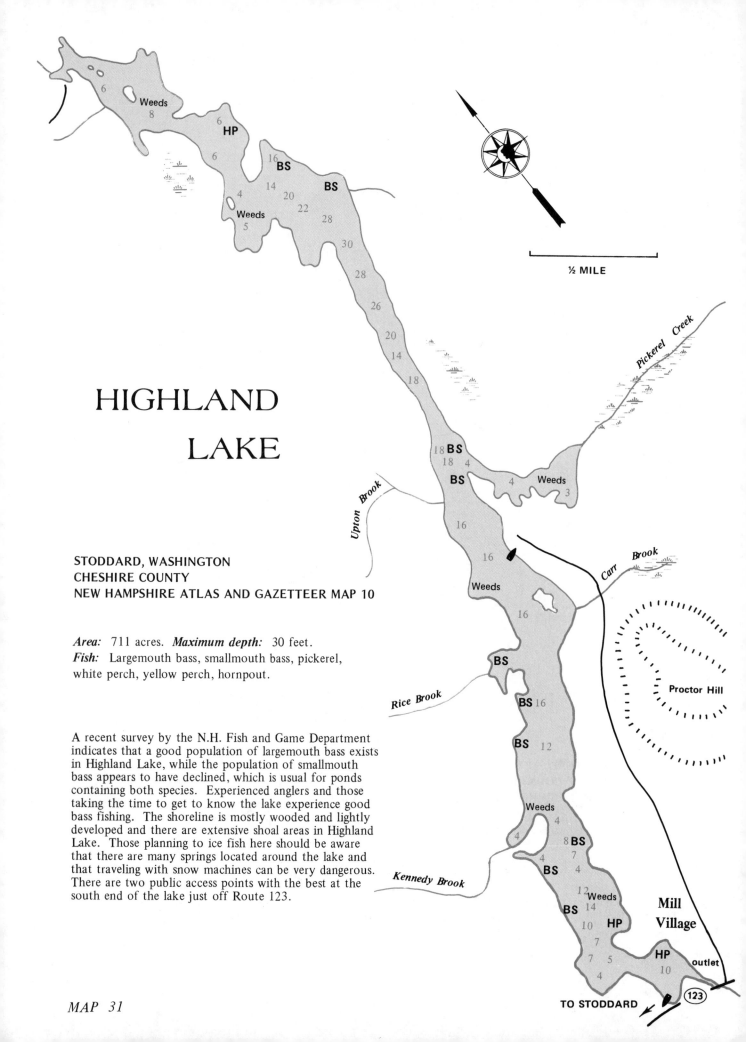

HIGHLAND

LAKE

STODDARD, WASHINGTON
CHESHIRE COUNTY
NEW HAMPSHIRE ATLAS AND GAZETTEER MAP 10

Area: 711 acres. *Maximum depth:* 30 feet.
Fish: Largemouth bass, smallmouth bass, pickerel,
white perch, yellow perch, hornpout.

A recent survey by the N.H. Fish and Game Department
indicates that a good population of largemouth bass exists
in Highland Lake, while the population of smallmouth
bass appears to have declined, which is usual for ponds
containing both species. Experienced anglers and those
taking the time to get to know the lake experience good
bass fishing. The shoreline is mostly wooded and lightly
developed and there are extensive shoal areas in Highland
Lake. Those planning to ice fish here should be aware
that there are many springs located around the lake and
that traveling with snow machines can be very dangerous.
There are two public access points with the best at the
south end of the lake just off Route 123.

MAP 31

½ MILE

Weeds
8
6
HP
6
16
BS
14
BS
20
22
28
Weeds
5
4
30
28
26
20
14
18

Pickerel Creek

18 BS
18 4
Upton Brook
BS
Weeds
3
4
16
16
Weeds
16

Carr Brook

Proctor Hill

BS
Rice Brook
BS 16
BS 12

Weeds
4
4
8 BS
7
4
BS
4
Kennedy Brook
12
Weeds
14
BS
10
HP
7
HP
5
7
4
10 outlet

**Mill
Village**

TO STODDARD
123

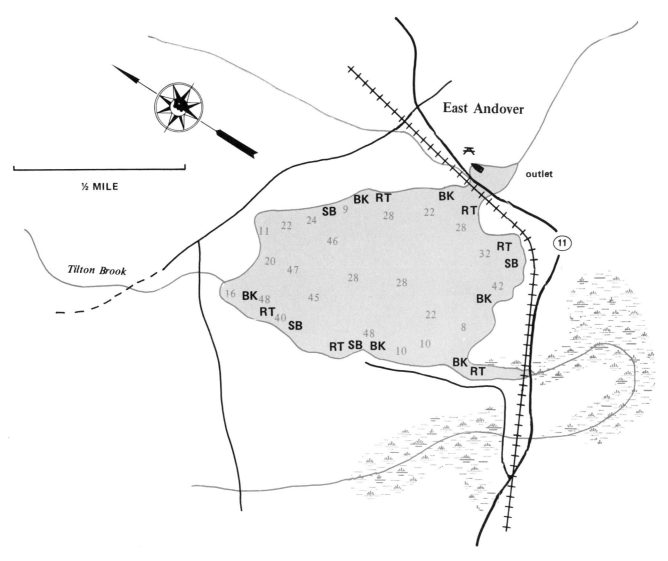

HIGHLAND LAKE

ANDOVER
MERRIMACK COUNTY
NEW HAMPSHIRE ATLAS AND GAZETTEER MAP 27

Area: 211 acres. *Maximum depth:* 48 feet.
Fish: Rainbow trout, brook trout, smallmouth bass.

Highland Lake is an excellent trout and smallmouth bass lake located off Route 11 in Andover. The lake is periodically stocked by the N.H. Fish and Game Department with rainbow and brook trout. Trout anglers often hook smallmouth bass here and when they do they are treated to a fine display of the bass' fighting abilities. The bottom of the lake is composed of sand, muck and clay. The shoreline is a combination of wood and meadow. There is a good paved boat ramp just off Route 11. A fee has been charged in the past. Ice-out is usually around the last week of April.

MAP 32

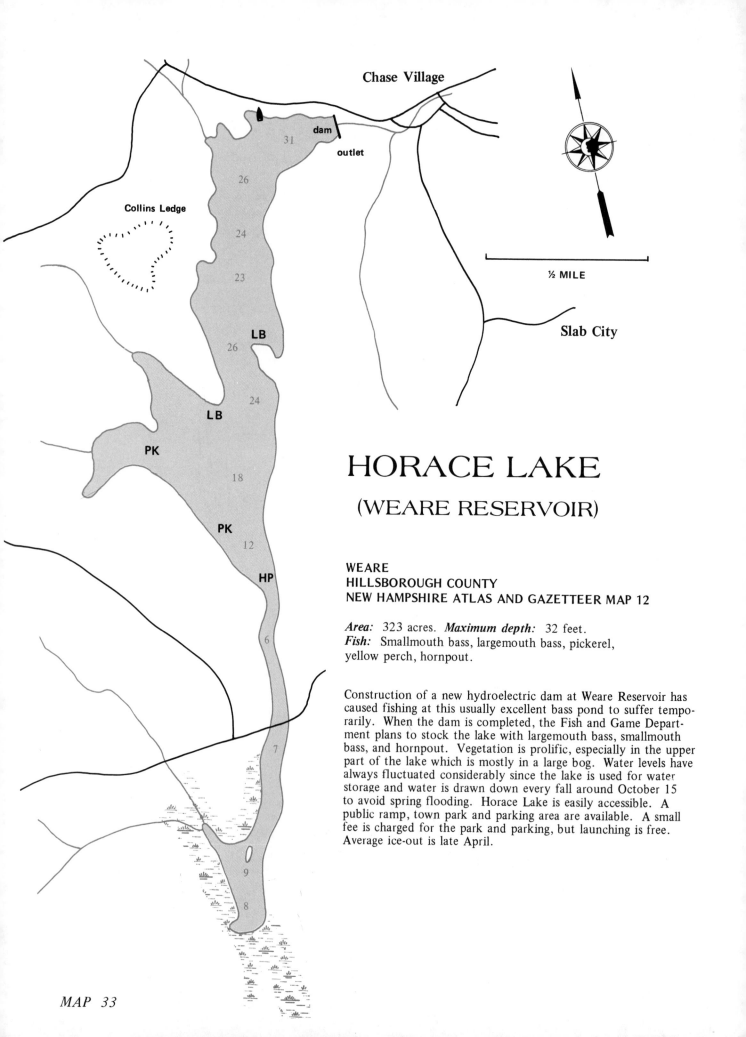

Chase Village

dam

outlet

31

26

Collins Ledge

24

23

LB

26

24

LB

PK

18

PK

12

HP

6

½ MILE

Slab City

HORACE LAKE

(WEARE RESERVOIR)

**WEARE
HILLSBOROUGH COUNTY
NEW HAMPSHIRE ATLAS AND GAZETTEER MAP 12**

Area: 323 acres. *Maximum depth:* 32 feet.
Fish: Smallmouth bass, largemouth bass, pickerel,
yellow perch, hornpout.

Construction of a new hydroelectric dam at Weare Reservoir has
caused fishing at this usually excellent bass pond to suffer tempo-
rarily. When the dam is completed, the Fish and Game Department plans to stock the lake with largemouth bass, smallmouth
bass, and hornpout. Vegetation is prolific, especially in the upper
part of the lake which is mostly in a large bog. Water levels have
always fluctuated considerably since the lake is used for water
storage and water is drawn down every fall around October 15
to avoid spring flooding. Horace Lake is easily accessible. A
public ramp, town park and parking area are available. A small
fee is charged for the park and parking, but launching is free.
Average ice-out is late April.

7

9

8

MAP 33

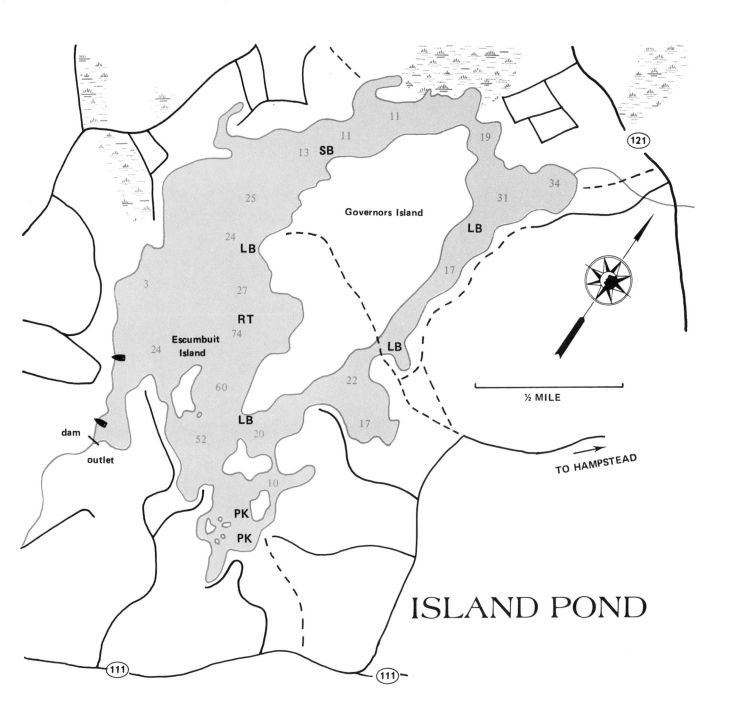

ISLAND POND

DERRY, ATKINSON, HAMPSTEAD
ROCKINGHAM COUNTY
NEW HAMPSHIRE ATLAS AND
GAZETTEER MAP 6

Area: 510 acres.
Maximum depth: 79 feet.
Fish: Brown trout, rainbow trout,
 largemouth bass, smallmouth bass,
 pickerel, yellow perch, hornpout,
 smelt.

Island Pond is a natural body of water with a large island in the middle and several smaller islands scattered about. The islands dramatically increase the fishing shoreline of this warm water bass fishing spot. The state also stocks the pond with rainbow trout and good catches have been reported. Experienced anglers here report catches of sometimes large rainbow trout. The moderately developed shoreline is mostly wooded with some swampy areas. Access to the pond is sometimes a problem because the launch site near the dam is not always open.
Average ice-out is late April.

MAP 34

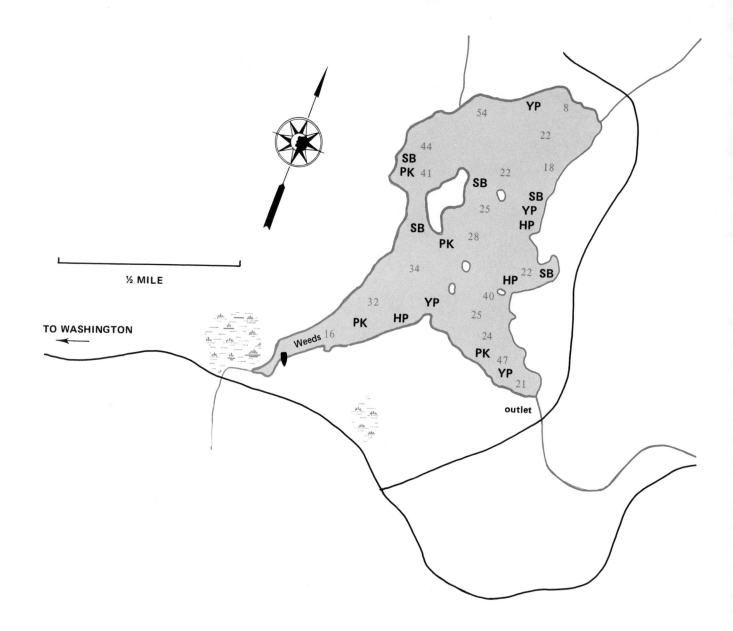

½ MILE

TO WASHINGTON

54   YP   8

22

44

SB
PK   41   SB
22
18

SB
22   YP
25   HP

SB
PK   28

34   HP   22   SB

32   YP   40

PK   HP   25

24

Weeds 16   PK   47
YP
21

outlet

ISLAND POND

WASHINGTON
SULLIVAN COUNTY
NEW HAMPSHIRE ATLAS AND GAZETTEER MAP 19

Area: 202 acres. *Maximum depth:* 54 feet.
Fish: Largemouth bass, pickerel, hornpout, yellow perch.

Located in the town of Washington off Route 31 and
south of Pillsbury State Park, Island Pond is best known
for its good bass fishing. There is only one access point
for boat launching. Launching is free, but the ramp is
in poor condition. Average ice-out is May 1.

MAP 35

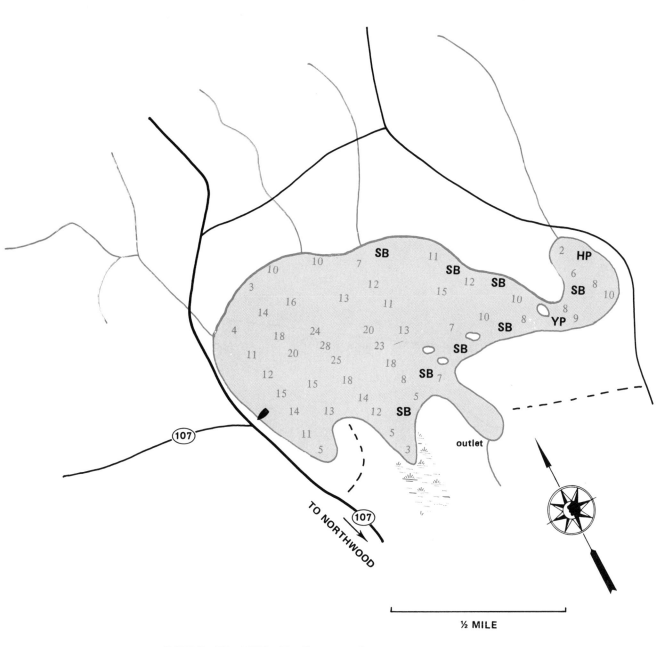

JENNESS POND

NORTHWOOD, PITTSFIELD
ROCKINGHAM COUNTY
NEW HAMPSHIRE ATLAS AND GAZETTEER MAP 22

Area: 243 acres. *Maximum depth:* 28 feet.
Fish: Smallmouth bass, pickerel, hornpout.

Jenness Pond is located just off Route 107 in Northwood. Access may
be made at a public, no-fee launch where there is a good, unpaved ramp
with some vegetation obstructing it. The shoreline is wooded with
light development and a bottom that ranges from mud to sand. The
fish are reported to be small in size due to suspected lack of feed.

MAP 36

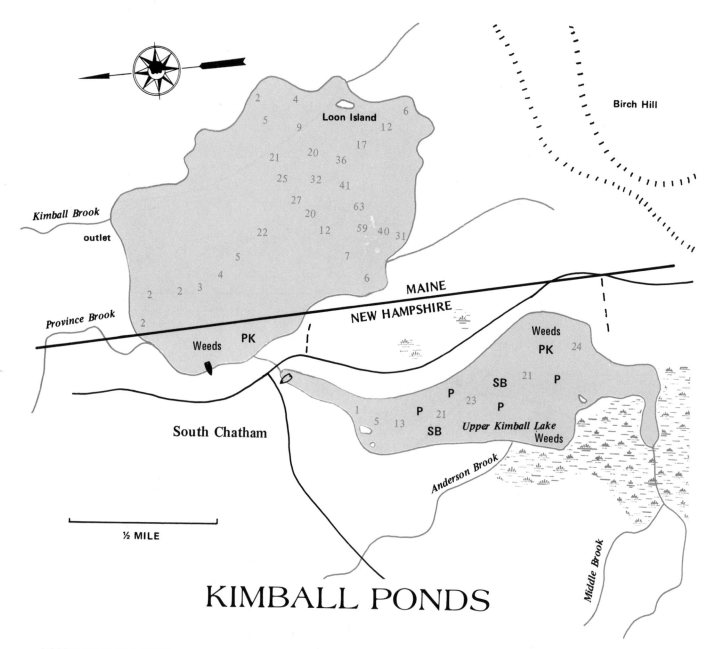

KIMBALL PONDS

**UPPER KIMBALL POND
CHATHAM, N. H.
CARROLL COUNTY
NEW HAMPSHIRE ATLAS AND GAZETTEER MAPS 42, 47**

**LOWER KIMBALL POND
FRYEBURG, MAINE
OXFORD COUNTY
MAINE ATLAS AND GAZETTEER MAP 10**

Area: 388 acres. *Maximum Depth:* 62 feet.
Fish: Smallmouth bass, white perch, pickerel, yellow perch.

Upper Kimball Pond, in South Chatham in the White Mountain National
Forest, can be reached by traveling east on the scenic Hurricane Mountain
Road from North Conway. The shoreline is undeveloped and heavily
wooded. The rugged, beautiful mountain scenery nearby makes it a very
nice spot for fishing and boating. There are also many good little trout
streams in the area which can be easily located with a topo map or by a
little exploring.

MAP 37

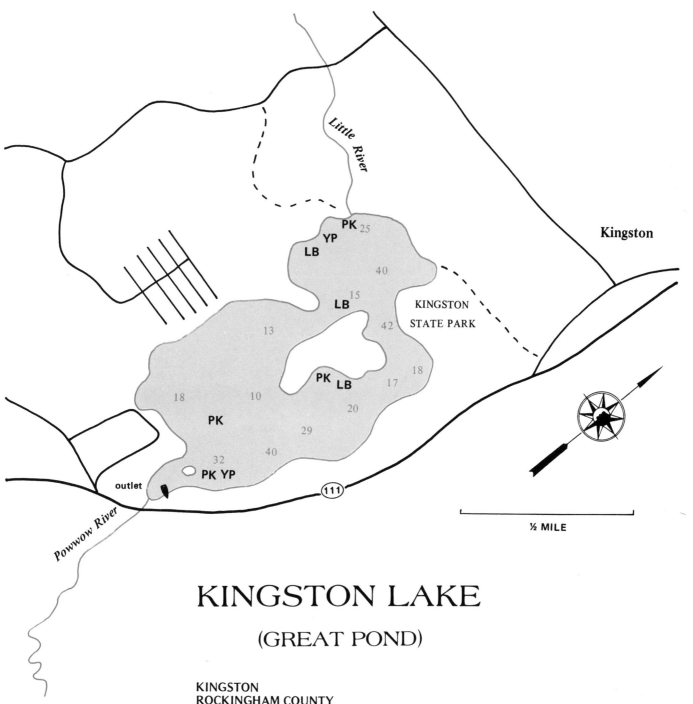

KINGSTON LAKE

(GREAT POND)

KINGSTON
ROCKINGHAM COUNTY
NEW HAMPSHIRE ATLAS AND GAZETTEER MAPS 7, 15

Area: 204 acres. *Maximum depth:* 44 feet.
Fish: Largemouth bass, pickerel, yellow perch, hornpout.

Along with Country Pond and Powwow River, Kingston Lake (also known as Great Pond) offers the bass angler some of the best bass fishing in southern N.H. Any of these three bodies of water, all in Kingston, can produce exceptional fishing and large fish. Popular Kingston State Park offers public facilities and excellent swimming. There is a free, unpaved public boat launch at the outlet. The shoreline is moderately-to-heavily developed. Average ice-out is at the end of April.

MAP 38

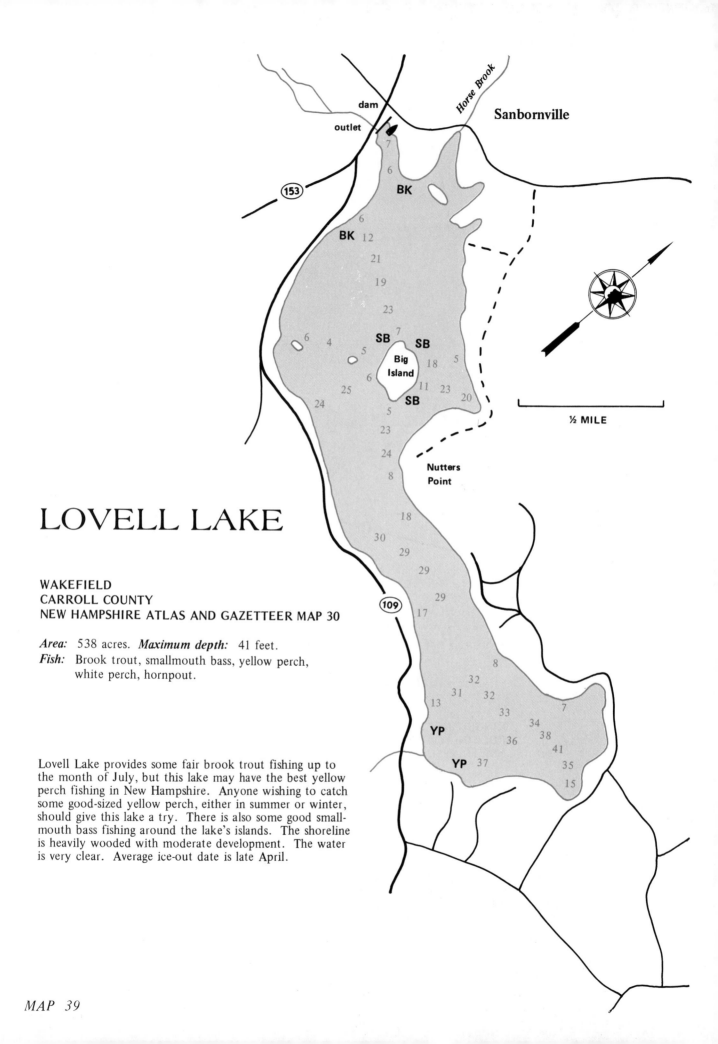

LOVELL LAKE

WAKEFIELD
CARROLL COUNTY
NEW HAMPSHIRE ATLAS AND GAZETTEER MAP 30

Area: 538 acres. *Maximum depth:* 41 feet.
Fish: Brook trout, smallmouth bass, yellow perch,
white perch, hornpout.

Lovell Lake provides some fair brook trout fishing up to
the month of July, but this lake may have the best yellow
perch fishing in New Hampshire. Anyone wishing to catch
some good-sized yellow perch, either in summer or winter,
should give this lake a try. There is also some good smallmouth bass fishing around the lake's islands. The shoreline
is heavily wooded with moderate development. The water
is very clear. Average ice-out date is late April.

½ MILE

Sanbornville

Horse Brook

dam
outlet

153

BK

BK

SB

SB
Big Island
SB

Nutters
Point

109

YP

YP

MAP 39

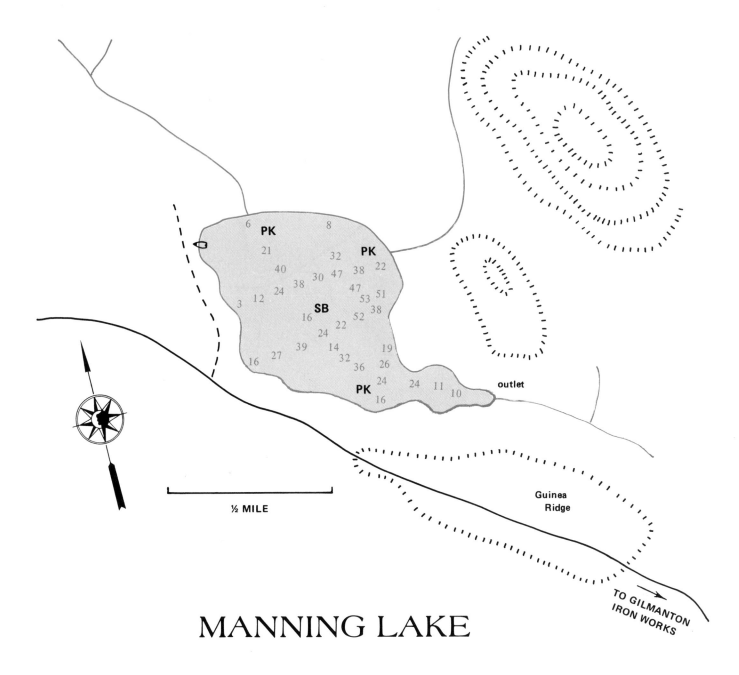

MANNING LAKE

GILMANTON
BELKNAP COUNTY
NEW HAMPSHIRE ATLAS AND GAZETTEER MAP 29

Area: 202 acres. *Maximum depth:* 56 feet.
Fish: Smallmouth bass, largemouth bass, pickerel, yellow perch, hornpout.

A natural pond near Gilmanton Iron Works, fishing in Manning Lake is confined to warm-water species. After ice-out in early May, angling picks up as the water warms and the bass begin to spawn. This is a good pond for anglers with canoes and car-top boats and for those who prefer to fish a small body of water. The shoreline is rocky and mostly undeveloped.

MAP 40

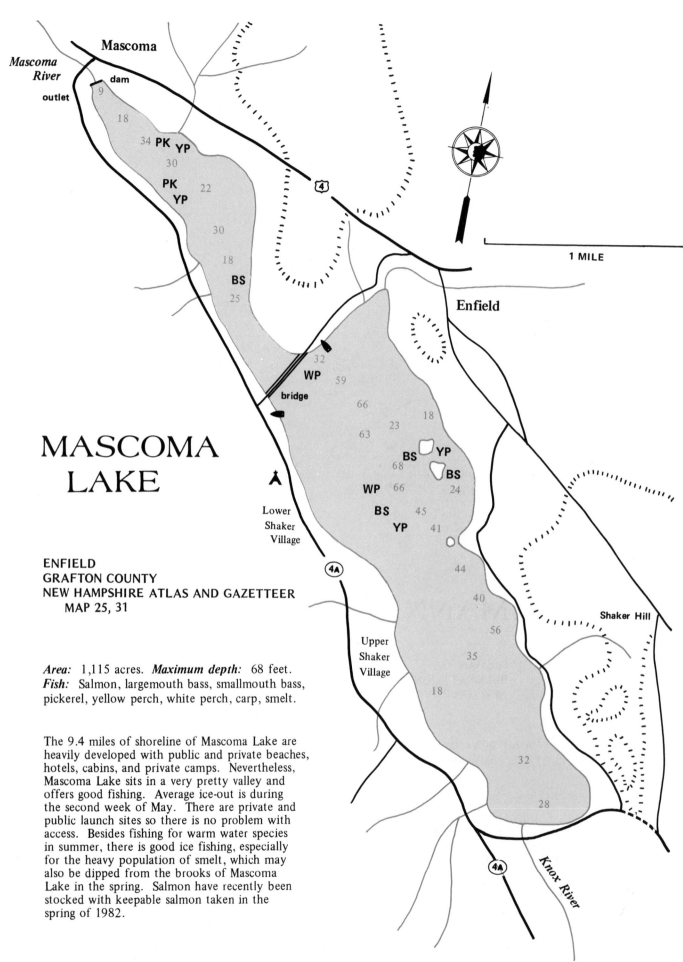

Mascoma

Mascoma River

outlet
dam
9
18
34 **PK** **YP**
30
PK
YP
22
30
18
BS
25

4

1 MILE

Enfield

32
WP 59
66
18
63 23
BS **YP**
68 **BS**
WP 66
24
BS 45
YP 41
44
40
56
Shaker Hill
35
18
32
28

bridge

MASCOMA LAKE

Lower Shaker Village

4A

Upper Shaker Village

ENFIELD
GRAFTON COUNTY
NEW HAMPSHIRE ATLAS AND GAZETTEER
MAP 25, 31

Area: 1,115 acres. *Maximum depth:* 68 feet.
Fish: Salmon, largemouth bass, smallmouth bass,
pickerel, yellow perch, white perch, carp, smelt.

The 9.4 miles of shoreline of Mascoma Lake are
heavily developed with public and private beaches,
hotels, cabins, and private camps. Nevertheless,
Mascoma Lake sits in a very pretty valley and
offers good fishing. Average ice-out is during
the second week of May. There are private and
public launch sites so there is no problem with
access. Besides fishing for warm water species
in summer, there is good ice fishing, especially
for the heavy population of smelt, which may
also be dipped from the brooks of Mascoma
Lake in the spring. Salmon have recently been
stocked with keepable salmon taken in the
spring of 1982.

4A

Knox River

MAP 41

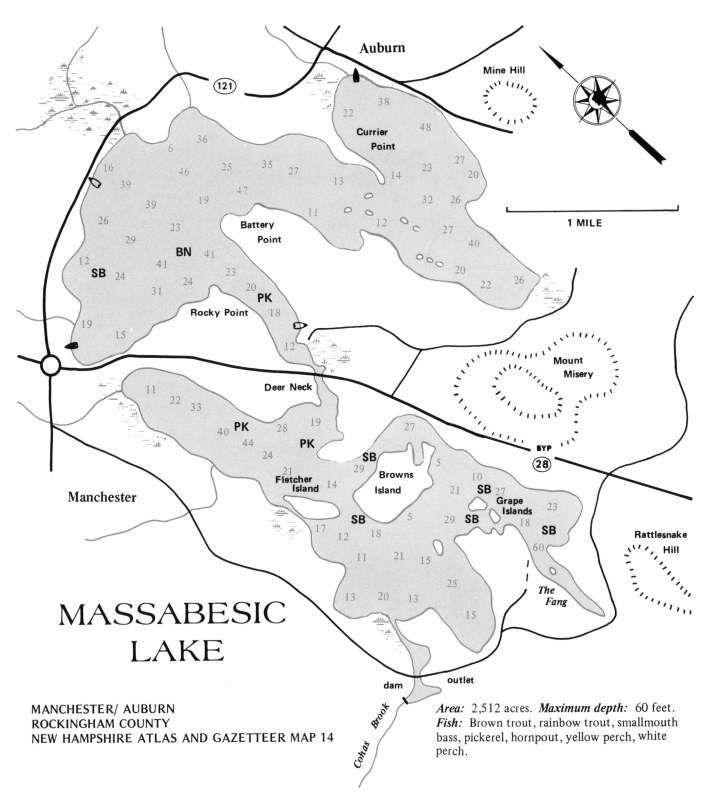

Auburn

Mine Hill

(121)

38

22

Currier
Point

48

36

6

25   35   27

16

39   46   13   14   23   27

26   39   19   47   11   12   32   26

23   Battery
Point

29   BN   41   12   27

12   SB   41   24   23   20   22

24   31   24   20   PK   18   26

19   Rocky Point   12

15

1 MILE

Mount
Misery

11   Deer Neck

22   33

40   PK   28   19   27

44   PK   24   BYP

21   SB   5   (28)

Fletcher   14   29   Browns   10

Island   Island   21   SB   27

17   SB   5   29   SB   23

12   18   18   SB

11   21   15   60   Grape
Islands

Rattlesnake
Hill

25

The
Fang

13   20   13

15

MASSABESIC
LAKE

Manchester

dam   outlet

MANCHESTER/ AUBURN
ROCKINGHAM COUNTY
NEW HAMPSHIRE ATLAS AND GAZETTEER MAP 14

Cohas Brook

Area: 2,512 acres. *Maximum depth:* 60 feet.
Fish: Brown trout, rainbow trout, smallmouth
bass, pickerel, hornpout, yellow perch, white
perch.

Massabesic Lake, located partly within N.H.'s largest city, Manchester, serves as both water supply and
scenic place to fish. The shore is undeveloped, the lake is surrounded by hills, and the water is extremely clean and clear. The rocky shore and bottom account for the above-average smallmouth bass fishing
here. Massabesic has an excellent reputation as a top-notch bass lake. The best time to fish for smallmouth bass here is in early spring just after ice-out, but good fishing is available throughout the summer.
There is also a good pickerel fishery and many large pickerel are taken here each year. Massabesic was
one of the first lakes in the state to be stocked and over the years it has been filled with everything from
lake trout to salmon. Today the only remaining cold water fish is brown trout. There are several access
points and launch sites around the lake. The lake is large enough to support many fishermen, but the
fishing pressure is very light on most days. Average ice-out date is late April.

MAP 42

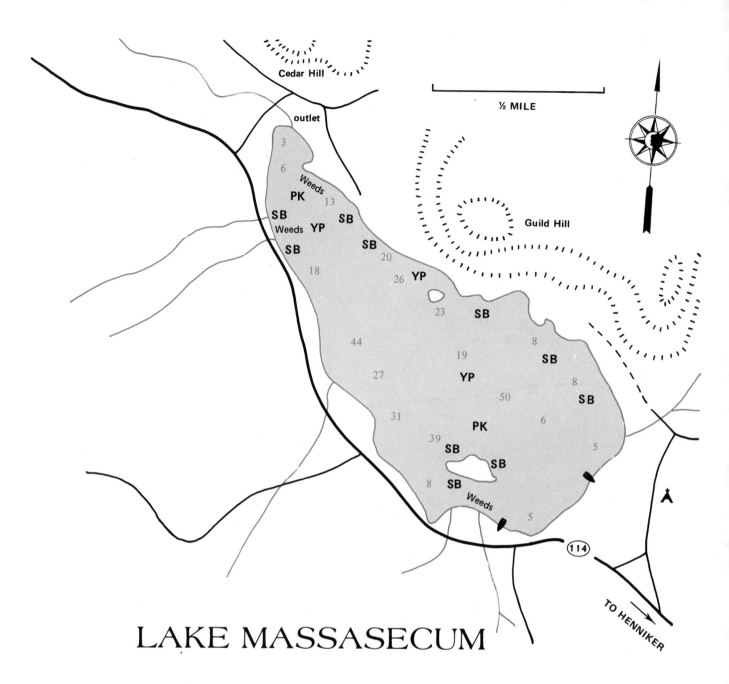

LAKE MASSASECUM

**BRADFORD
MERRIMACK COUNTY
NEW HAMPSHIRE ATLAS AND GAZETTEER MAP 19**

Area: 402 acres. *Maximum depth:* 50 feet.
Fish: Smallmouth bass, pickerel, yellow perch.

Massasecum Lake is a natural body of water just south of Bradford on Route 114. Smallmouth bass fishing here is excellent and fishermen seeking this sporty game fish should give this lake a try. With partly rocky and partly swampy shore and muddy and swampy bottom, fishing opportunities are varied. The diverse conditions and the lake's depth give good fishing all year. There is a commercial launch and a free public launch

MAP 43

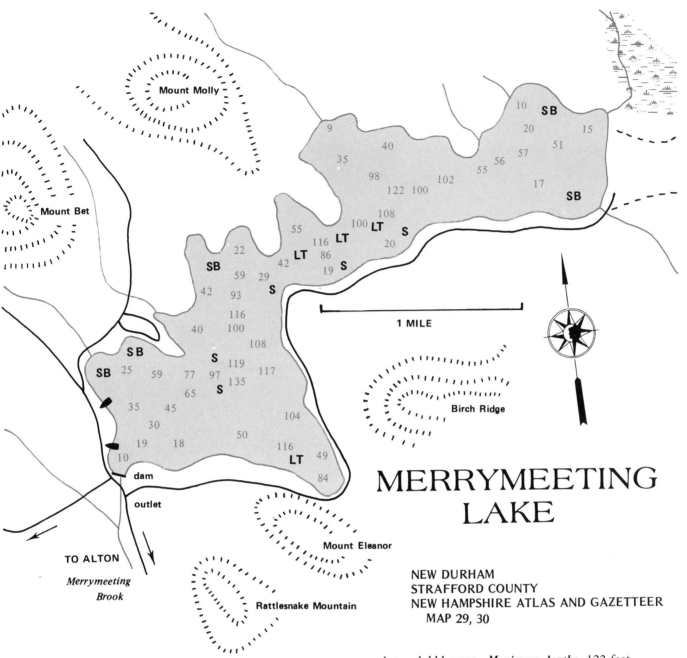

MERRYMEETING LAKE

NEW DURHAM
STRAFFORD COUNTY
NEW HAMPSHIRE ATLAS AND GAZETTEER
MAP 29, 30

Area: 1,111 acres. *Maximum depth:* 122 feet.
Fish: Salmon, lake trout, smallmouth bass, pickerel,
yellow perch, hornpout, smelt.

Located in the rugged mountains of New Durham, Merrymeeting Lake has long enjoyed
an excellent reputation as an outstanding lake for trout, salmon and smallmouth bass
fishing. Sometimes overshadowed by large Lake Winnipesaukee, Merrymeeting Lake is
often overlooked by anglers unfamiliar with its fine fishing. Average ice-out date is
late April, the best time for anglers to fish for trout and salmon. The water is cool and
the fish close to the surface in the spring so salmon and trout may be taken on light
tackle. Popular methods of taking these fish include trolling streamer flies, sewed-on
smelt and small silver and gold spoons. Anglers catching trout or salmon with a trolled
streamer fly on a fly rod will have plenty of excitement. Merrymeeting Lake also has
a good population of smallmouth bass which may be taken as the water warms in the
spring. The water transparency exceeds 22 feet and aquatic vegetation is scarce. Shoreline development is moderate.

MAP 44

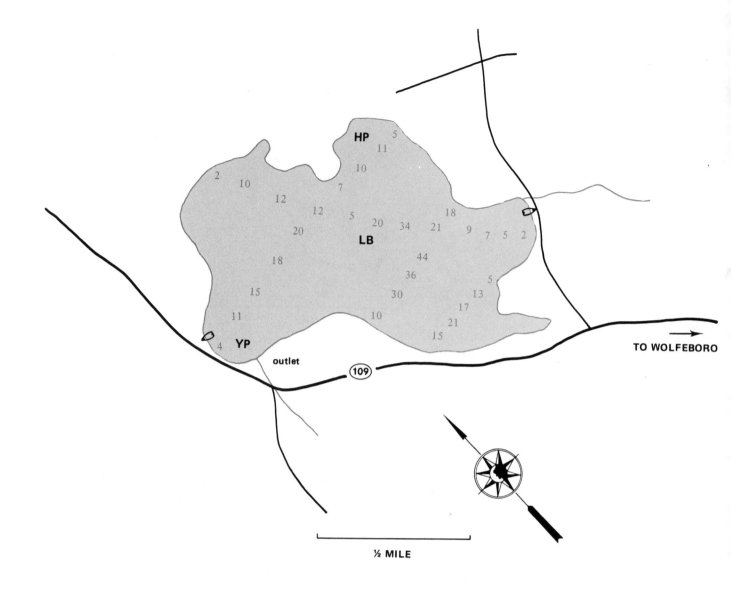

½ MILE

MIRROR LAKE

**TUFTONBORO, WOLFEBORO
CARROLL COUNTY
NEW HAMPSHIRE ATLAS AND GAZETTEER MAP 29, 35**

Area: 377 acres. *Maximum depth:* 44 feet.
Fish: Largemouth bass, yellow perch, hornpout.

Located within sight of Lake Winnipesaukee, Mirror Lake receives little
attention from fishermen. But this smaller body of water offers good
largemouth bass fishing and easy access. There are two public access
points on the lake, one of which is on Route 109. The shoreline is
moderately developed and heavily wooded. Average ice-out is late April.

MAP 45

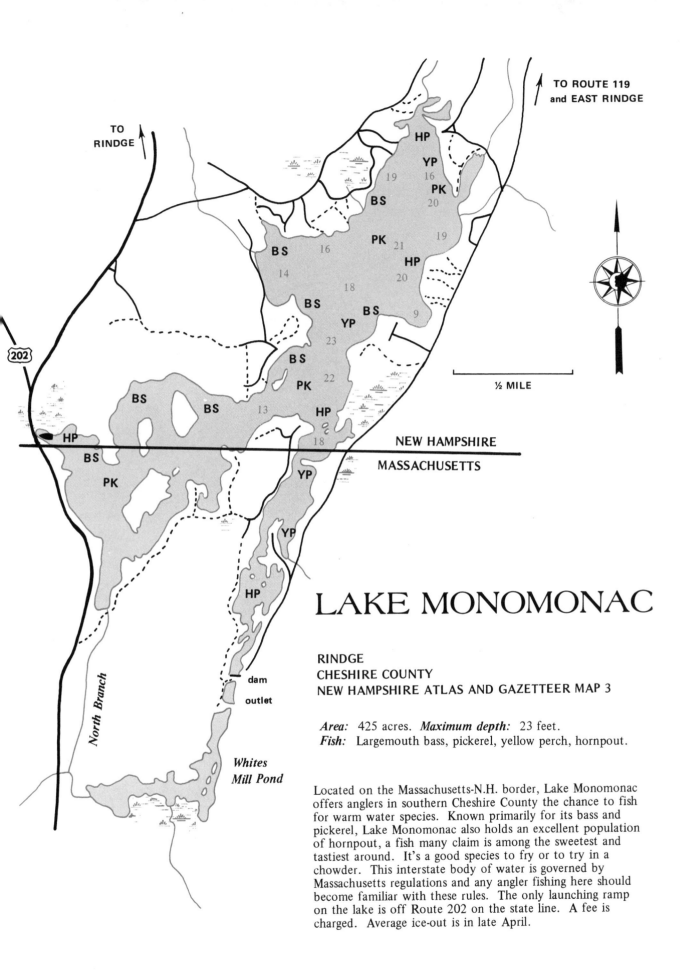

TO RINDGE

TO ROUTE 119 and EAST RINDGE

HP
YP 16
PK 20
BS 19
PK 21
HP 20
BS 19
9
BS 16
BS 14
18
BS
YP
BS 23
BS
PK 22
HP
13
BS
BS
HP 18

202

NEW HAMPSHIRE
MASSACHUSETTS

BS
PK
HP
YP

YP

HP

½ MILE

North Branch

dam

outlet

Whites Mill Pond

LAKE MONOMONAC

RINDGE
CHESHIRE COUNTY
NEW HAMPSHIRE ATLAS AND GAZETTEER MAP 3

Area: 425 acres. *Maximum depth:* 23 feet.
Fish: Largemouth bass, pickerel, yellow perch, hornpout.

Located on the Massachusetts-N.H. border, Lake Monomonac offers anglers in southern Cheshire County the chance to fish for warm water species. Known primarily for its bass and pickerel, Lake Monomonac also holds an excellent population of hornpout, a fish many claim is among the sweetest and tastiest around. It's a good species to fry or to try in a chowder. This interstate body of water is governed by Massachusetts regulations and any angler fishing here should become familiar with these rules. The only launching ramp on the lake is off Route 202 on the state line. A fee is charged. Average ice-out is in late April.

MAP 46

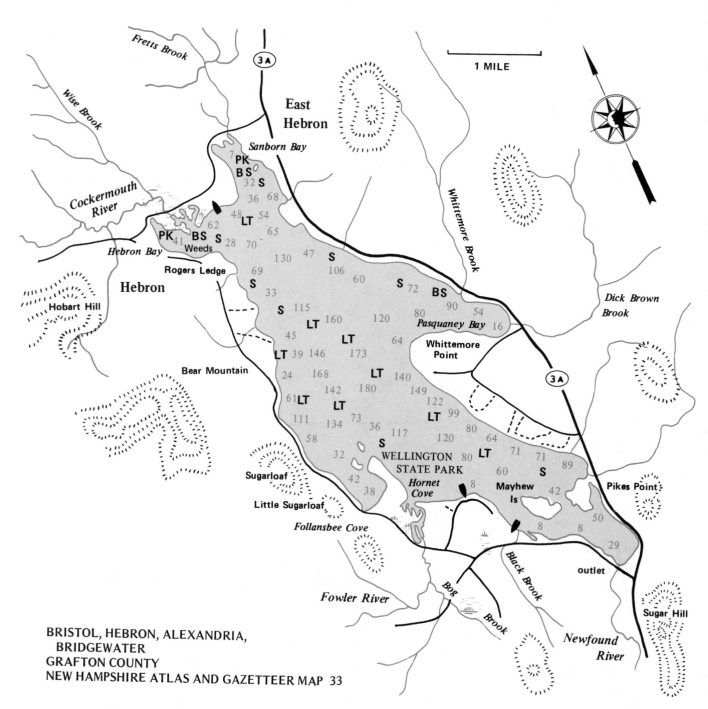

BRISTOL, HEBRON, ALEXANDRIA,
    BRIDGEWATER
GRAFTON COUNTY
NEW HAMPSHIRE ATLAS AND GAZETTEER MAP 33

Area: 4,105 acres. *Maximum depth:* 183 feet.
Fish: Salmon, lake trout, brook trout, smallmouth bass,
pickerel, yellow perch, shad, suckers, rock bass, white fish,
cusk, smelt.

NEWFOUND LAKE

Newfound Lake is one of the best-known salmon and lake trout lakes in N.H. The lake
was first stocked with salmon in 1866. The water is well-known for its exceptionally
large lake trout, and the record lake trout for the state was caught here. The waters are
crystal clear and run up to 183 feet in the center. Best fishing for lake trout and salmon
is in the upper end of the lake. The 20-mile shoreline of this natural body of water is
moderately developed; the bottom is rocky and sandy. There are three commercial boat
launches. Average ice-out is April 15.

MAP 47

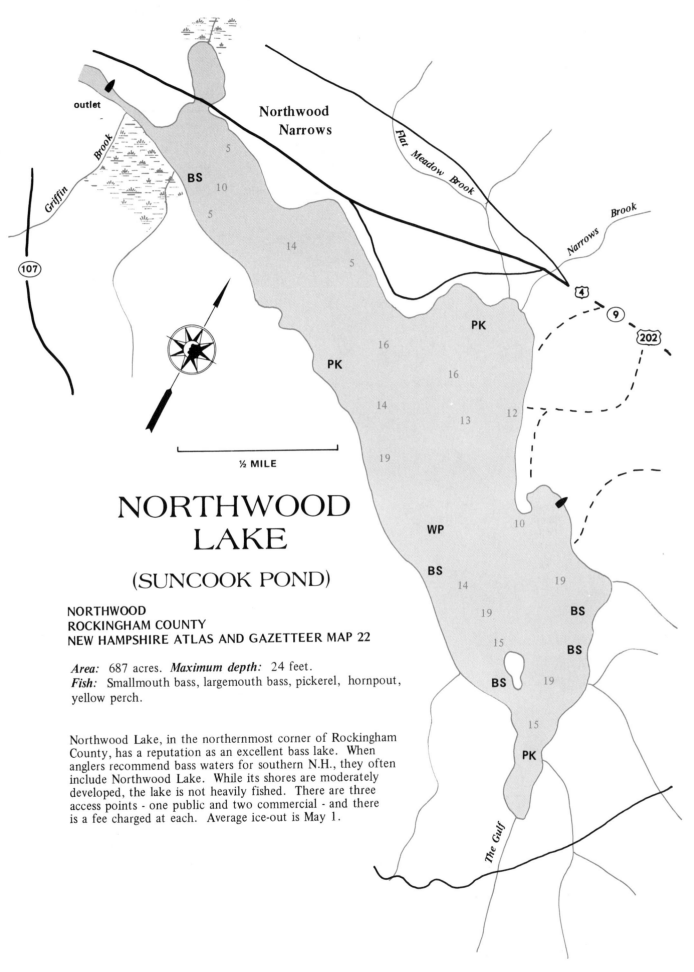

NORTHWOOD LAKE

(SUNCOOK POND)

**NORTHWOOD
ROCKINGHAM COUNTY
NEW HAMPSHIRE ATLAS AND GAZETTEER MAP 22**

Area: 687 acres. *Maximum depth:* 24 feet.
Fish: Smallmouth bass, largemouth bass, pickerel, hornpout, yellow perch.

Northwood Lake, in the northernmost corner of Rockingham County, has a reputation as an excellent bass lake. When anglers recommend bass waters for southern N.H., they often include Northwood Lake. While its shores are moderately developed, the lake is not heavily fished. There are three access points - one public and two commercial - and there is a fee charged at each. Average ice-out is May 1.

½ MILE

MAP 48

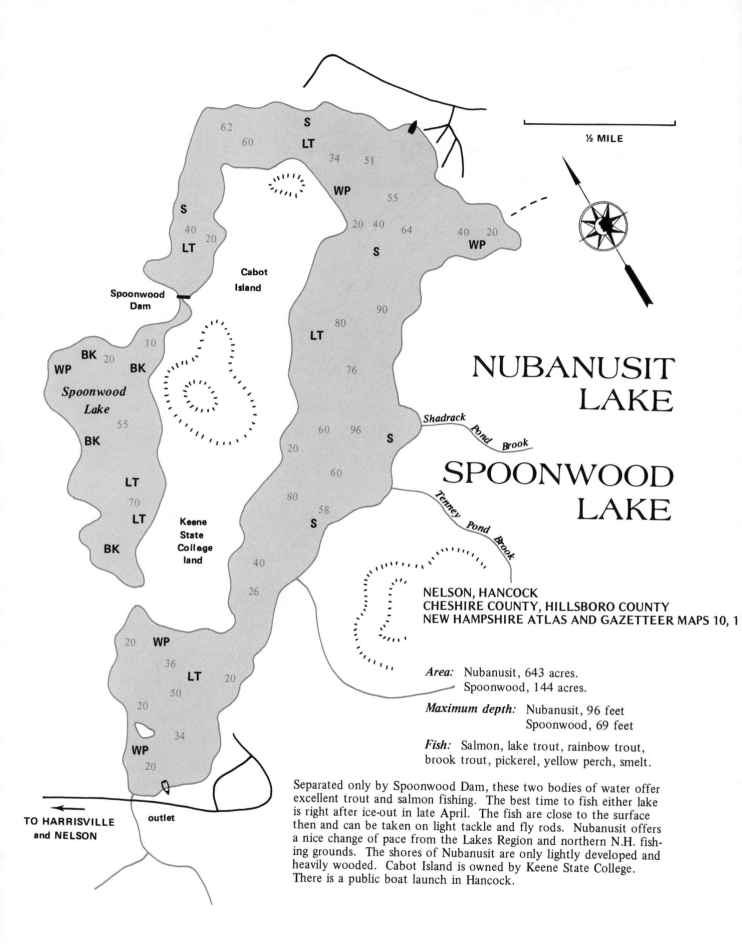

½ MILE

62
60

S
LT

34   51

WP

55

S
LT
40   20

20   40   64

S

40   20
WP

Cabot
Island

Spoonwood
Dam

90

80

LT

76

NUBANUSIT
LAKE

10

BK
20
WP   BK

Spoonwood
Lake

55

BK

Shadrack   *Pond*   *Brook*

60   96
S

60   96
20

60

LT
70

LT

BK

Keene
State
College
land

80
58
S

Tenney   Pond   Brook

SPOONWOOD
LAKE

40

26

NELSON, HANCOCK
CHESHIRE COUNTY, HILLSBORO COUNTY
NEW HAMPSHIRE ATLAS AND GAZETTEER MAPS 10, 1

20   WP

36
LT   20
50

20

34

WP

20

Area: Nubanusit, 643 acres.
Spoonwood, 144 acres.

Maximum depth: Nubanusit, 96 feet
Spoonwood, 69 feet

Fish: Salmon, lake trout, rainbow trout,
brook trout, pickerel, yellow perch, smelt.

TO HARRISVILLE
and NELSON

outlet

Separated only by Spoonwood Dam, these two bodies of water offer
excellent trout and salmon fishing. The best time to fish either lake
is right after ice-out in late April. The fish are close to the surface
then and can be taken on light tackle and fly rods. Nubanusit offers
a nice change of pace from the Lakes Region and northern N.H. fishing grounds. The shores of Nubanusit are only lightly developed and
heavily wooded. Cabot Island is owned by Keene State College.
There is a public boat launch in Hancock.

MAP 49

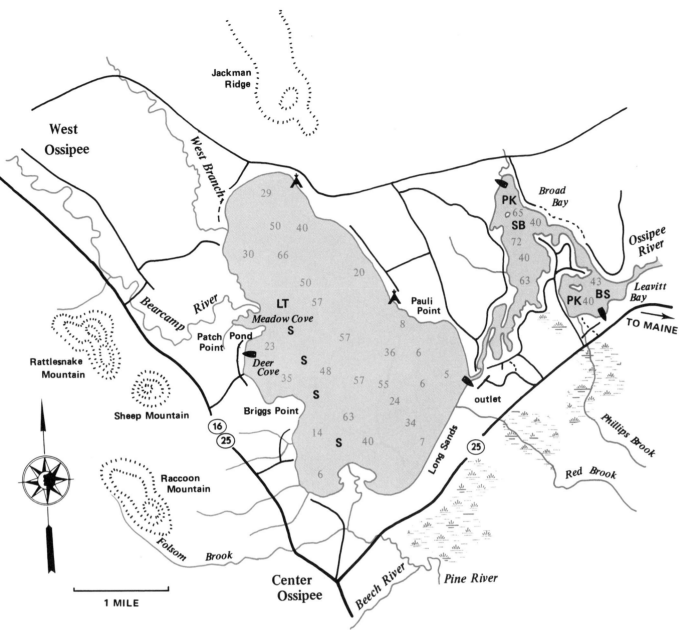

OSSIPEE LAKE

OSSIPEE, FREEDOM
CARROLL COUNTY
NEW HAMPSHIRE ATLAS AND GAZETTEER MAP 36

Area: 3,092 acres. *Maximum depth:* 61 feet.
Fish: Salmon, lake trout, brook trout, pickerel, smallmouth bass, cusk, yellow perch, suckers, hornpout, smelt.

Ossipee Lake, Leavitt Bay and Broad Bay may be best described as a large sandbowl filled with water. This lake is known primarily for its good salmon fishing, but also has good populations of warm water game fish. Good salmon fishing may be had in the spring off the Bearcamp River because of the large run of smelt in the river in early to mid-April. During the summer, drifted bait in the center of the lake will take salmon. While Leavitt Bay and Broad Bay do have some lake trout, the fishing is poor. Trout fishing is best confined to Ossipee Lake itself. However, the two bays offer good fishing for perch and pickerel. Pickerel and perch fishing is also good in the 600-acre shoal in the southern portion of Ossipee Lake. There is a public launch site on the eastern shore of the lake. A fee is charged for parking. Average ice-out is mid-April.

MAP 50

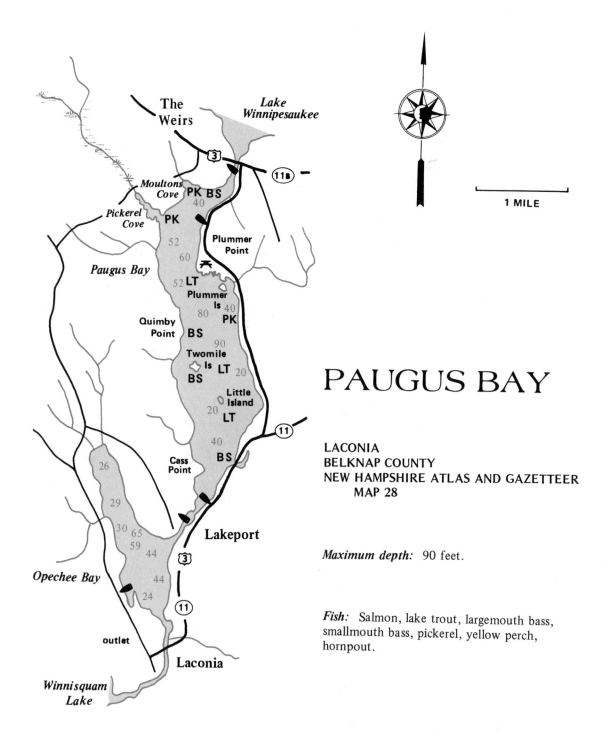

PAUGUS BAY

LACONIA
BELKNAP COUNTY
NEW HAMPSHIRE ATLAS AND GAZETTEER
MAP 28

Maximum depth: 90 feet.

Fish: Salmon, lake trout, largemouth bass, smallmouth bass, pickerel, yellow perch, hornpout.

Paugus Bay sits between Lake Winnipesaukee to the north and Winnisquam Lake to the south, connected to each by a narrow neck of water. Although it is called a bay, Paugus's size and depth would qualify it as a lake. Its uniformly deep, well-oxygenated waters provide lake trout and salmon fishing. In the summer, Paugus is used heavily for recreational boating. To avoid traffic, fish early in the morning and late in the evening. The best time to fish Paugus for lake trout and salmon is spring just after ice-out in late April. Bass fishing holds up all year. Because ice-out on Paugus is a little earlier than on neighboring waters, it ranks as a popular place to catch that first trout or salmon of the season. Located in the heart of the Lakes Region, accommodations, services and supplies are readily available in the area. Access points to the bay are plentiful.

MAP 51

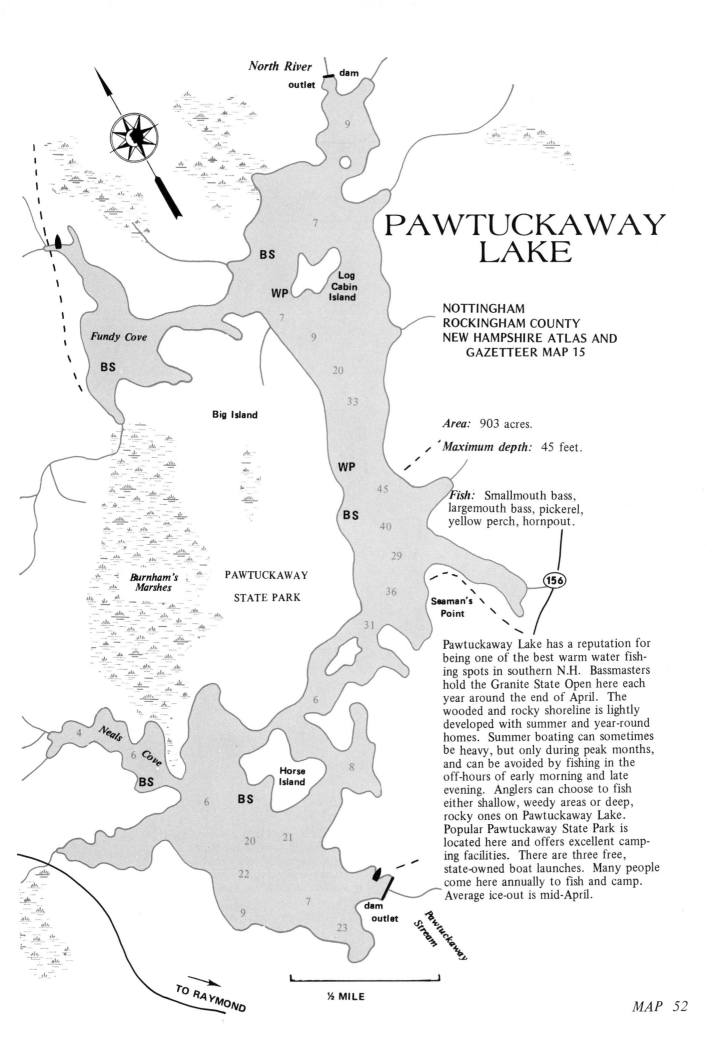

North River
outlet — dam

9

PAWTUCKAWAY LAKE

NOTTINGHAM
ROCKINGHAM COUNTY
NEW HAMPSHIRE ATLAS AND
GAZETTEER MAP 15

7

BS

WP

Log
Cabin
Island

7

9

20

33

Fundy Cove

BS

Big Island

Area: 903 acres.

Maximum depth: 45 feet.

WP

45

BS

40

29

36

31

Fish: Smallmouth bass,
largemouth bass, pickerel,
yellow perch, hornpout.

156

Seaman's
Point

Burnham's
Marshes

PAWTUCKAWAY
STATE PARK

6

Pawtuckaway Lake has a reputation for
being one of the best warm water fishing spots in southern N.H. Bassmasters
hold the Granite State Open here each
year around the end of April. The
wooded and rocky shoreline is lightly
developed with summer and year-round
homes. Summer boating can sometimes
be heavy, but only during peak months,
and can be avoided by fishing in the
off-hours of early morning and late
evening. Anglers can choose to fish
either shallow, weedy areas or deep,
rocky ones on Pawtuckaway Lake.
Popular Pawtuckaway State Park is
located here and offers excellent camping facilities. There are three free,
state-owned boat launches. Many people
come here annually to fish and camp.
Average ice-out is mid-April.

4

Neals

6

Cove

BS

Horse
Island

8

6

BS

20

21

22

7

9

23

dam
outlet

Pawtuckaway Stream

TO RAYMOND

½ MILE

MAP 52

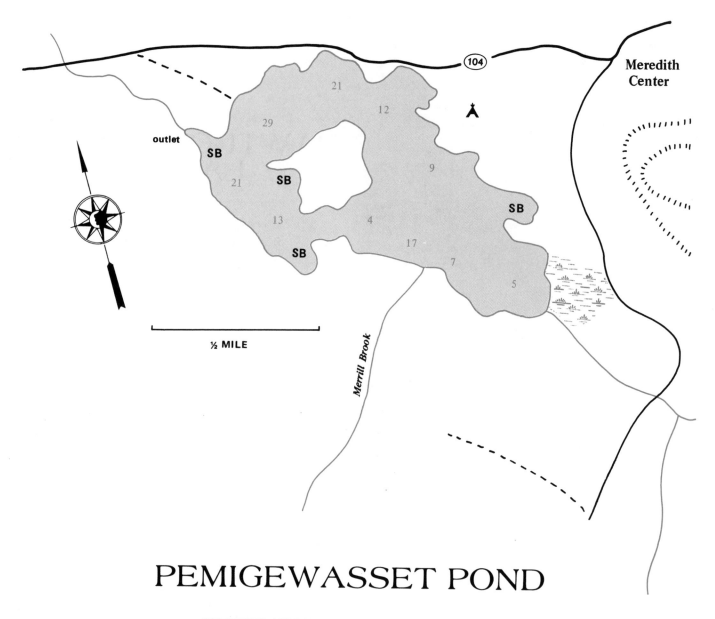

PEMIGEWASSET POND

MEREDITH, NEW HAMPTON
BELKNAP COUNTY
NEW HAMPSHIRE ATLAS AND GAZETTEER MAP 28

Area: 241 acres. *Maximum depth:* 30 feet.
Fish: Smallmouth bass, pickerel, yellow perch, hornpout.

Located in the heart of the New Hampshire Lakes Region, Pemigewasset Pond is noted for its above-average bass fishing. The pond is located off Route 104 between Interstate 93 and the town of Meredith. It can be easily fished by canoe, car-top boat or larger, trailered boats if the angler desires. Fishing remains good throughout the entire fishing season, beginning in May and ending around October.

MAP 53

PINE RIVER POND

WAKEFIELD
CARROLL COUNTY
NEW HAMPSHIRE ATLAS AND GAZETTEER MAPS 30, 36

Area: 593 acres. *Maximum depth:* 61 feet.
Fish: Pickerel, yellow perch, hornpout.

Pine River Pond was formed when a dam was
placed on Pine River. Although Pine River is
noted for being a top-notch brook trout stream,
the pond is probably one of the best pickerel
ponds in the state. The best fishing is found in
the lower eastern portion of the pond. Although
pickerel may be taken by many means, slowly
trolled lures have been successful on this pond.
Pickerel up to three feet long and weighing
six to seven pounds have been caught here.

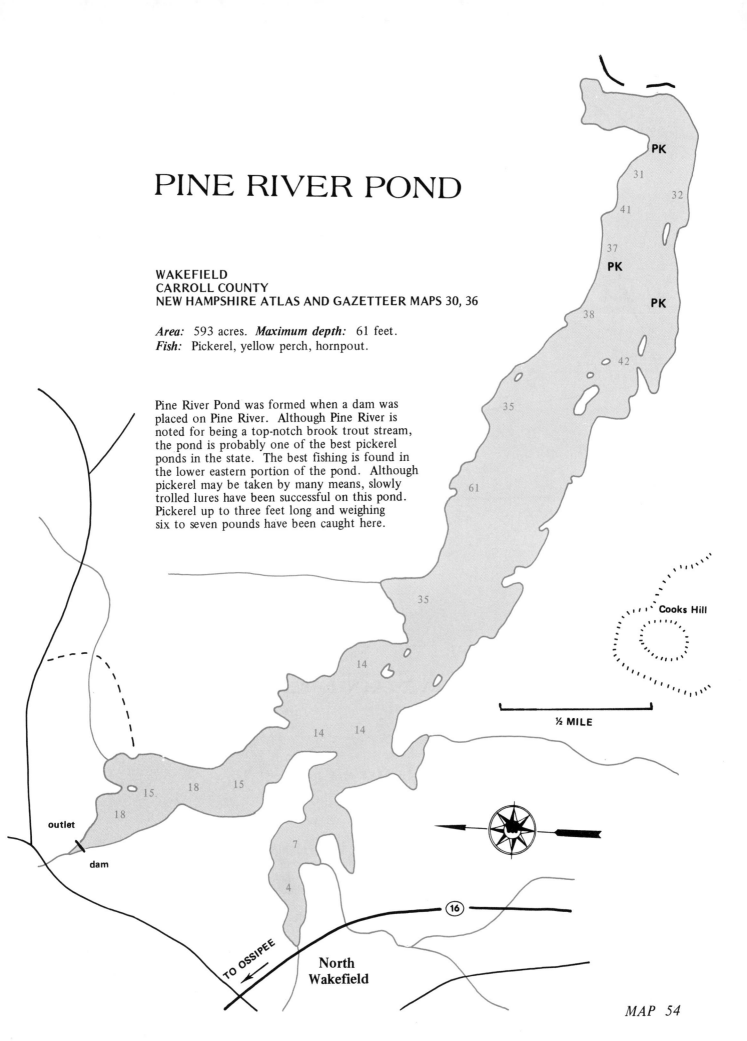

PK

31

32

41

37

PK

PK

38

42

35

61

35

14

14

14

15

18

15

15

18

outlet

dam

7

4

Cooks Hill

½ MILE

16

**North
Wakefield**

TO OSSIPEE

MAP 54

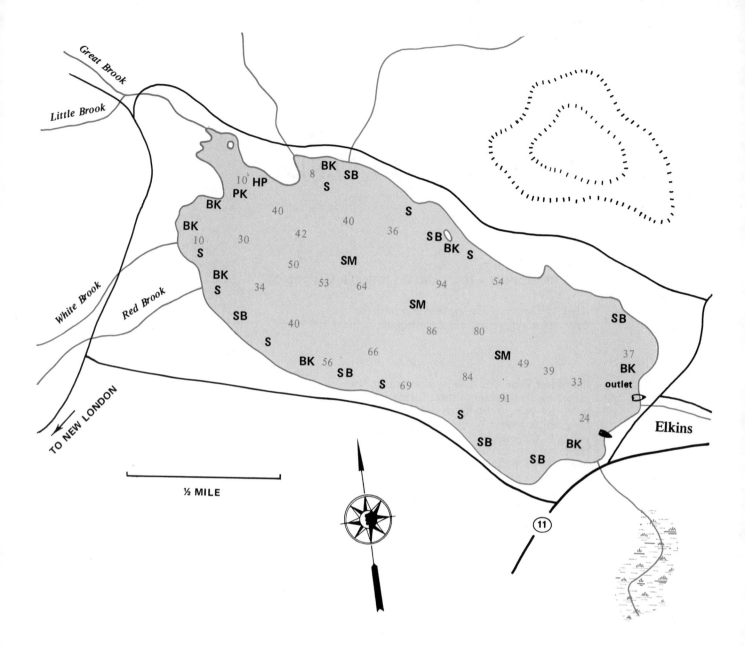

PLEASANT LAKE

NEW LONDON
MERRIMACK COUNTY
NEW HAMPSHIRE ATLAS AND GAZETTEER MAP 26

Area: 606 acres. *Maximum depth:* 91 feet.
Fish: Salmon, brook trout, smallmouth bass, pickerel, yellow perch, hornpout, smelt.

Pleasant Lake is one of the best trout and salmon waters in the state. The current New Hampshire records for both salmon and brook trout have come from Pleasant Lake. And, in the past, this lake also held the smallmouth bass record. This is certainly a distinction for any body of water and indicates the lake's excellent fishing potential. The 4.5-mile shoreline is wooded and rocky and moderately developed. There is a commercial launch site with gas and concessions and a free, state-owned launch. Average ice-out is May 1.

MAP 55

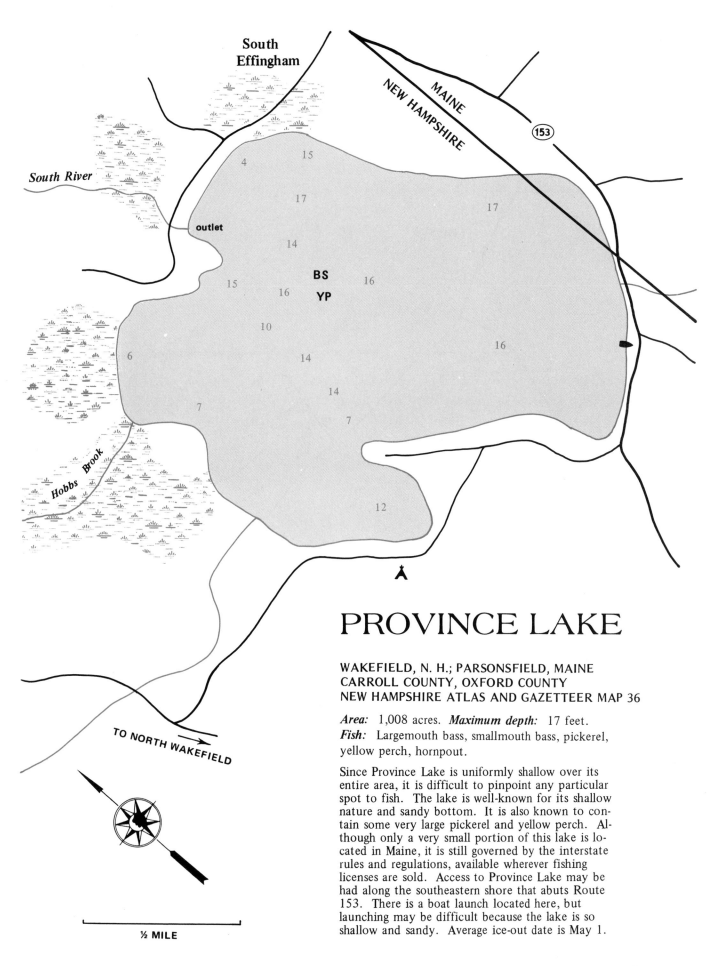

South
Effingham

MAINE

NEW HAMPSHIRE

153

South River

4   15

17

outlet

17

14

BS
YP

15

16   16

10

16

6

14

7

14

14

7

Hobbs Brook

16

12

TO NORTH WAKEFIELD

½ MILE

PROVINCE LAKE

WAKEFIELD, N. H.; PARSONSFIELD, MAINE
CARROLL COUNTY, OXFORD COUNTY
NEW HAMPSHIRE ATLAS AND GAZETTEER MAP 36

Area: 1,008 acres. *Maximum depth:* 17 feet.
Fish: Largemouth bass, smallmouth bass, pickerel, yellow perch, hornpout.

Since Province Lake is uniformly shallow over its entire area, it is difficult to pinpoint any particular spot to fish. The lake is well-known for its shallow nature and sandy bottom. It is also known to contain some very large pickerel and yellow perch. Although only a very small portion of this lake is located in Maine, it is still governed by the interstate rules and regulations, available wherever fishing licenses are sold. Access to Province Lake may be had along the southeastern shore that abuts Route 153. There is a boat launch located here, but launching may be difficult because the lake is so shallow and sandy. Average ice-out date is May 1.

MAP 56

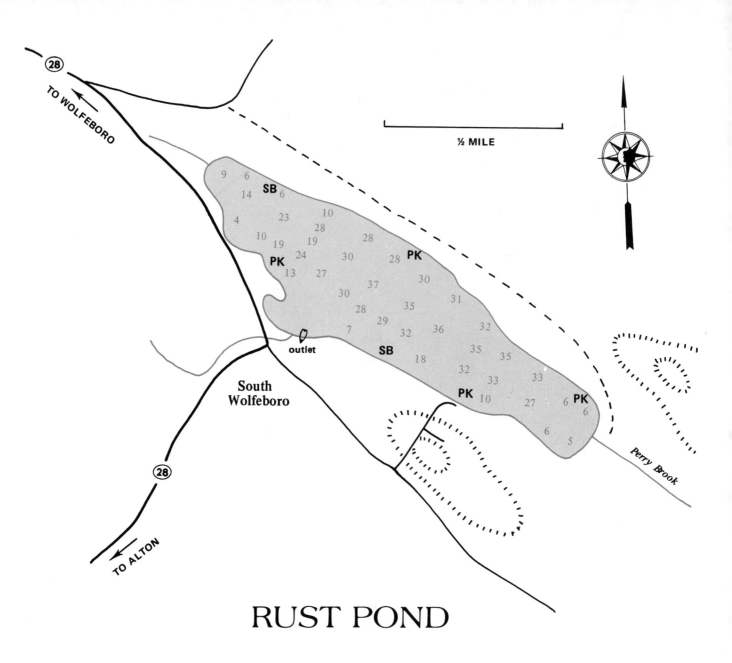

RUST POND

RUST POND
WOLFEBORO
CARROLL COUNTY
NEW HAMPSHIRE ATLAS AND GAZETTEER MAP 29, 30

Area: 210 acres. *Maximum depth:* 39 feet.
Fish: Smallmouth bass, pickerel, yellow perch.

Rust Pond is a good alternative to busy Lake Winnipesaukee and Lake Wentworth which are often very windy and heavily laden with boat traffic. Located south of Wolfeboro on Route 28 between the two larger lakes, Rust Pond is a good place to fish for smallmouth bass and pickerel from a canoe or small, car-top boat. The lightly developed shoreline is mostly wooded, but there are some meadows. There is public access to this pond at South Wolfeboro. Average ice-out is by late April.

MAP 57

SILVER LAKE

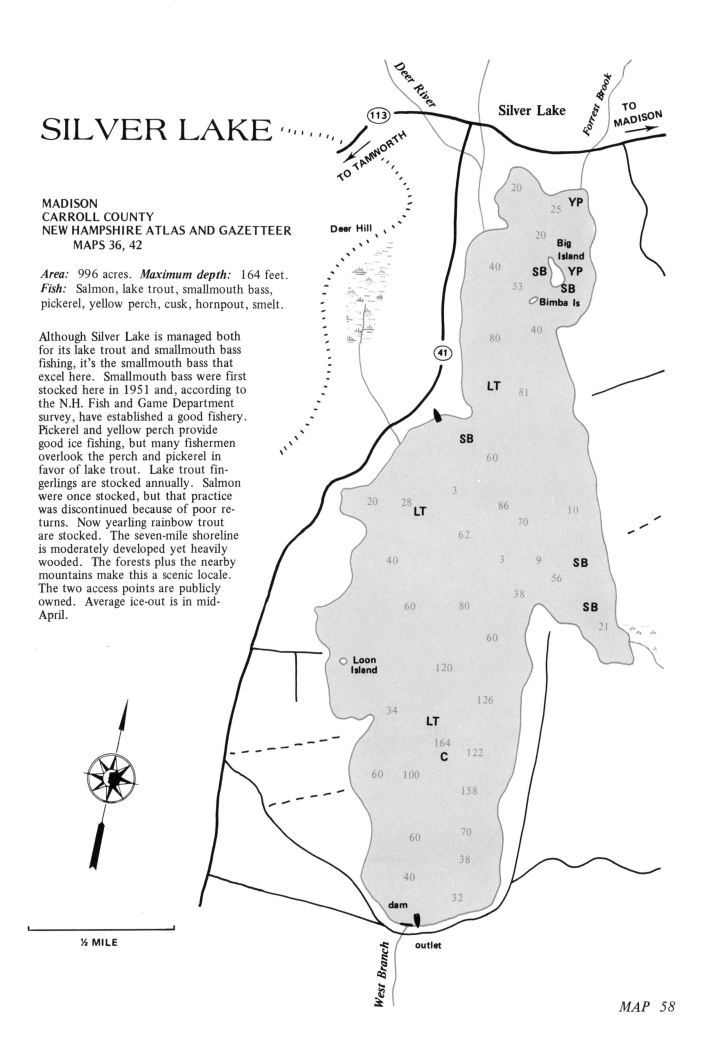

MADISON
CARROLL COUNTY
NEW HAMPSHIRE ATLAS AND GAZETTEER
MAPS 36, 42

Area: 996 acres. *Maximum depth:* 164 feet.
Fish: Salmon, lake trout, smallmouth bass,
pickerel, yellow perch, cusk, hornpout, smelt.

Although Silver Lake is managed both
for its lake trout and smallmouth bass
fishing, it's the smallmouth bass that
excel here. Smallmouth bass were first
stocked here in 1951 and, according to
the N.H. Fish and Game Department
survey, have established a good fishery.
Pickerel and yellow perch provide
good ice fishing, but many fishermen
overlook the perch and pickerel in
favor of lake trout. Lake trout fin-
gerlings are stocked annually. Salmon
were once stocked, but that practice
was discontinued because of poor returns. Now yearling rainbow trout
are stocked. The seven-mile shoreline
is moderately developed yet heavily
wooded. The forests plus the nearby
mountains make this a scenic locale.
The two access points are publicly
owned. Average ice-out is in mid-
April.

½ MILE

Deer River

113

TO TAMWORTH

Deer Hill

41

Silver Lake

Forrest Brook

TO MADISON

20
25 YP
20
40 Big Island
SB YP
53 SB
Bimba Is
40
80
LT 81
SB
60
20 28 LT 3
86 10
70
62
40 3 9 SB
56
38 SB
60 80 21
60
Loon Island
120
126
34
LT
164
C 122
60 100
158
60 70
38
40
32
dam
outlet
West Branch

MAP 58

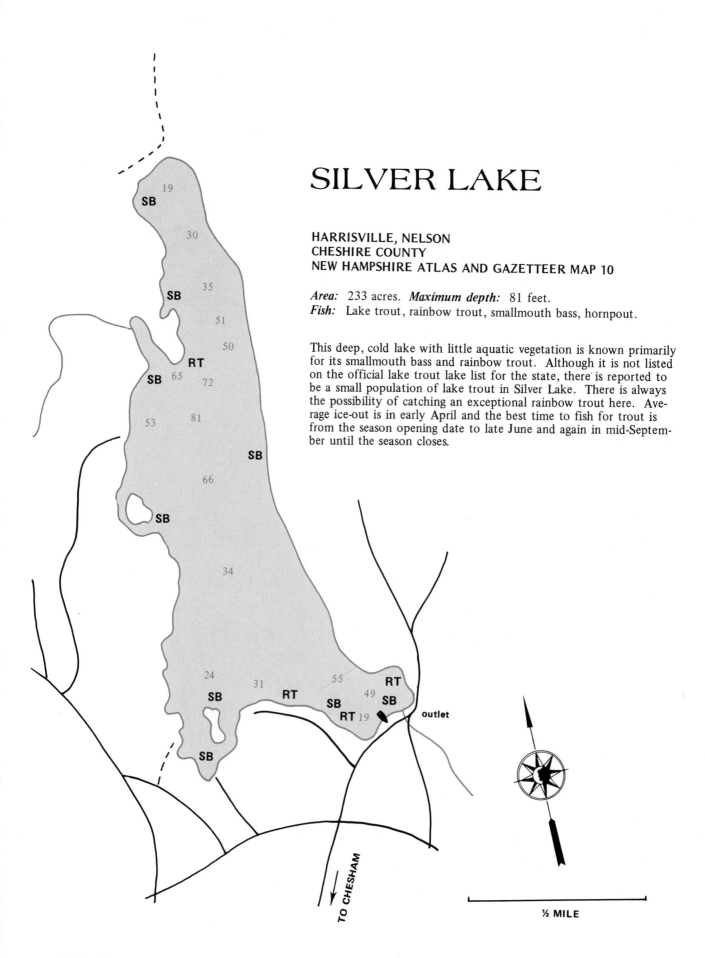

SILVER LAKE

HARRISVILLE, NELSON
CHESHIRE COUNTY
NEW HAMPSHIRE ATLAS AND GAZETTEER MAP 10

Area: 233 acres. *Maximum depth:* 81 feet.
Fish: Lake trout, rainbow trout, smallmouth bass, hornpout.

This deep, cold lake with little aquatic vegetation is known primarily for its smallmouth bass and rainbow trout. Although it is not listed on the official lake trout lake list for the state, there is reported to be a small population of lake trout in Silver Lake. There is always the possibility of catching an exceptional rainbow trout here. Average ice-out is in early April and the best time to fish for trout is from the season opening date to late June and again in mid-September until the season closes.

outlet

TO CHESHAM

½ MILE

MAP 59

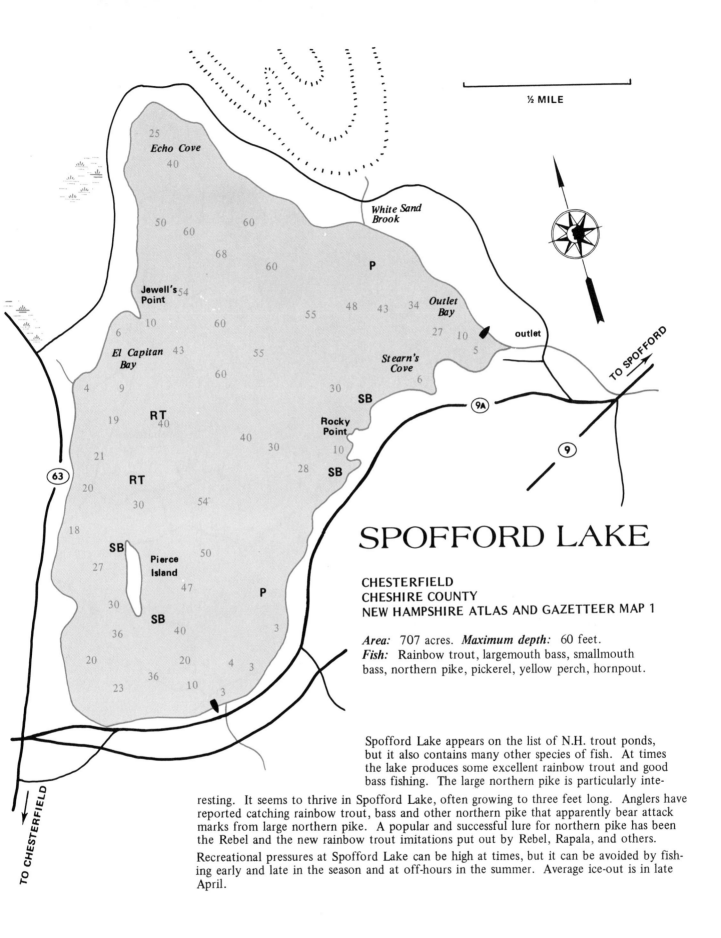

SPOFFORD LAKE

CHESTERFIELD
CHESHIRE COUNTY
NEW HAMPSHIRE ATLAS AND GAZETTEER MAP 1

Area: 707 acres. *Maximum depth:* 60 feet.
Fish: Rainbow trout, largemouth bass, smallmouth
bass, northern pike, pickerel, yellow perch, hornpout.

Spofford Lake appears on the list of N.H. trout ponds,
but it also contains many other species of fish. At times
the lake produces some excellent rainbow trout and good
bass fishing. The large northern pike is particularly inte-
resting. It seems to thrive in Spofford Lake, often growing to three feet long. Anglers have
reported catching rainbow trout, bass and other northern pike that apparently bear attack
marks from large northern pike. A popular and successful lure for northern pike has been
the Rebel and the new rainbow trout imitations put out by Rebel, Rapala, and others.

Recreational pressures at Spofford Lake can be high at times, but it can be avoided by fishing early and late in the season and at off-hours in the summer. Average ice-out is in late
April.

MAP 60

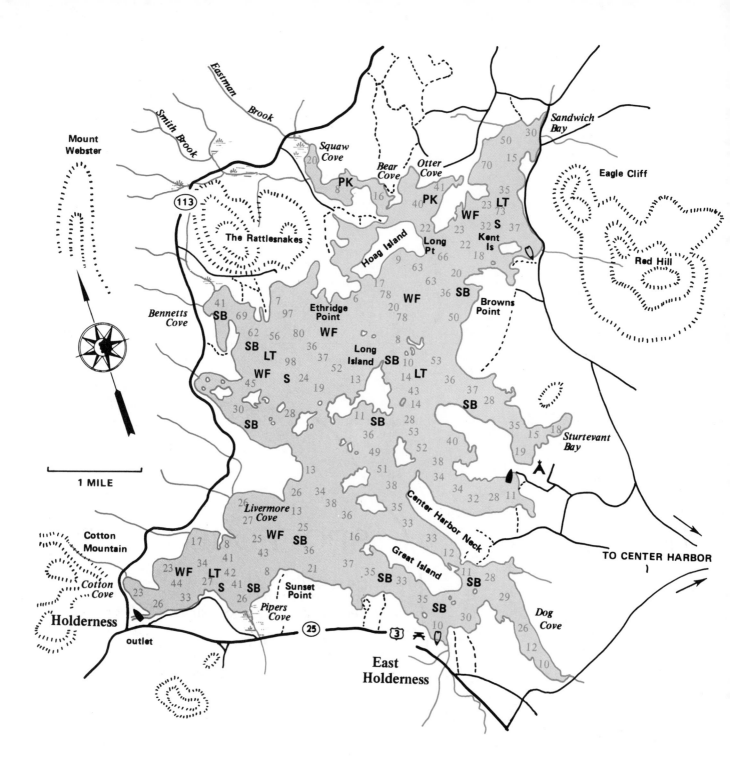

SQUAM LAKE

HOLDERNESS, CENTER HARBOR, SANDWICH,
  MOULTONBORO
CARROLL COUNTY, GRAFTON COUNTY
NEW HAMPSHIRE ATLAS AND GAZETTEER
  MAP 34

Area: 6,765 acres. *Maximum depth:* 98 feet.
Fish: Salmon, lake trout, smallmouth bass,
    pickerel, white perch, yellow perch,
    hornpout, whitefish, cusk, smelt.

Squam Lake is known for its salmon and lake trout.
There are also good populations of smallmouth bass
and pickerel in the shallow areas. The lake is a natural body of water raised by a dam on the Little
Squam River. The 61-mile shoreline is rocky and
wooded with moderate development. The bottom
is typical of a northern, cold water lake - sandy,
gravelly, and rocky. Squam is a picturesque lake
and, in summer, it is busy with boat traffic. There
are several launch sites.

MAP 61

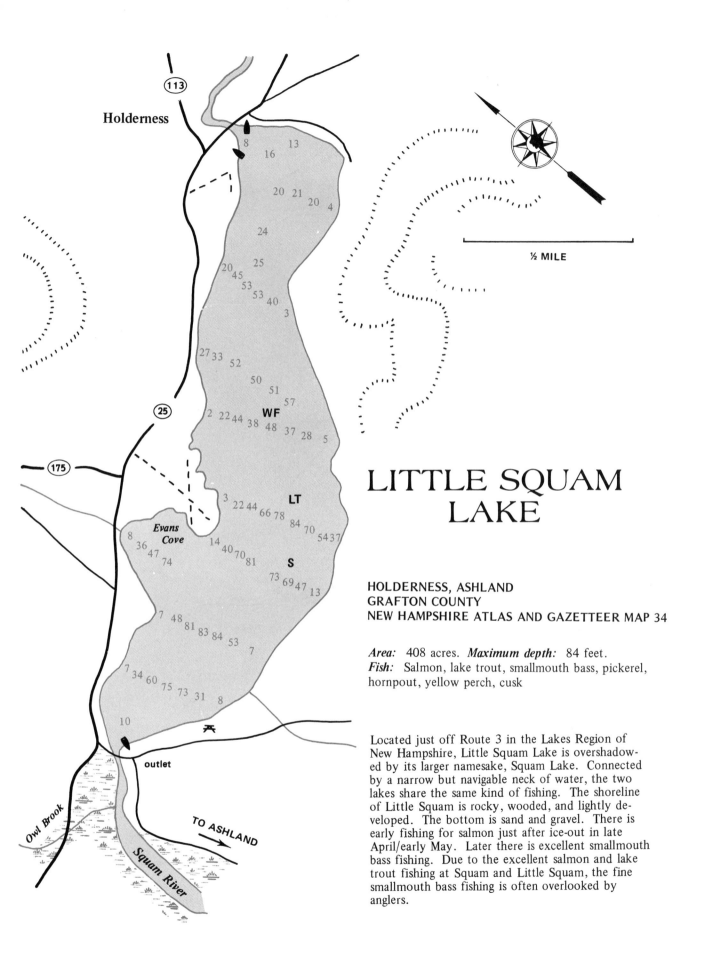

LITTLE SQUAM LAKE

**HOLDERNESS, ASHLAND
GRAFTON COUNTY
NEW HAMPSHIRE ATLAS AND GAZETTEER MAP 34**

Area: 408 acres. *Maximum depth:* 84 feet.
Fish: Salmon, lake trout, smallmouth bass, pickerel, hornpout, yellow perch, cusk

Located just off Route 3 in the Lakes Region of New Hampshire, Little Squam Lake is overshadowed by its larger namesake, Squam Lake. Connected by a narrow but navigable neck of water, the two lakes share the same kind of fishing. The shoreline of Little Squam is rocky, wooded, and lightly developed. The bottom is sand and gravel. There is early fishing for salmon just after ice-out in late April/early May. Later there is excellent smallmouth bass fishing. Due to the excellent salmon and lake trout fishing at Squam and Little Squam, the fine smallmouth bass fishing is often overlooked by anglers.

MAP 62

STINSON LAKE

RUMNEY, ELLSWORTH
GRAFTON COUNTY
NEW HAMPSHIRE ATLAS AND GAZETTEER MAP 39

Area: 346 acres. *Maximum depth:* 75 feet.
Fish: Rainbow trout, brook trout, lake trout, cusk, smelt, yellow perch, pickerel, smallmouth bass, white suckers, fallfish.

Located in the White Mountain National Forest, Stinson Lake is nevertheless accessible from Interstate 93 or Route 25. Access to the lake is by a private, paved boat ramp. A fee is charged. The lake shore is entirely wooded and there is no development. Ice-out can be expected in late April/early May. Stinson Lake is open for ice fishing and gives the angler an opportunity to seek trout, yellow perch, and pickerel through the ice. Excellent results have been reported. It is usually illegal to use powered boats in White Mountain National Forest waters, but Stinson Lake is an exception.

MAP 63

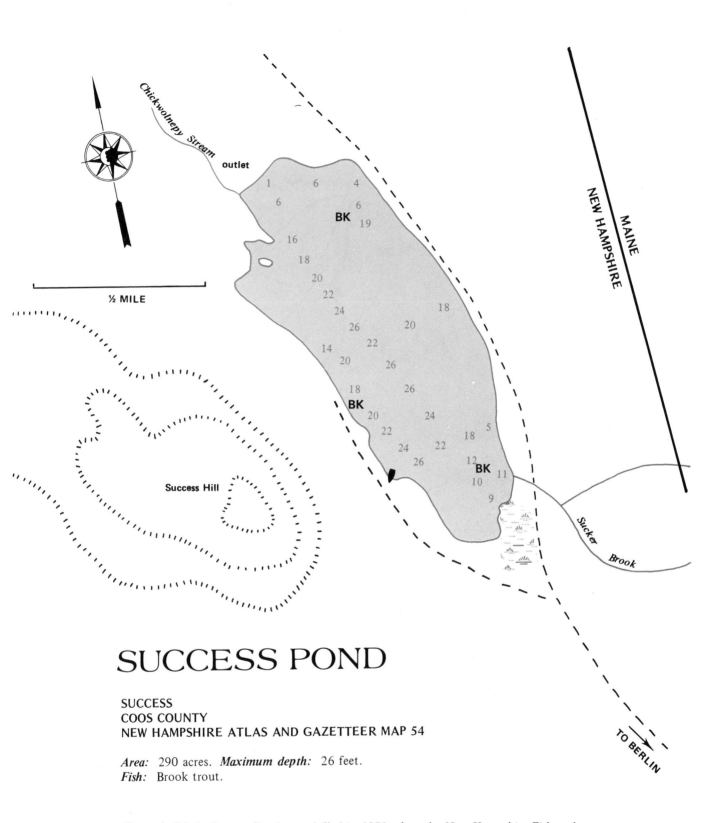

SUCCESS POND

SUCCESS
COOS COUNTY
NEW HAMPSHIRE ATLAS AND GAZETTEER MAP 54

Area: 290 acres. *Maximum depth:* 26 feet.
Fish: Brook trout.

All rough fish in Success Pond were killed in 1972 when the New Hampshire Fish and Game Department reclaimed the pond. It used to contain pickerel, hornpout, suckers and smelt, but is now being managed solely for brook trout. The best fishing is early in the season, just after ice-out in early May, and the best spots to fish are around the inlets of brooks and along the drop offs. Fishing remains fairly good throughout the year, and improves in the fall when the water cools. Success Pond is surrounded by wooded hills, with a few camps along the shoreline. There is a public launch on the southwest shore. Average ice-out date is May 1.

MAP 64

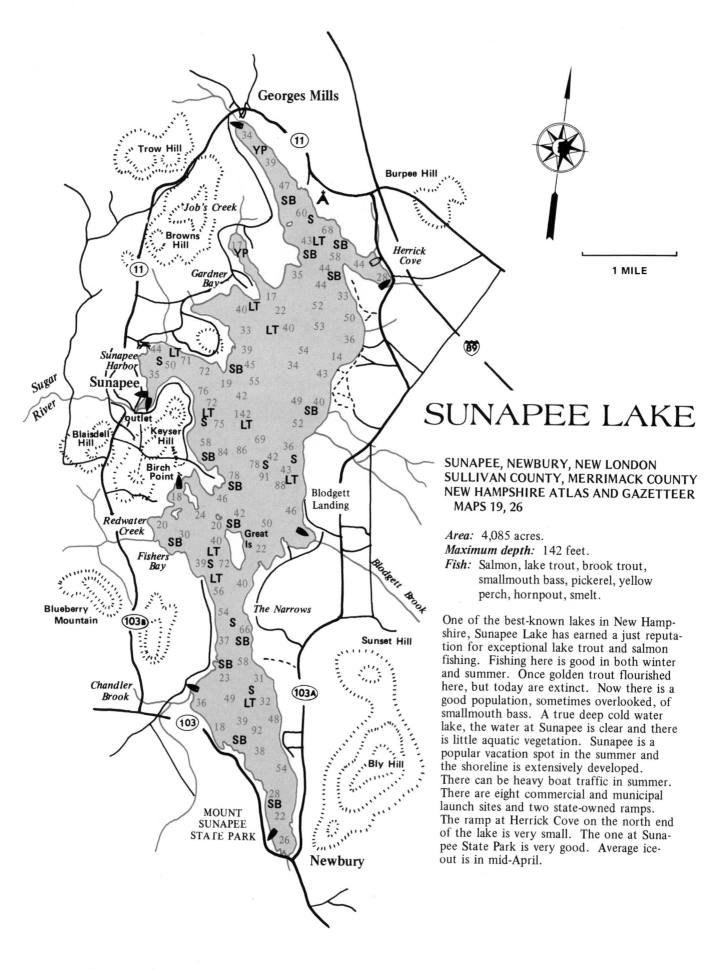

SUNAPEE LAKE

**SUNAPEE, NEWBURY, NEW LONDON
SULLIVAN COUNTY, MERRIMACK COUNTY
NEW HAMPSHIRE ATLAS AND GAZETTEER
MAPS 19, 26**

Area: 4,085 acres.
Maximum depth: 142 feet.
Fish: Salmon, lake trout, brook trout,
    smallmouth bass, pickerel, yellow
    perch, hornpout, smelt.

One of the best-known lakes in New Hampshire, Sunapee Lake has earned a just reputation for exceptional lake trout and salmon fishing. Fishing here is good in both winter and summer. Once golden trout flourished here, but today are extinct. Now there is a good population, sometimes overlooked, of smallmouth bass. A true deep cold water lake, the water at Sunapee is clear and there is little aquatic vegetation. Sunapee is a popular vacation spot in the summer and the shoreline is extensively developed. There can be heavy boat traffic in summer. There are eight commercial and municipal launch sites and two state-owned ramps. The ramp at Herrick Cove on the north end of the lake is very small. The one at Sunapee State Park is very good. Average ice-out is in mid-April.

Georges Mills

Trow Hill

Job's Creek

Browns Hill

Burpee Hill

Herrick Cove

Gardner Bay

Sunapee Harbor

Sunapee

Sugar River

Blaisdell Hill

Keyser Hill

Birch Point

outlet

Redwater Creek

Fishers Bay

Blueberry Mountain

Chandler Brook

Blodgett Landing

Great Is

The Narrows

Sunset Hill

Bly Hill

Blodgett Brook

MOUNT SUNAPEE STATE PARK

Newbury

1 MILE

MAP 65

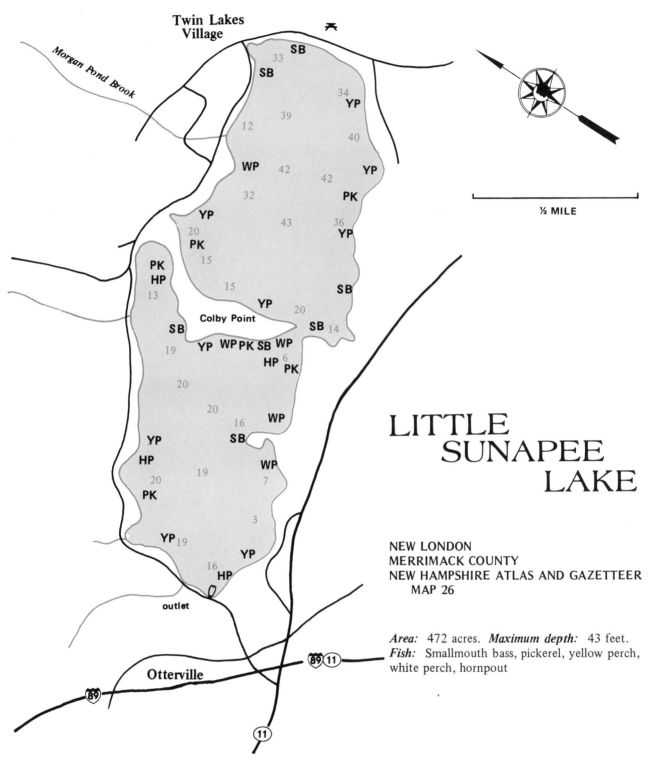

Twin Lakes Village

Morgan Pond Brook

SB
33
SB
34
YP
12   39
40
WP   42
42   YP
32   PK
YP   43   36
20   YP
PK
PK   15
HP   15
13   SB
SB   YP   20
19   SB 14
Colby Point
YP WP PK SB WP
HP 6 PK
YP
HP   WP
20   16
PK   SB
YP   WP
HP   19   7
20
PK   3
YP 19
YP
16
HP

outlet

½ MILE

LITTLE SUNAPEE LAKE

NEW LONDON
MERRIMACK COUNTY
NEW HAMPSHIRE ATLAS AND GAZETTEER
   MAP 26

Area: 472 acres. *Maximum depth:* 43 feet.
Fish: Smallmouth bass, pickerel, yellow perch,
white perch, hornpout

Otterville   89 11

89

11

Little Sunapee Lake is just north of Sunapee Lake and within minutes of Interstate 89. Because of Sunapee's popularity, Little Sunapee is often overlooked by many anglers, but this water offers good fishing for smallmouth bass, pickerel and, of special note, white perch. There should also be some good ice fishing here. The shores are entirely wooded and there is a free, state-owned launch site. Average ice-out is in late April.

MAP 66

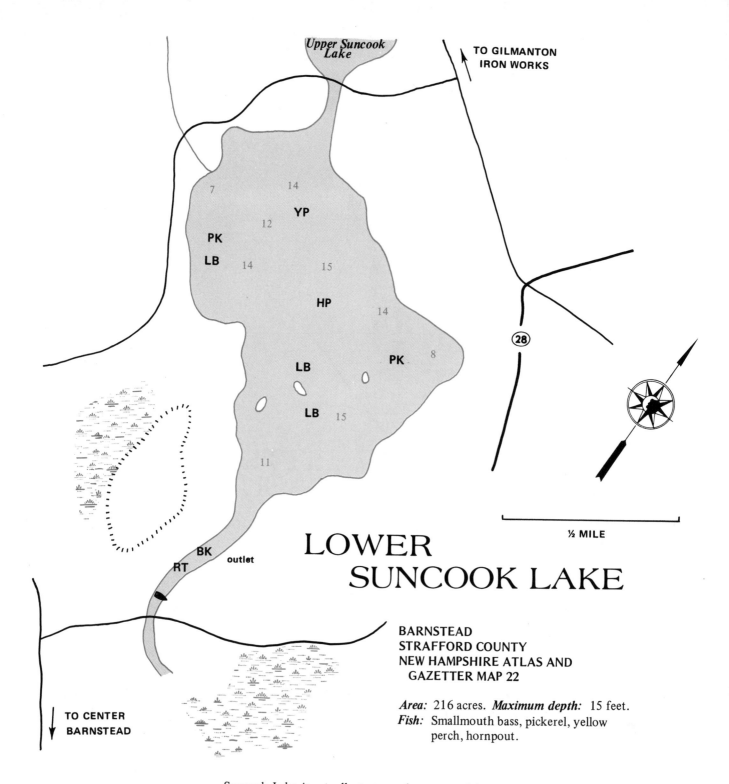

Upper Suncook Lake

TO GILMANTON
IRON WORKS

7
14
YP
12
PK
LB
14
15
HP
14
28
LB
PK
8
LB
LB
15
11

½ MILE

BK
RT
outlet

LOWER
SUNCOOK LAKE

BARNSTEAD
STRAFFORD COUNTY
NEW HAMPSHIRE ATLAS AND
GAZETTER MAP 22

Area: 216 acres. *Maximum depth:* 15 feet.
Fish: Smallmouth bass, pickerel, yellow
perch, hornpout.

TO CENTER
BARNSTEAD

Suncook Lake is actually two ponds connected by a
narrow strait. It now suffers from an overabundance
of yellow perch which seems to have stunted the size
of the fish. If it persists, this perch problem will un-
doubtably have an effect on the pickerel and bass fishing. Suncook has several islands and the shoreline is
wooded and only lightly developed. There are two
free public launches; sometimes parking is a problem.
Average ice-out is in late April.

MAP 67

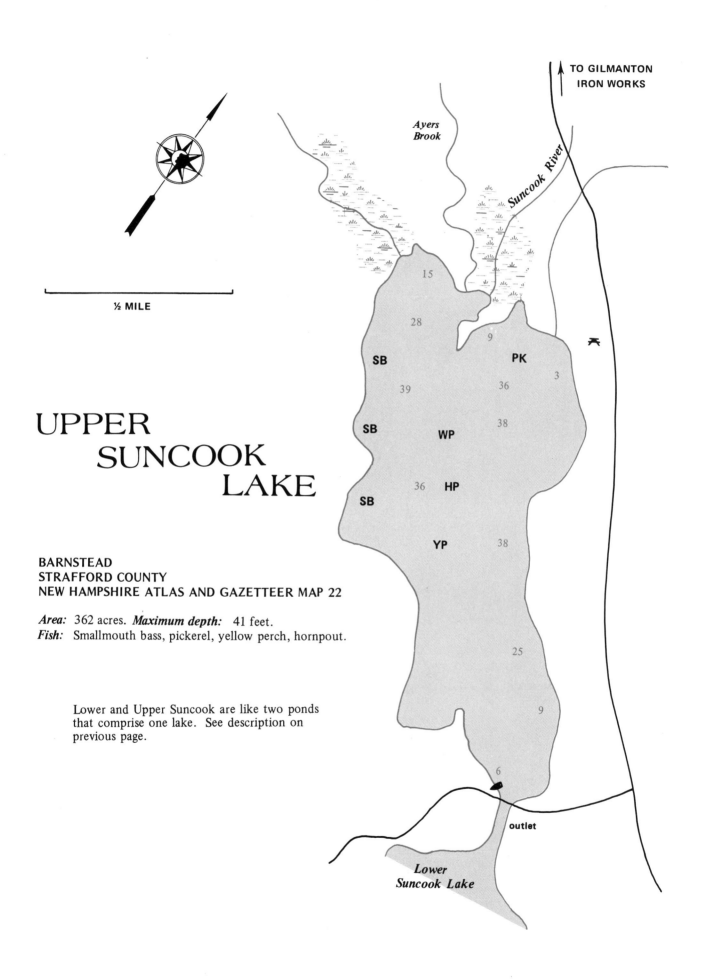

½ MILE

TO GILMANTON
IRON WORKS

Ayers
Brook

Suncook River

15

28

9

SB

PK

39

36

3

SB

WP

38

36

HP

SB

YP

38

25

9

6

outlet

Lower
Suncook Lake

UPPER
SUNCOOK
LAKE

BARNSTEAD
STRAFFORD COUNTY
NEW HAMPSHIRE ATLAS AND GAZETTEER MAP 22

Area: 362 acres. *Maximum depth:* 41 feet.
Fish: Smallmouth bass, pickerel, yellow perch, hornpout.

Lower and Upper Suncook are like two ponds
that comprise one lake. See description on
previous page.

MAP 68

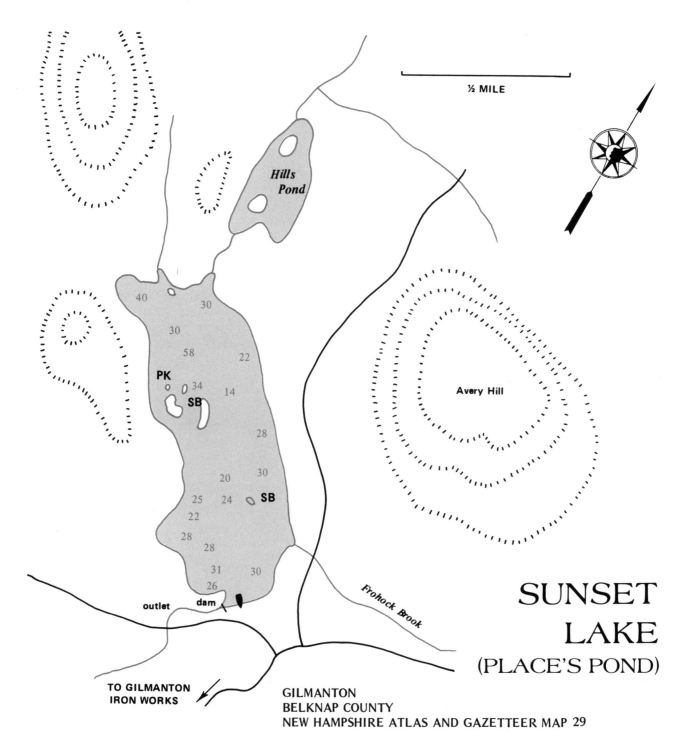

½ MILE

Hills
Pond

40
30
30
58   22
PK
34   14
SB
28
20   30
25   24   SB
22
28
28
31   30
26
outlet   dam

Avery Hill

Frohock Brook

TO GILMANTON
IRON WORKS

SUNSET
LAKE
(PLACE'S POND)

GILMANTON
BELKNAP COUNTY
NEW HAMPSHIRE ATLAS AND GAZETTEER MAP 29

Area: 206 acres. *Maximum depth:* 62 feet.
Fish: Smallmouth bass, pickerel, yellow perch, hornpout.

A natural body of water raised by a dam, Sunset Lake sits at the headwaters of Suncook River. A rocky-bottomed lake with an entirely wooded shoreline that is lightly developed, Sunset Lake is a pretty body of water. Containing the usual assortment of warm water fish, this lake is known for its good smallmouth bass fishing. There is a poor, unpaved, state-owned launch near a small beach. Sunset Lake is an easy body of water to fish with good access for small boats.

MAP 69

SWAINS POND
(UNION POND)

BARRINGTON
STRAFFORD COUNTY
NEW HAMPSHIRE ATLAS AND GAZETTEER MAP 23

½ MILE

Area: 520 acres. *Maximum depth:* 29 feet.
Fish: Largemouth bass, smallmouth bass, pickerel, yellow perch, hornpout, white perch.

With a crooked, irregular shoreline, Swains Pond, enlarged by a dam on the Bellamy River, offers bass fishing opportunities galore. Although it is noted primarily for its largemouth bass fishing, the pond also has smallmouth bass. The angler will find the rocky shoreline attractive and lightly developed.

Bellamy River

outlet

dam

TO ROUTE 9

Rocks

LB

LB

YP

YP

Mica
Point

Peaked
Hill

SB

South
Barrington

MAP 70

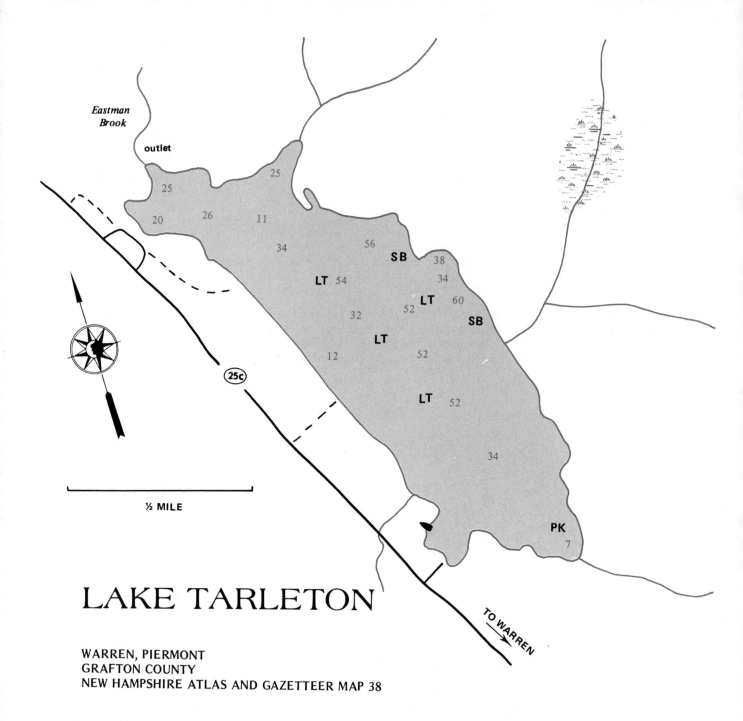

Eastman
Brook

outlet

25

25

20 26 11

34 56

SB

38

LT 54 34

LT 60

32 52

SB

LT

12 52

LT 52

34

25c

½ MILE

PK
7

TO WARREN

LAKE TARLETON

WARREN, PIERMONT
GRAFTON COUNTY
NEW HAMPSHIRE ATLAS AND GAZETTEER MAP 38

Area: 315 acres. *Maximum depth:* 60 feet.
Fish: Salmon, lake trout, brook trout, smallmouth bass, yellow perch,
pickerel, hornpout, smelt.

Lake Tarleton borders the White Mountain National Forest and is accessible off Route 25C. A natural
body of water with wooded, undeveloped shoreline, it is a beautiful lake with exceptionally good fishing. The lake contains both warm water and cold water fish. Smallmouth bass fishing can be explosive
at times. Area anglers commonly troll streamers and wet flies for these exciting fish. There is only one
access point for boats - a dirt launch which may prove troublesome for heavy or large boats. Average
ice-out is in mid-May.

MAP 71

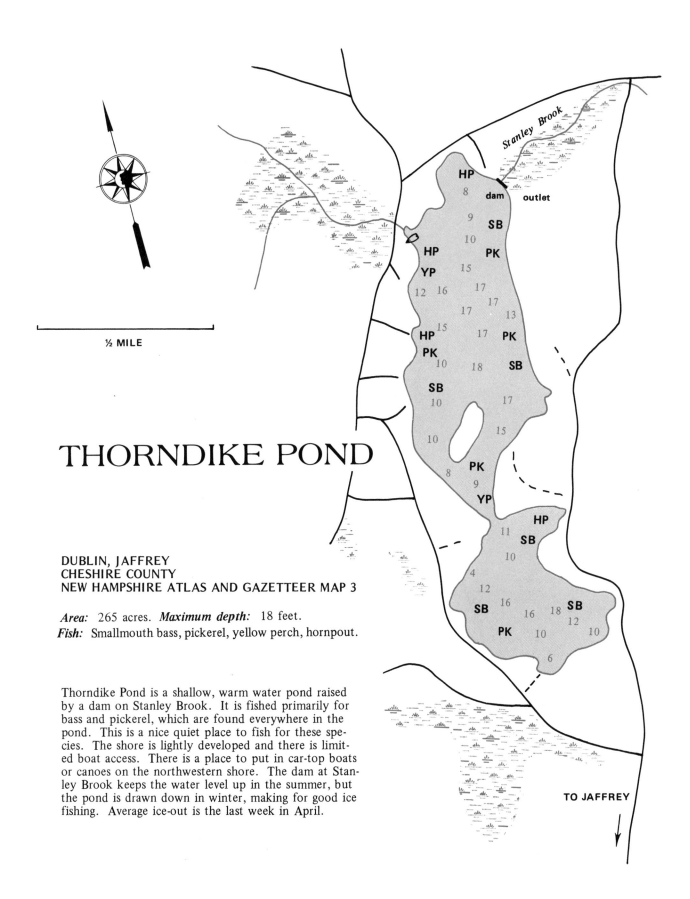

THORNDIKE POND

**DUBLIN, JAFFREY
CHESHIRE COUNTY
NEW HAMPSHIRE ATLAS AND GAZETTEER MAP 3**

Area: 265 acres. *Maximum depth:* 18 feet.
Fish: Smallmouth bass, pickerel, yellow perch, hornpout.

Thorndike Pond is a shallow, warm water pond raised by a dam on Stanley Brook. It is fished primarily for bass and pickerel, which are found everywhere in the pond. This is a nice quiet place to fish for these species. The shore is lightly developed and there is limited boat access. There is a place to put in car-top boats or canoes on the northwestern shore. The dam at Stanley Brook keeps the water level up in the summer, but the pond is drawn down in winter, making for good ice fishing. Average ice-out is the last week in April.

½ MILE

Stanley Brook

HP
dam outlet
SB
PK
HP
YP
SB
PK
HP
PK
SB
SB
PK
YP
HP
SB
SB
SB
PK

TO JAFFREY

MAP 72

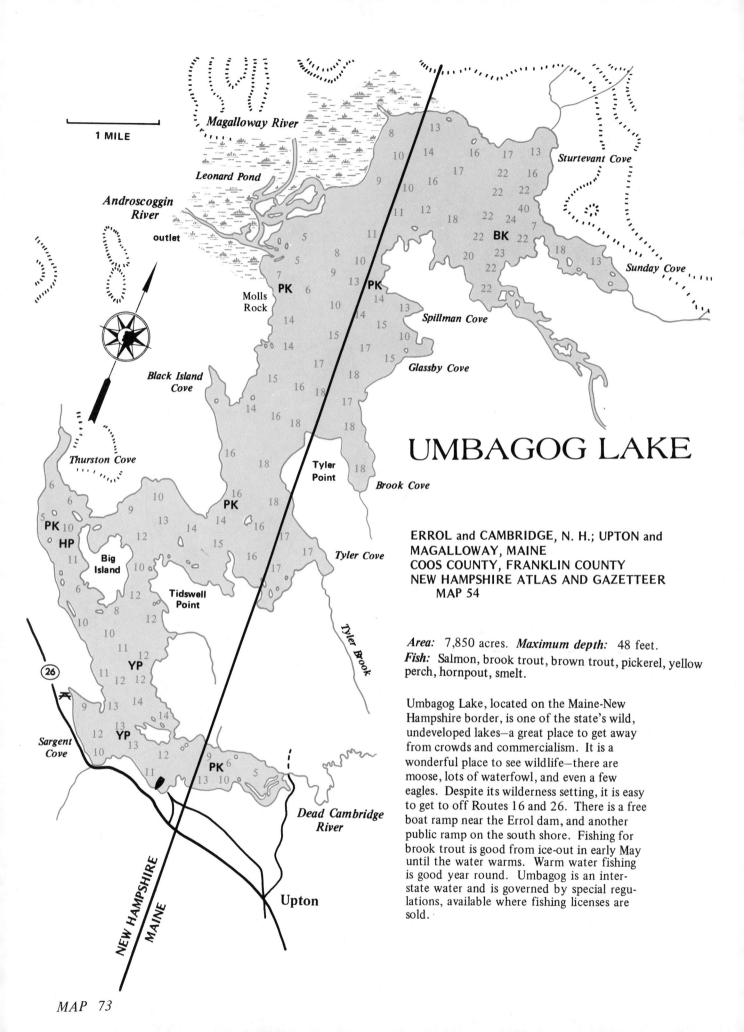

1 MILE

Magalloway River

Leonard Pond

Androscoggin River

outlet

Sturtevant Cove

8   13

10   14   16   17   13

9   17   22   16

10   16   22   22

11   12   18   22   24   40
            22   23   **BK**   7
        20   22
                22
                22

Sunday Cove

Molls Rock

PK   5
    5   6
    7
    14
    14

8
9
10
    13   **PK**
        14
    13
    14   15
        10
    15

Spillman Cove

Glassby Cove

Black Island Cove

15   16   17
    14   16   18
        17
        18

18   13   22

18

Thurston Cove

UMBAGOG LAKE

6
6
5   **PK**   10
    HP
11
    Big Island
6
    8
10   12
    10
    11
    YP   12
11   12   13
    12   14   14
9   13   13   14
    12   **YP**   13
10   13   12
    11   13   10

16
    PK
14   16
    16
    17
18   17   17

Tyler Point

Brook Cove

Tyler Cove

Tyler Brook

ERROL and CAMBRIDGE, N. H.; UPTON and
MAGALLOWAY, MAINE
COOS COUNTY, FRANKLIN COUNTY
NEW HAMPSHIRE ATLAS AND GAZETTEER
MAP 54

Area: 7,850 acres. *Maximum depth:* 48 feet.
Fish: Salmon, brook trout, brown trout, pickerel, yellow
perch, hornpout, smelt.

Umbagog Lake, located on the Maine-New
Hampshire border, is one of the state's wild,
undeveloped lakes—a great place to get away
from crowds and commercialism. It is a
wonderful place to see wildlife—there are
moose, lots of waterfowl, and even a few
eagles. Despite its wilderness setting, it is easy
to get to off Routes 16 and 26. There is a free
boat ramp near the Errol dam, and another
public ramp on the south shore. Fishing for
brook trout is good from ice-out in early May
until the water warms. Warm water fishing
is good year round. Umbagog is an interstate water and is governed by special regulations, available where fishing licenses are
sold.

Sargent Cove

26

PK   6
    5
13   10

Dead Cambridge River

Tidswell Point

NEW HAMPSHIRE
MAINE

Upton

MAP 73

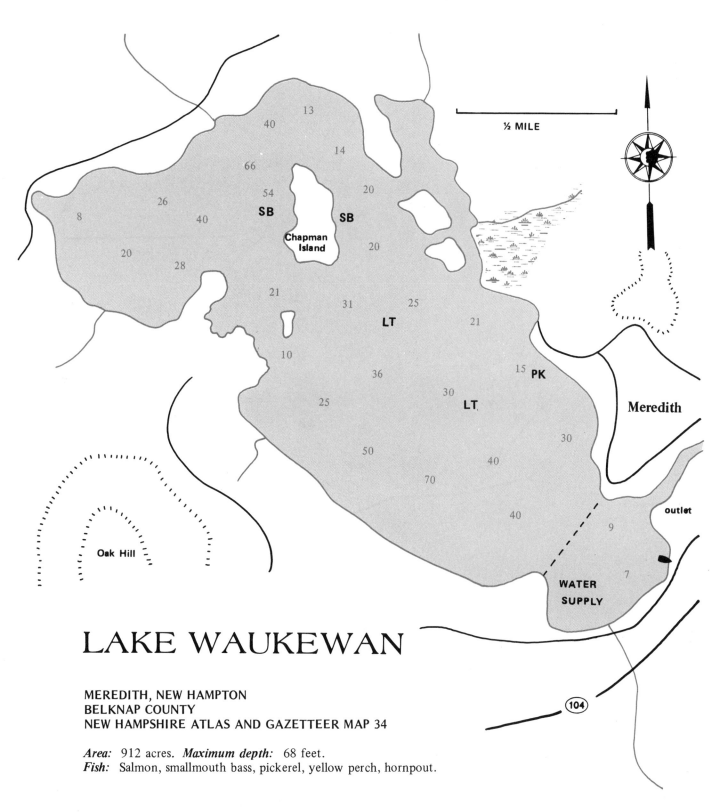

LAKE WAUKEWAN

MEREDITH, NEW HAMPTON
BELKNAP COUNTY
NEW HAMPSHIRE ATLAS AND GAZETTEER MAP 34

Area: 912 acres. *Maximum depth:* 68 feet.
Fish: Salmon, smallmouth bass, pickerel, yellow perch, hornpout.

A good smallmouth fishery exists at Waukewan Lake, a water once managed for salmon. Annual stocking of salmon, begun in 1954, was discontinued in 1964 because the lake's limited supply of deep water made it more suitable to bass management. A recent survey by the New Hampshire Fish and Game Department revealed a good distribution of bass, with many large fish and an abundant supply of crayfish for bass food. The rocky, gravelly bottom of Waukewan is well suited for smallmouth bass nesting and anglers fishing here will observe many nests along the shore. The Fish and Game Department is considering stocking Waukewan with splake or brook trout and this is something anglers might want to watch for. Average ice-out is in late April.

MAP 74

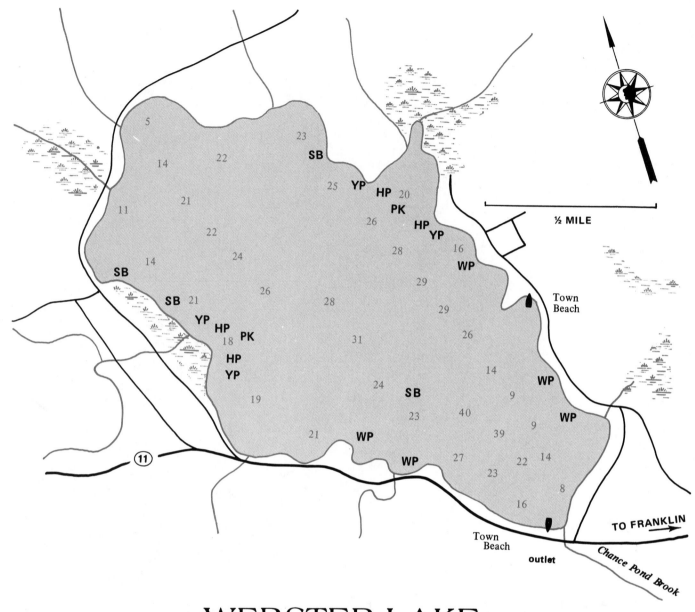

WEBSTER LAKE

FRANKLIN
MERRIMACK COUNTY
NEW HAMPSHIRE ATLAS AND GAZETTEER MAP 27

Area: 612 acres. *Maximum depth:* 40 feet.
Fish: Smallmouth bass, pickerel, yellow perch, white perch, hornpout

Webster Lake has an excellent population of warm water fish. This natural body
of water, located just west of Franklin off Route 11, has a moderately wooded
shoreline that is lightly developed. There are two public beaches on Webster Lake
and a boat ramp at the outlet on the town beach. Picnic tables, fireplaces, and
concessions are available. A fee is charged for use of the launch.

MAP 75

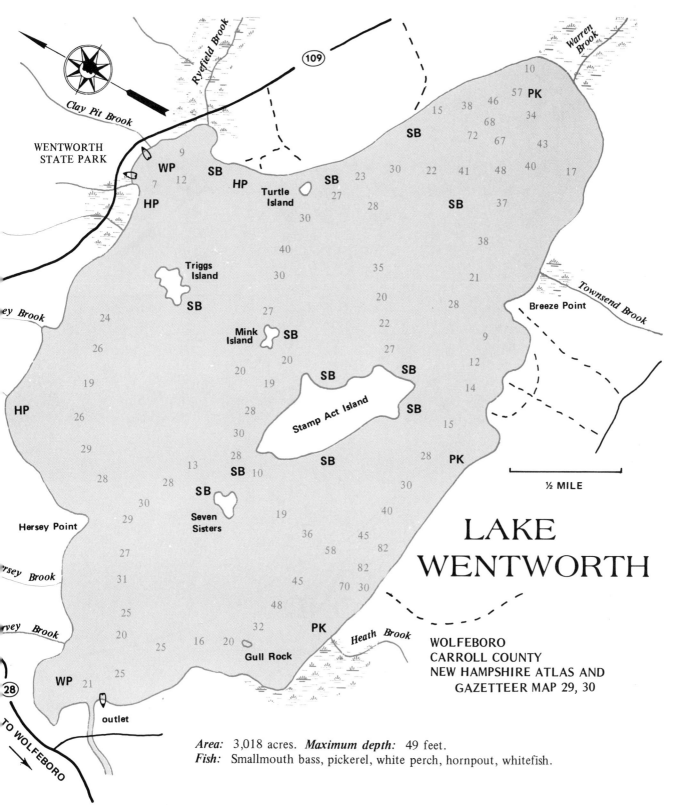

LAKE WENTWORTH

WOLFEBORO
CARROLL COUNTY
NEW HAMPSHIRE ATLAS AND
GAZETTEER MAP 29, 30

½ MILE

Area: 3,018 acres. *Maximum depth:* 49 feet.
Fish: Smallmouth bass, pickerel, white perch, hornpout, whitefish.

When anyone writes about or lists the premier smallmouth bass lakes In New England, or the best place to fish in the state, Lake Wentworth is nearly always near the top. With nearly 14 miles of shoreline, a rocky bottom and numerous islands, there are plenty of places to fish. Wentworth is noted primarily for its smallmouth bass but, as an added bonus, there are large schools of white perch which the New Hampshire Fish and Game Department encourages anglers to pursue. If you come across a school of white perch, the fishing can be fast and furious. There are many summer cottages and homes along the shores and the lake is heavily used in the summer. But the angler who fishes early in the spring and in the evenings during the summer can avoid the crowds. Fishing pressure on the whole is very light, considering the lake's potential. Access to the lake may be made with car-top boats or canoes off Route 109 at Claypit Brook. Trailered boats can be launched at Wentworth State Park. A small fee is charged for launching and parking. Average ice-out date is May 1.

MAP 76

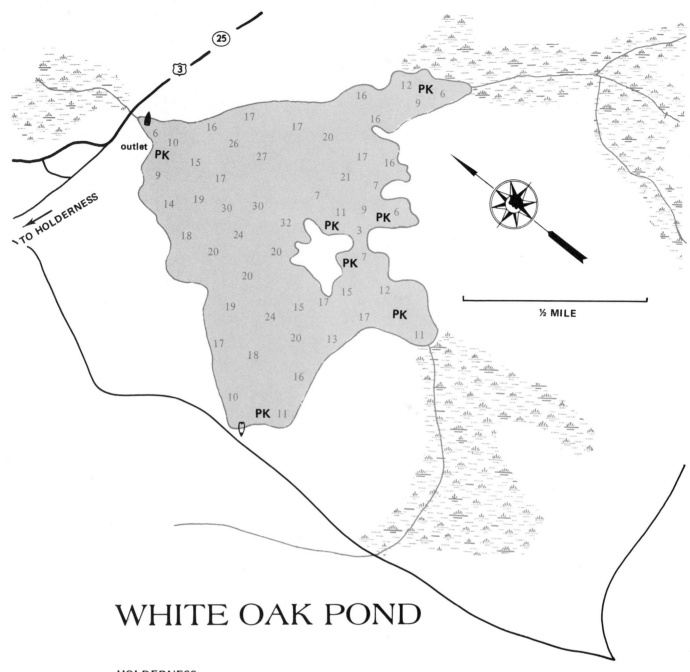

WHITE OAK POND

HOLDERNESS
GRAFTON COUNTY
NEW HAMPSHIRE ATLAS AND GAZETTEER MAP 34

Area: 291 acres. *Maximum depth:* 32 feet.
Fish: Pickerel, yellow perch, hornpout.

A relatively shallow pond located in the Lakes Region of New Hampshire, White Oak Pond is noted for its pickerel fishing. Being a warm water fish, pickerel fishing should be good throughout the summer. Those seeking a change from the pursuit of lake trout through the ice in the Lakes Region would do well to try White Oak Pond with excellent pickerel fishing reported in the winter. There are two launching sites and during the winter there should be no problem gaining access for ice fishing. No outboard motor over 7½ horsepower is permitted on this pond. Average ice-out date is May 1.

MAP 77

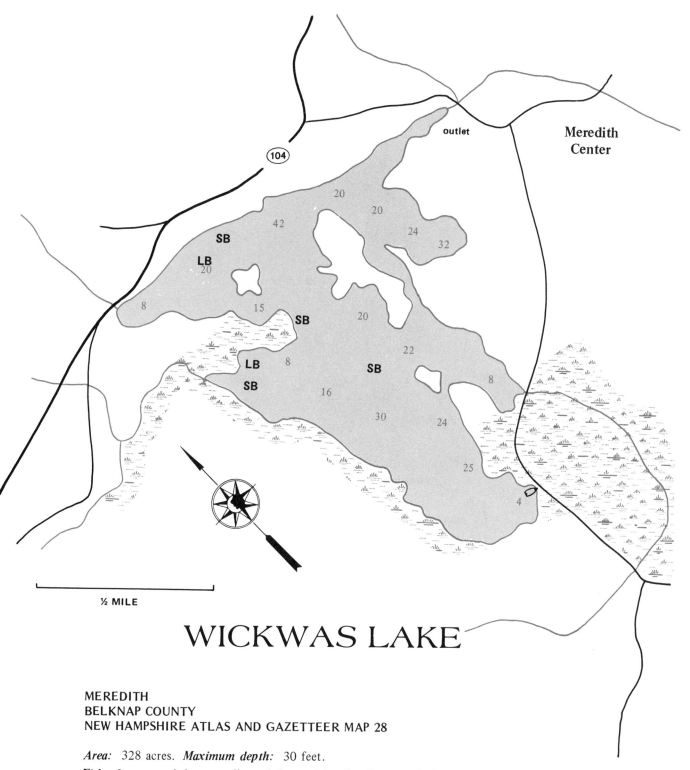

WICKWAS LAKE

**MEREDITH
BELKNAP COUNTY
NEW HAMPSHIRE ATLAS AND GAZETTEER MAP 28**

Area: 328 acres. *Maximum depth:* 30 feet.
Fish: Largemouth bass, smallmouth bass, pickerel, yellow perch, hornpout.

When anglers think of Meredith, they think of lake trout and salmon fishing in the well-known waters of Lake Winnipesaukee, Winnisquam Lake and Squam Lake. Most anglers are surprised to find out that there are also two excellent bass fishing lakes in Meredith - Wickwas Lake and Pemigewasset Lake, located within a few miles of each other. Bass fishing at Wickwas is exceptional from May right through October. Spinnerbaits seem to be the most successful in spring and fall, while purple, plastic worms are commonly used from June to September. Sometimes the popular crank-baits are good fish producers. The shores of Wickwas Lake are wooded and lightly developed. There is a public launch at the southeast end of the lake. Average ice-out is late April.

MAP 78

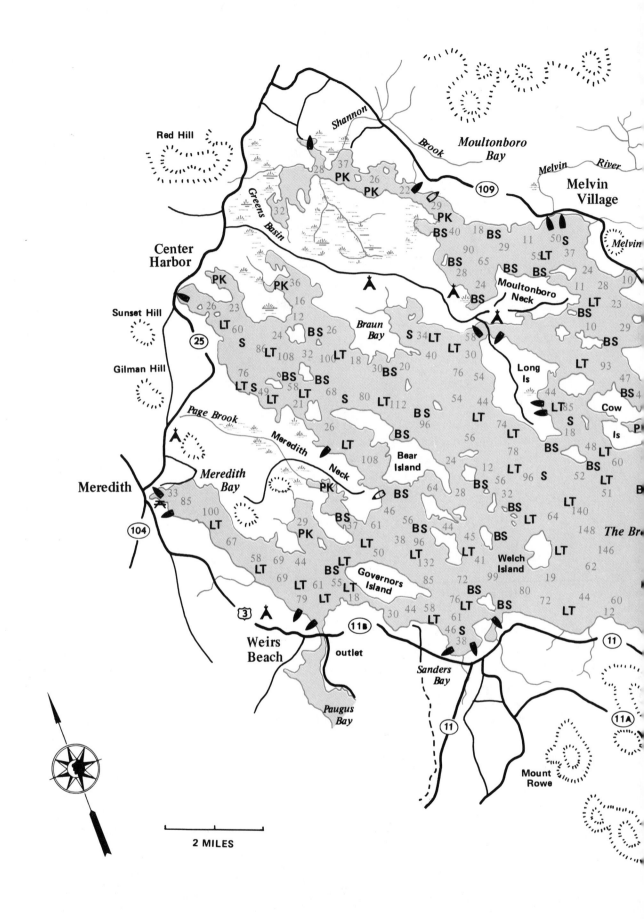

2 MILES

LAKE WINNIPESAUKEE

ALTON, CENTER HARBOR, GILFORD, LACONIA, MEREDITH, MOULTONBORO, TUFTONBORO
  AND WOLFEBORO
BELKNAP COUNTY, CARROLL COUNTY
NEW HAMPSHIRE ATLAS AND GAZETTEER MAPS 28, 29, 34, 35

Area: 44,586 acres. *Maximum depth:* 168 feet.
Fish: Salmon, lake trout, smallmouth bass, largemouth bass, pickerel, yellow perch, hornpout, cusk, smelt, whitefish.

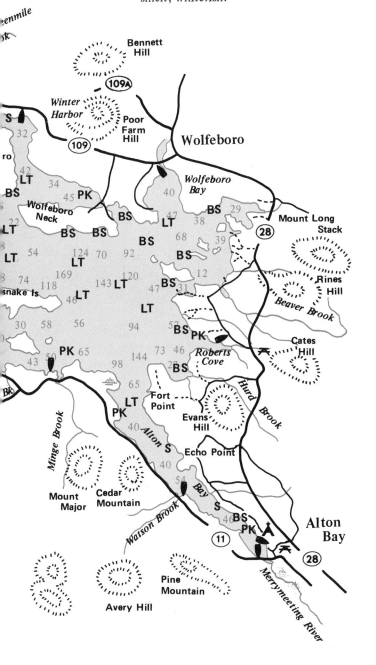

Lake Winnipesaukee, New Hampshire's largest and most famous lake, is a longtime favorite vacation and fishing spot. Winnipesaukee - with 70 square miles of water, 250 islands, and 240 miles of shoreline - offers great cold and warm water fishing. It is undoubtedly one of the best lake trout and salmon fishing waters in New England and is appealing for its large size, unlimited access, and varied fishing conditions and habitat.

At ice-out in late April/early May and when the season opens, Alton Bay and Merrymeeting River are local hot spots for salmon. As the ice leaves, lake trout and salmon may be taken by trolling streamer flies, lures and sewed-on bait, such as smelt, near the surface. A popular local method of taking trout and salmon is with live smelt. As the season progresses, trout and salmon are taken in deeper water by trolling with weighted line and downriggers.

Though sometimes overlooked by anglers, there is excellent smallmouth bass fishing here in the rocky areas on all shores. Bass fishing is particularly good during the spring nesting period from May to July 1. The shoreline of the lake is highly developed with summer camps and an ever-increasing number of year-round homes and condominiums. Recreational boat traffic is quite heavy in the summer, but fishermen can still find plenty of room for fishing all season. Camps, motels, fishing supplies, bait and food are widely available in the area, as are launch sites.

MAP 79

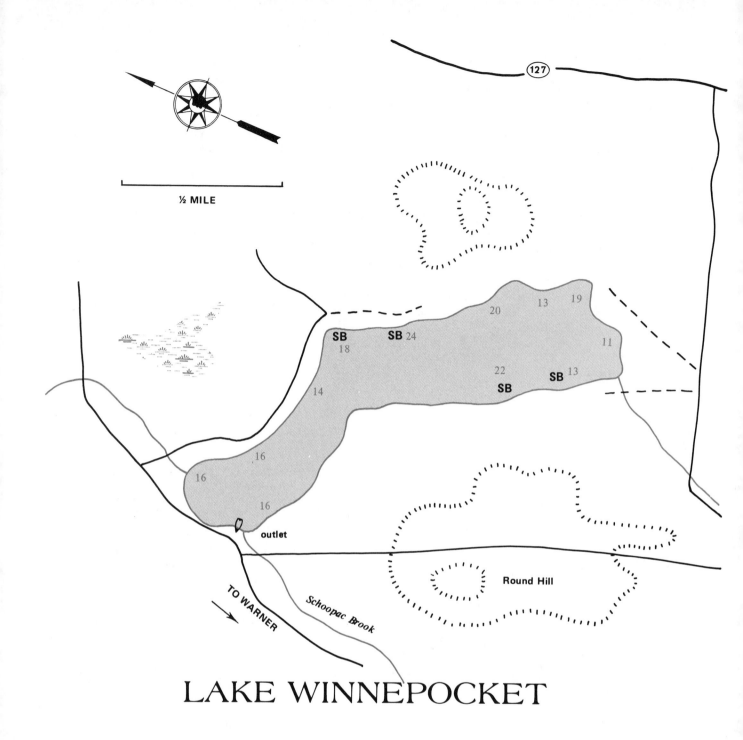

LAKE WINNEPOCKET

WEBSTER
MERRIMACK COUNTY
NEW HAMPSHIRE ATLAS AND GAZETTEER MAP 20

Area: 227 acres. *Maximum depth:* 55 feet.
Fish: Smallmouth bass, pickerel, hornpout, yellow perch.

The water at Winnepocket Lake is very clear and provides excellent smallmouth bass fishing. Anglers here report good luck using cranks or spinnerbaits for bass. There is excellent fishing as the water warms following ice-out in early May and the fish begin to spawn in spring. There is a good boat launch at the outlet.

MAP 80

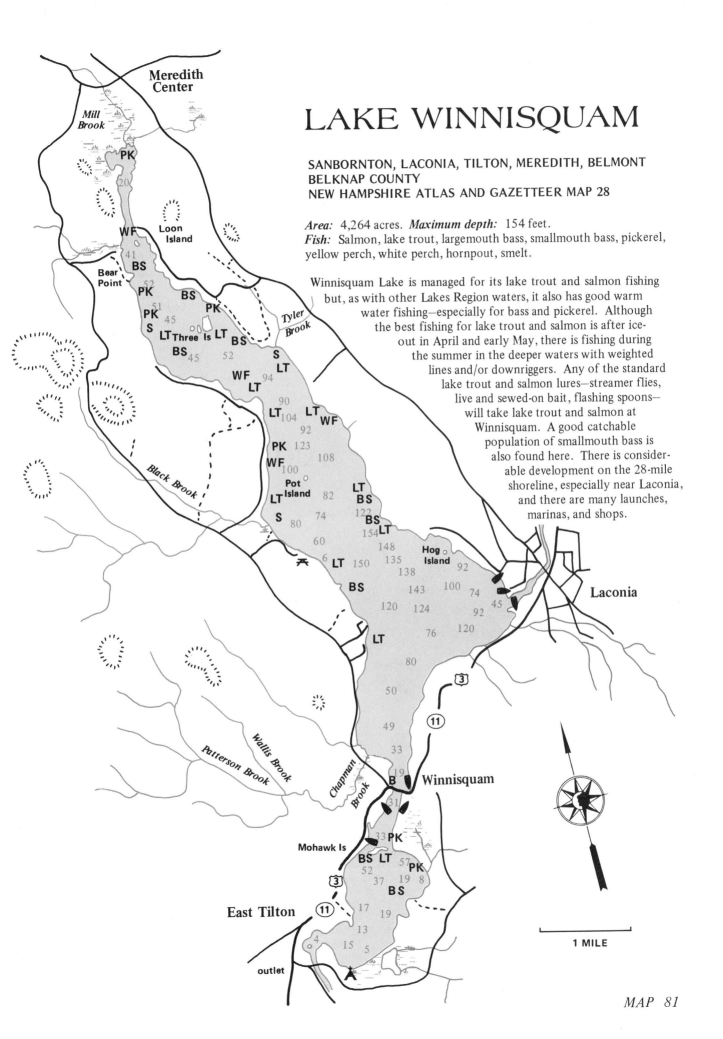

LAKE WINNISQUAM

SANBORNTON, LACONIA, TILTON, MEREDITH, BELMONT
BELKNAP COUNTY
NEW HAMPSHIRE ATLAS AND GAZETTEER MAP 28

Area: 4,264 acres. *Maximum depth:* 154 feet.
Fish: Salmon, lake trout, largemouth bass, smallmouth bass, pickerel, yellow perch, white perch, hornpout, smelt.

Winnisquam Lake is managed for its lake trout and salmon fishing but, as with other Lakes Region waters, it also has good warm water fishing—especially for bass and pickerel. Although the best fishing for lake trout and salmon is after ice-out in April and early May, there is fishing during the summer in the deeper waters with weighted lines and/or downriggers. Any of the standard lake trout and salmon lures—streamer flies, live and sewed-on bait, flashing spoons—will take lake trout and salmon at Winnisquam. A good catchable population of smallmouth bass is also found here. There is considerable development on the 28-mile shoreline, especially near Laconia, and there are many launches, marinas, and shops.

1 MILE

MAP 81

Towns Mountain +

Dalton Mountain +

Connecticut River

Gardner Mountain +

2 MILES

Walker Mountain +

Littleton ○

302

Ogontz Brook

TO WHITEFIELD

10

Osborn Hill +

Pettyboro Brook

Lisbon ○

Gale River

Baker Brook

Barrett Brook

Beech Hill +

VERMONT

Childs Brook

Salmon Hole Brook

Garnet + Mountain

Mount + Agassiz

Bath ○

Mill Brook

Ore Hill +

Ammonoosuc River

Wells River ○

93

Big Bickford Mountain +

+ Green Mountain

Waterman Brook

Bowen Brook

North Haverhill ○

Cobble Mountain +

Morse Brook

AMMONOOSUC

Black Mountain +

RIVERS

10

25

Sugarloaf Mountain +

Whitcher Brook

Tunnel Brook

Mount Wolf +

Jeffers Mountain +

Wild Ammonoosuc River

Mount Moosilauke +

112

Length: Ammonoosuc, 55 miles.
    Wild Ammonoosuc, 15 miles.
Fish: Brook trout, rainbow trout.

118

TO NORTH WOODSTOCK

TO WARREN

CARROLL to WOODSVILLE
GRAFTON COUNTY
NEW HAMPSHIRE ATLAS AND
GAZETTEER MAPS 43, 44, 45

The Ammonoosuc River originates at Lake of Clouds on Mount Washington in the heart of the White Mountain National Forest, then flows west for 55 miles before entering the Connecticut River at Haverhill.

The river is managed for its brook trout and is heavily stocked by the state.

The upper Ammonoosuc River above Bethlehem is a fast-moving river that runs cool even in summer. There is easy access from Route 302 which parallels the river. This section is the best for brook trout fishing. Fishing pressure is spotty.

The lower section of the Ammonoosuc, a series of long pools separated by riffles, runs through farmland. There are five dams on this stretch; the Littleton dam sometimes shuts water off

and disrupts fishing. The best fishing here is from June through August. That is also the period of highest fishing pressure. There are many places to camp out or spend the night in this area.

The Wild Ammonoosuc, originating near Kinsman Notch in the White Mountain National Forest, is a typical, fast-flowing mountain stream. It runs 15 miles along Route 112 before joining the Ammonoosuc in Bath. The upper 6 miles of the river supply water for Woodsville. The remainder of the river is heavily stocked. Fishing pressure is spread out over the river's length. For some reason, this river is not heavily fished by tourists. The best fishing here is from the season opening through June.

MAP 82

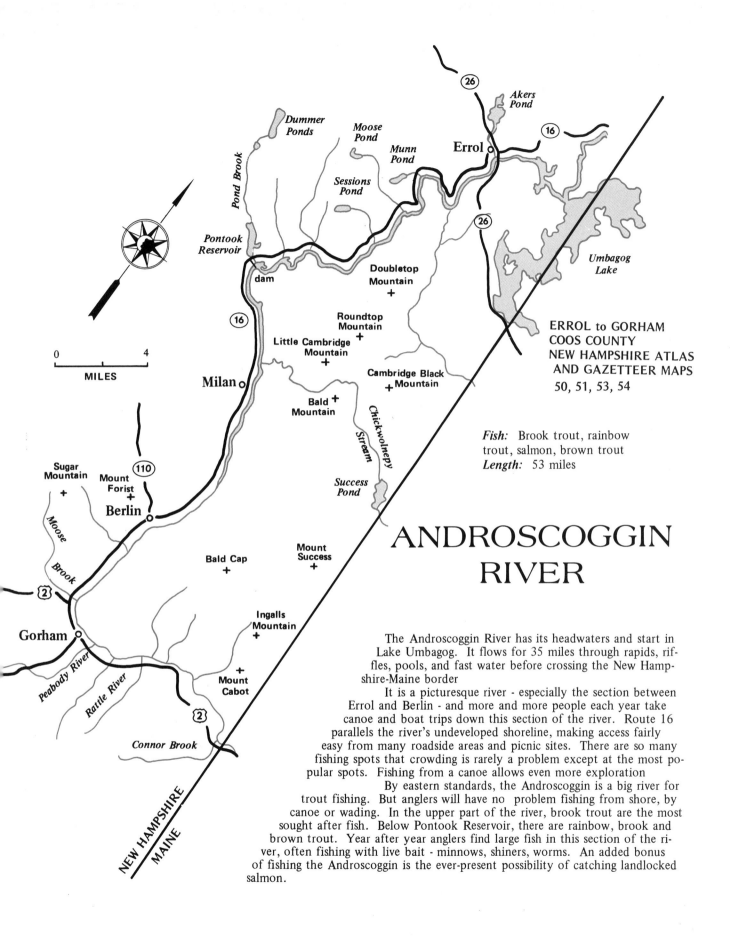

Dummer Ponds

Moose Pond

Munn Pond

Akers Pond

(26)

(16)

Errol

Pond Brook

Sessions Pond

Pontook Reservoir

(26)

dam

Doubletop Mountain +

Umbagog Lake

(16)

Roundtop Mountain +

ERROL to GORHAM
COOS COUNTY
NEW HAMPSHIRE ATLAS
AND GAZETTEER MAPS
50, 51, 53, 54

Little Cambridge Mountain +

Cambridge Black Mountain +

Milan o

Bald Mountain +

Chickwolnepy Stream

Fish: Brook trout, rainbow trout, salmon, brown trout
Length: 53 miles

Success Pond

0   4
MILES

Sugar Mountain +

Mount Forist +

(110)

Berlin o

Bald Cap +

Mount Success +

ANDROSCOGGIN RIVER

Moose Brook

(2)

Gorham o

Peabody River

Ratile River

Ingalls Mountain +

Mount Cabot +

(2)

Connor Brook

NEW HAMPSHIRE

MAINE

The Androscoggin River has its headwaters and start in Lake Umbagog. It flows for 35 miles through rapids, riffles, pools, and fast water before crossing the New Hampshire-Maine border

It is a picturesque river - especially the section between Errol and Berlin - and more and more people each year take canoe and boat trips down this section of the river. Route 16 parallels the river's undeveloped shoreline, making access fairly easy from many roadside areas and picnic sites. There are so many fishing spots that crowding is rarely a problem except at the most popular spots. Fishing from a canoe allows even more exploration

By eastern standards, the Androscoggin is a big river for trout fishing. But anglers will have no problem fishing from shore, by canoe or wading. In the upper part of the river, brook trout are the most sought after fish. Below Pontook Reservoir, there are rainbow, brook and brown trout. Year after year anglers find large fish in this section of the river, often fishing with live bait - minnows, shiners, worms. An added bonus of fishing the Androscoggin is the ever-present possibility of catching landlocked salmon.

MAP 83

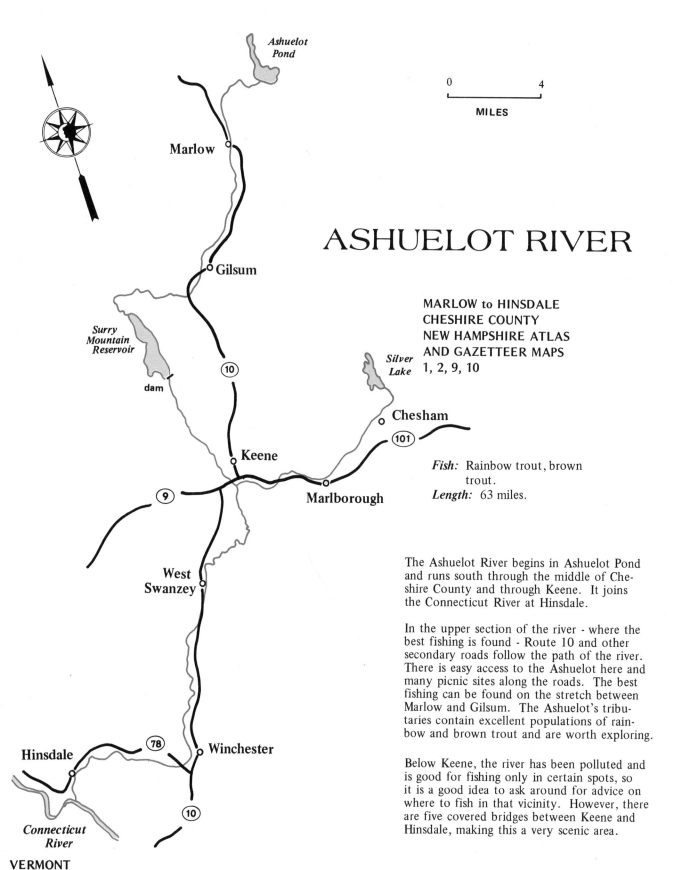

Ashuelot Pond

Marlow

0   4

MILES

ASHUELOT RIVER

**MARLOW to HINSDALE
CHESHIRE COUNTY
NEW HAMPSHIRE ATLAS
AND GAZETTEER MAPS
1, 2, 9, 10**

Gilsum

*Surry
Mountain
Reservoir*

*Silver
Lake*

(10)

dam

○ **Chesham**

(101)

Keene

Fish: Rainbow trout, brown
          trout.
Length: 63 miles.

(9)

Marlborough

The Ashuelot River begins in Ashuelot Pond
and runs south through the middle of Cheshire County and through Keene. It joins
the Connecticut River at Hinsdale.

**West
Swanzey**

In the upper section of the river - where the
best fishing is found - Route 10 and other
secondary roads follow the path of the river.
There is easy access to the Ashuelot here and
many picnic sites along the roads. The best
fishing can be found on the stretch between
Marlow and Gilsum. The Ashuelot's tributaries contain excellent populations of rainbow and brown trout and are worth exploring.

Hinsdale

(78) **Winchester**

(10)

Below Keene, the river has been polluted and
is good for fishing only in certain spots, so
it is a good idea to ask around for advice on
where to fish in that vicinity. However, there
are five covered bridges between Keene and
Hinsdale, making this a very scenic area.

*Connecticut
River*

VERMONT

MAP 84

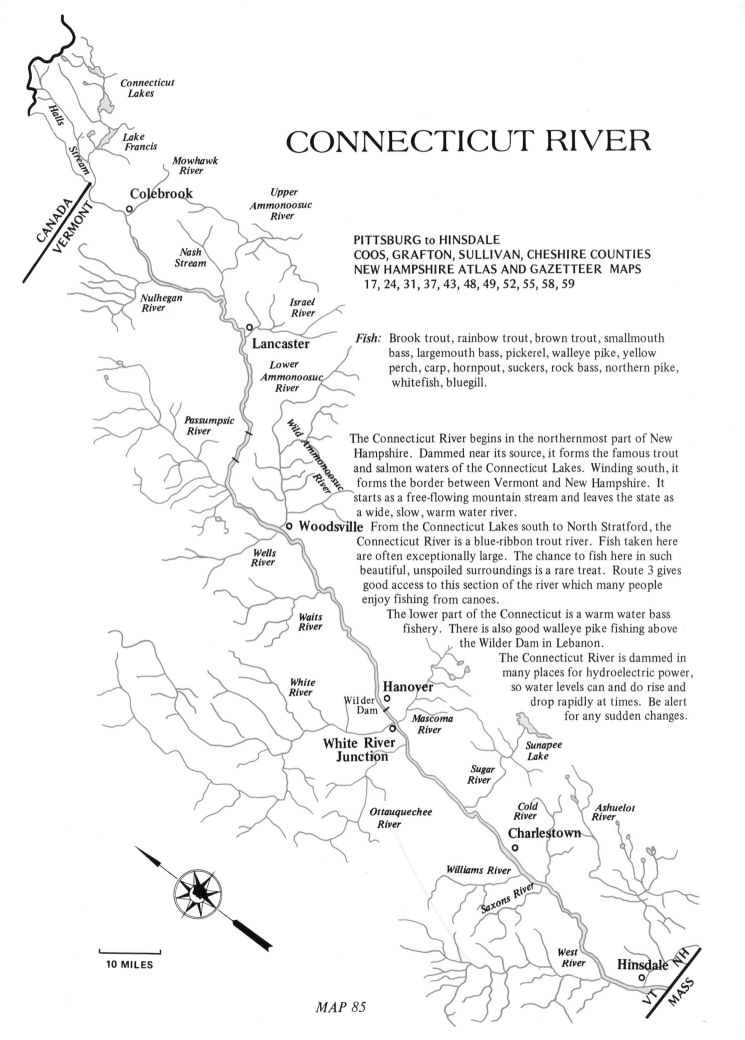

CONNECTICUT RIVER

Connecticut Lakes

Halls Stream

Lake Francis

Mowhawk River

CANADA
VERMONT

Upper Ammonoosuc River

Colebrook

Nash Stream

Nulhegan River

Israel River

Lancaster

Lower Ammonoosuc River

Passumpsic River

Wild Ammonoosuc River

PITTSBURG to HINSDALE
COOS, GRAFTON, SULLIVAN, CHESHIRE COUNTIES
NEW HAMPSHIRE ATLAS AND GAZETTEER MAPS
17, 24, 31, 37, 43, 48, 49, 52, 55, 58, 59

Fish: Brook trout, rainbow trout, brown trout, smallmouth bass, largemouth bass, pickerel, walleye pike, yellow perch, carp, hornpout, suckers, rock bass, northern pike, whitefish, bluegill.

The Connecticut River begins in the northernmost part of New Hampshire. Dammed near its source, it forms the famous trout and salmon waters of the Connecticut Lakes. Winding south, it forms the border between Vermont and New Hampshire. It starts as a free-flowing mountain stream and leaves the state as a wide, slow, warm water river.

Woodsville From the Connecticut Lakes south to North Stratford, the Connecticut River is a blue-ribbon trout river. Fish taken here are often exceptionally large. The chance to fish here in such beautiful, unspoiled surroundings is a rare treat. Route 3 gives good access to this section of the river which many people enjoy fishing from canoes.

The lower part of the Connecticut is a warm water bass fishery. There is also good walleye pike fishing above the Wilder Dam in Lebanon.

The Connecticut River is dammed in many places for hydroelectric power, so water levels can and do rise and drop rapidly at times. Be alert for any sudden changes.

Wells River

Waits River

White River

Hanover

Wilder Dam

Mascoma River

Sunapee Lake

White River Junction

Sugar River

Ottauquechee River

Cold River

Ashuelot River

Charlestown

Williams River

Saxons River

West River

Hinsdale

VT
MASS
NH

10 MILES

MAP 85

EXETER RIVER

CHESTER to NEWMARKET
ROCKINGHAM COUNTY
NEW HAMPSHIRE ATLAS AND GAZETTEER
MAPS 14, 15, 16

Fish: Brook trout, rainbow trout, brown trout, smallmouth bass, largemouth bass, yellow perch, pickerel, hornpout, saltwater smelt.

Length: 35 miles.

A popular trout river in the seacoast area, the Exeter River offers good early fishing, mainly from stocked fish. The Exeter is generally slow-moving. Trout fishing is restricted to the faster sections. The warm-water fishery is found along the entire length of the river, though the best fishing spots are in the lower stretches where the river widens. Areas above Pickpocket Dam in Brentwood and between Route 108 and the dam in downtown Exeter are particularly good for bass and pickerel fishing.

During spring runoff the fast sections of the river are popular for whitewater canoeing and kayaking. The river is good canoe water and has sections long enough to offer good float trips. Although there are heavily populated areas nearby, the shoreline is undeveloped. There are two fishways on the Exeter. The coho salmon program has produced good fishing in the falls below the dam at Exeter. There is also a spring run of alewives and eels. The water below Exeter has become cleaner and saltwater smelt are now being caught upriver to the dam. The area from Exeter to Great Bay is tidal.

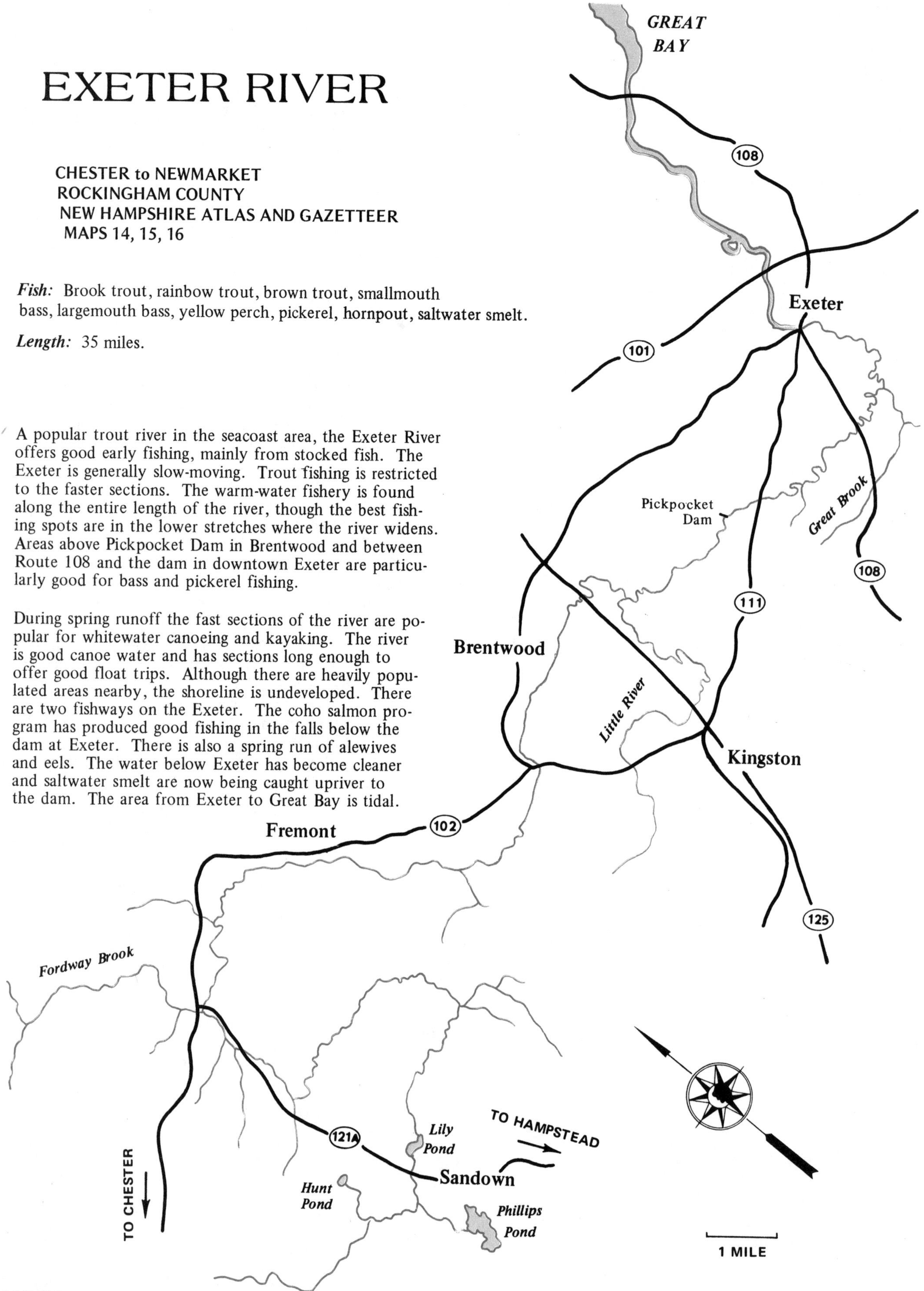

GREAT BAY

108

Exeter

101

Pickpocket Dam

Great Brook

108

111

Brentwood

Little River

Kingston

102

Fremont

125

Fordway Brook

121A

Lily Pond

TO HAMPSTEAD

TO CHESTER

Hunt Pond

Sandown

Phillips Pond

1 MILE

MAP 86

GALE RIVER

BETHLEHEM to FRANCONIA
GRAFTON COUNTY
NEW HAMPSHIRE ATLAS AND GAZETTEER
 MAPS 44, 45

Fish: Brook trout, brown trout
Length: 18 miles

The headwaters of the Gale River lie deep in the White
Mountain National Forest near Twin Mountain. From
there the river flows west through Franconia joining
the Ammonoosuc just below the town of Littleton.
The Gale River parallels Route 18 in several sections, and
is accessible from secondary roads in other areas.
There is good brook trout fishing over the entire length
of this fast-moving mountain stream which is periodically stocked by the New Hampshire Fish and Game
Department.

Beaver Brook

North Branch

Thompson Brook

Spruce Brook

Burnt Brook

South Branch

Scarface Brook

Priest Hill
+

Big Bickford
Mountain
+

Scarface
Mountain
+

Bickford
Mountain
+

3

93

Jordan Brook

Lafayette Brook

Franconia
Notch

Echo
Lake

+ Garnet
Mountain

Wiseman Brook

Black Brook

Indian Creek

Franconia

18

Tucker Brook

Meadow Brook

Ham Branch

Streeter
Pond

Garnet Hill
+

Ammonoosuc
River

1 MILE

MAP 87

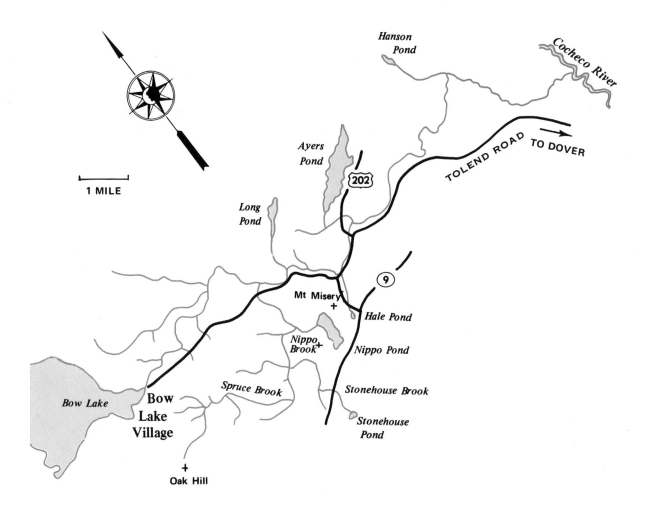

ISINGLASS RIVER

STRAFFORD to BARRINGTON
STRAFFORD COUNTY
NEW HAMPSHIRE ATLAS AND GAZETTEER MAP 23

Fish: Brook trout, rainbow trout

Length: 14 miles

From its source in Bow Lake in Strafford, the Isinglass River flows east, joining the Cocheco River south of Rochester. A road from Bow Lake parallels the river which crosses several state highways on its way to the Cocheco River. The state highway intersections are good access points to the river. Those willing to walk a short distance can gain access off the roads that parallel the river.

The Isinglass offers excellent trout fishing, though it is not a prime area like the streams and rivers in the northern part of the state. It is heavily stocked along its entire length. Best trout fishing spots are in the areas near roads, where stocking trucks have access. Anglers who fish the river by boat or canoe report good fishing because they are able to fish areas inaccessible by foot.

MAP 88

LAMPREY RIVER

DEERFIELD to NEWMARKET
ROCKINGHAM, STRAFFORD COUNTIES
NEW HAMPSHIRE ATLAS AND GAZETTEER MAP 14, 15, 16

Fish: Rainbow trout, brook trout, largemouth bass, yellow perch, hornpout, coho salmon, saltwater smelt, white perch.
Length: 43 miles.

The Lamprey is a truly exceptional river offering a vast variety of fishing. It contains every type of stream and river fish you could expect to find in New England. Undeveloped along its entire length, except at Newmarket, it is a pretty river to be on and to fish.

The state stocks the Lamprey heavily with trout and there is good to excellent trout fishing in the upper parts of the river around the Wiswall Dam and Packers Falls, and in the tributaries of the North and Little Rivers.

The Lamprey also boasts excellent bass fishing in its lower reaches, especially in the waters just above Wiswall Dam to the head of the tidewater in Newmarket. The section of Newmarket near Route 108 below Packers Falls is the best pickerel and bass ice fishing spot in southeastern New Hampshire. This is a good section to float with a boat or canoe. Easy access is available off many roads near the river.

Coho and Atlantic salmon are being stocked in the Lamprey. While cohos have established a sizeable population, Atlantics have not. The coho, some of them 10 to 12 pounds, sometimes jump clear out of the water, offering an unforgettable sight and one unduplicated anywhere in the state. The best place to see the coho is behind the mills at the head of the dam in Newmarket.

Anglers are still experimenting with lures for coho salmon and have reported some success with medium or large fluorescent wobbling plugs, especially the orange ones. Coho can also be taken on silver wobblers, red and white spoons and brightly colored flies. You may see many fish jumping, but you may have to spend hours to get any to strike. If you do land one, it may be the fish of a lifetime.

Saltwater smelt is another Lamprey River specialty. In winter, smelt ice fishing is popular, especially below the Newmarket Dam. Smelt may be taken as soon as the ice forms through March. The Lamprey also contains large numbers of white perch which may be taken through the ice with the same tackle and bait used for smelt.

There are many access points to the river and several places to park, buy bait and rent ice houses in the area.

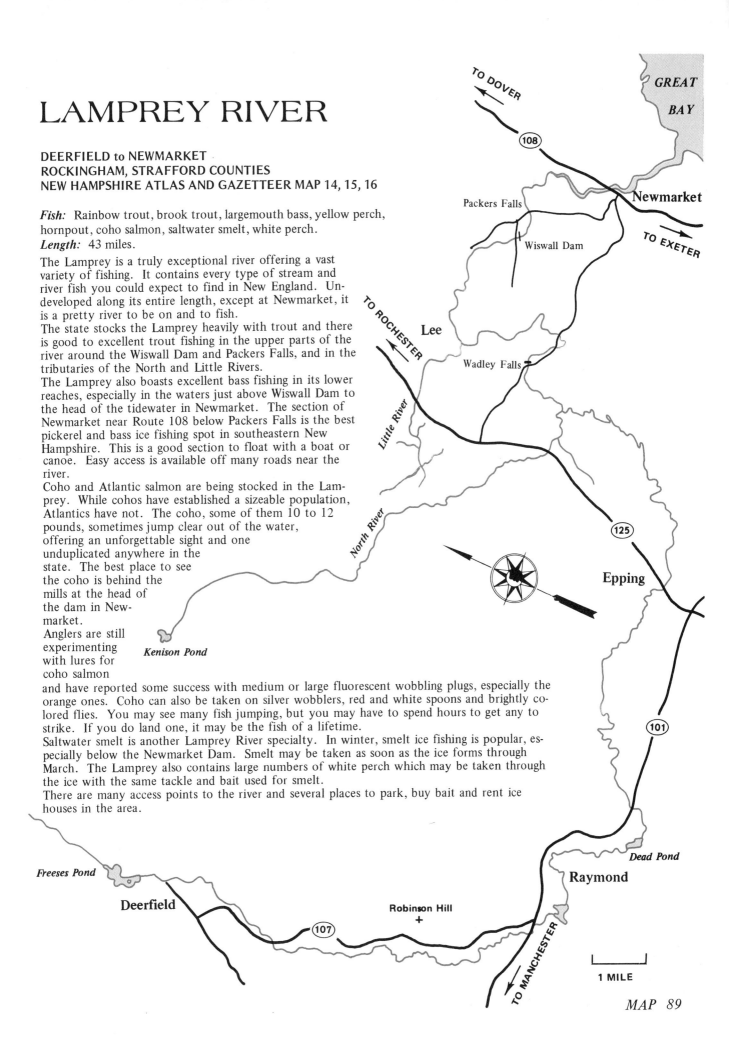

GREAT BAY

TO DOVER

108

Newmarket

Packers Falls

TO EXETER

Wiswall Dam

TO ROCHESTER

Lee

Wadley Falls

Little River

North River

125

Epping

Kenison Pond

101

Dead Pond

Freeses Pond

Raymond

Deerfield

Robinson Hill
+

107

TO MANCHESTER

1 MILE

MAP 89

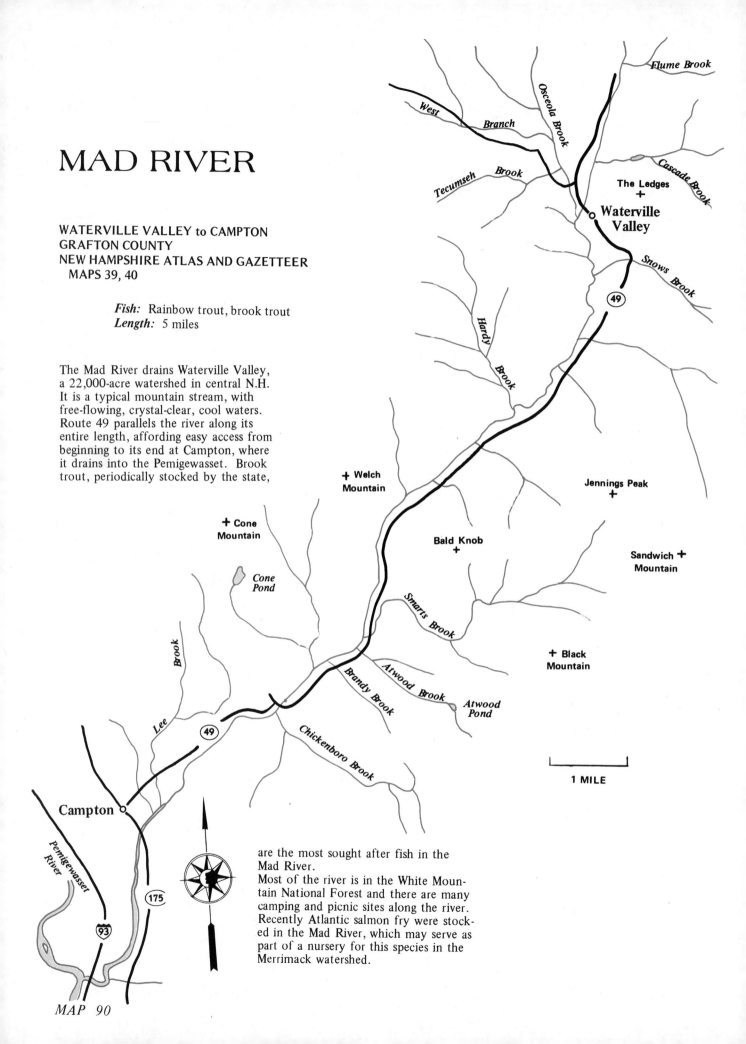

MAD RIVER

WATERVILLE VALLEY to CAMPTON
GRAFTON COUNTY
NEW HAMPSHIRE ATLAS AND GAZETTEER
MAPS 39, 40

Fish: Rainbow trout, brook trout
Length: 5 miles

The Mad River drains Waterville Valley, a 22,000-acre watershed in central N.H. It is a typical mountain stream, with free-flowing, crystal-clear, cool waters. Route 49 parallels the river along its entire length, affording easy access from beginning to its end at Campton, where it drains into the Pemigewasset. Brook trout, periodically stocked by the state, are the most sought after fish in the Mad River.

Most of the river is in the White Mountain National Forest and there are many camping and picnic sites along the river. Recently Atlantic salmon fry were stocked in the Mad River, which may serve as part of a nursery for this species in the Merrimack watershed.

MAP 90

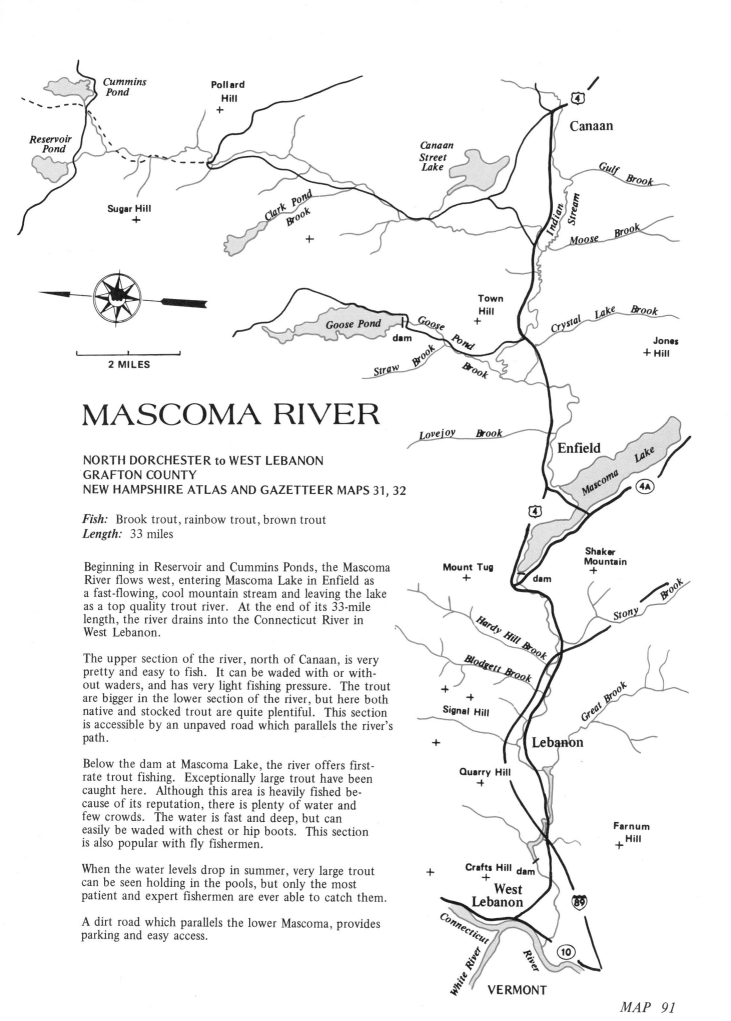

MASCOMA RIVER

NORTH DORCHESTER to WEST LEBANON
GRAFTON COUNTY
NEW HAMPSHIRE ATLAS AND GAZETTEER MAPS 31, 32

Fish: Brook trout, rainbow trout, brown trout
Length: 33 miles

Beginning in Reservoir and Cummins Ponds, the Mascoma River flows west, entering Mascoma Lake in Enfield as a fast-flowing, cool mountain stream and leaving the lake as a top quality trout river. At the end of its 33-mile length, the river drains into the Connecticut River in West Lebanon.

The upper section of the river, north of Canaan, is very pretty and easy to fish. It can be waded with or without waders, and has very light fishing pressure. The trout are bigger in the lower section of the river, but here both native and stocked trout are quite plentiful. This section is accessible by an unpaved road which parallels the river's path.

Below the dam at Mascoma Lake, the river offers first-rate trout fishing. Exceptionally large trout have been caught here. Although this area is heavily fished because of its reputation, there is plenty of water and few crowds. The water is fast and deep, but can easily be waded with chest or hip boots. This section is also popular with fly fishermen.

When the water levels drop in summer, very large trout can be seen holding in the pools, but only the most patient and expert fishermen are ever able to catch them.

A dirt road which parallels the lower Mascoma, provides parking and easy access.

MAP 91

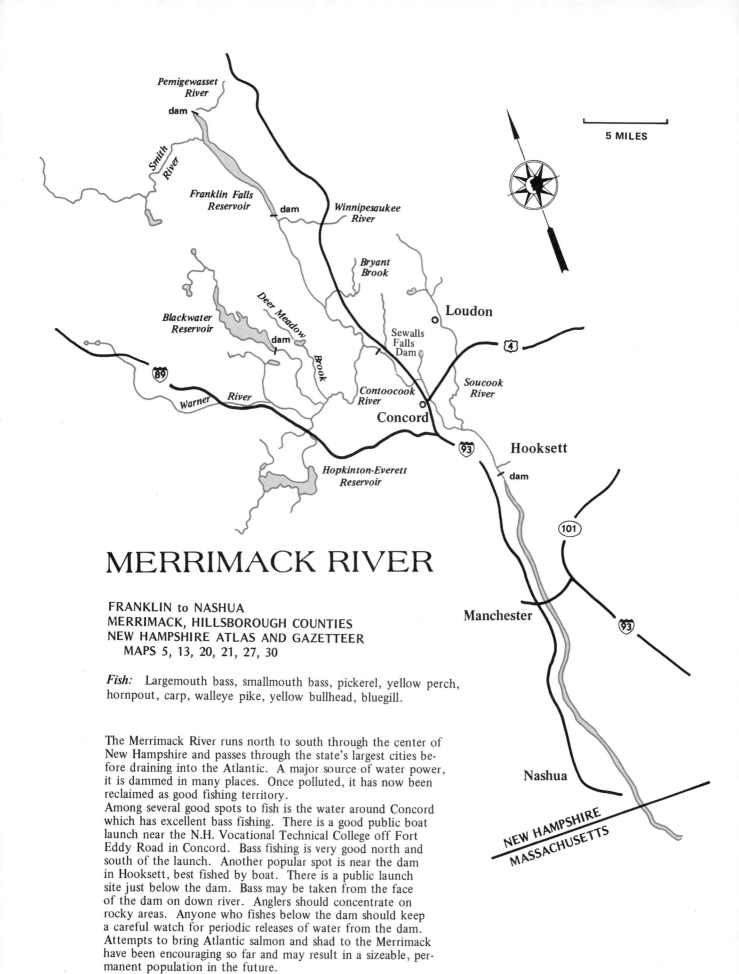

MERRIMACK RIVER

FRANKLIN to NASHUA
MERRIMACK, HILLSBOROUGH COUNTIES
NEW HAMPSHIRE ATLAS AND GAZETTEER
MAPS 5, 13, 20, 21, 27, 30

Fish: Largemouth bass, smallmouth bass, pickerel, yellow perch, hornpout, carp, walleye pike, yellow bullhead, bluegill.

The Merrimack River runs north to south through the center of New Hampshire and passes through the state's largest cities before draining into the Atlantic. A major source of water power, it is dammed in many places. Once polluted, it has now been reclaimed as good fishing territory.

Among several good spots to fish is the water around Concord which has excellent bass fishing. There is a good public boat launch near the N.H. Vocational Technical College off Fort Eddy Road in Concord. Bass fishing is very good north and south of the launch. Another popular spot is near the dam in Hooksett, best fished by boat. There is a public launch site just below the dam. Bass may be taken from the face of the dam on down river. Anglers should concentrate on rocky areas. Anyone who fishes below the dam should keep a careful watch for periodic releases of water from the dam. Attempts to bring Atlantic salmon and shad to the Merrimack have been encouraging so far and may result in a sizeable, permanent population in the future.

MAP 92

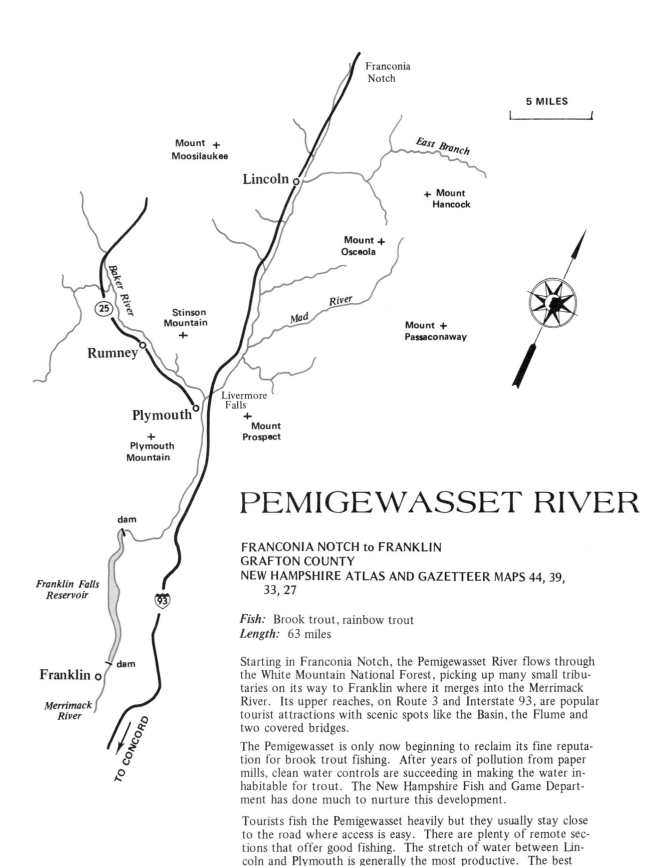

5 MILES

Franconia
Notch

East Branch

Mount +
Moosilaukee

Lincoln o

+ Mount
Hancock

Mount +
Osceola

Baker River

River

25

Mad

Stinson
Mountain
+

Mount +
Passaconaway

Rumney o

Livermore
Falls

Plymouth o

+
Mount
Prospect

+
Plymouth
Mountain

PEMIGEWASSET RIVER

FRANCONIA NOTCH to FRANKLIN
GRAFTON COUNTY
NEW HAMPSHIRE ATLAS AND GAZETTEER MAPS 44, 39,
33, 27

Fish: Brook trout, rainbow trout
Length: 63 miles

dam

Franklin Falls
Reservoir

93

Franklin o

dam

Merrimack
River

TO CONCORD

Starting in Franconia Notch, the Pemigewasset River flows through
the White Mountain National Forest, picking up many small tributaries on its way to Franklin where it merges into the Merrimack
River. Its upper reaches, on Route 3 and Interstate 93, are popular
tourist attractions with scenic spots like the Basin, the Flume and
two covered bridges.

The Pemigewasset is only now beginning to reclaim its fine reputation for brook trout fishing. After years of pollution from paper
mills, clean water controls are succeeding in making the water in-
habitable for trout. The New Hampshire Fish and Game Department has done much to nurture this development.

Tourists fish the Pemigewasset heavily but they usually stay close
to the road where access is easy. There are plenty of remote sections that offer good fishing. The stretch of water between Lincoln and Plymouth is generally the most productive. The best
fishing begins in late May/early June;

MAP 93

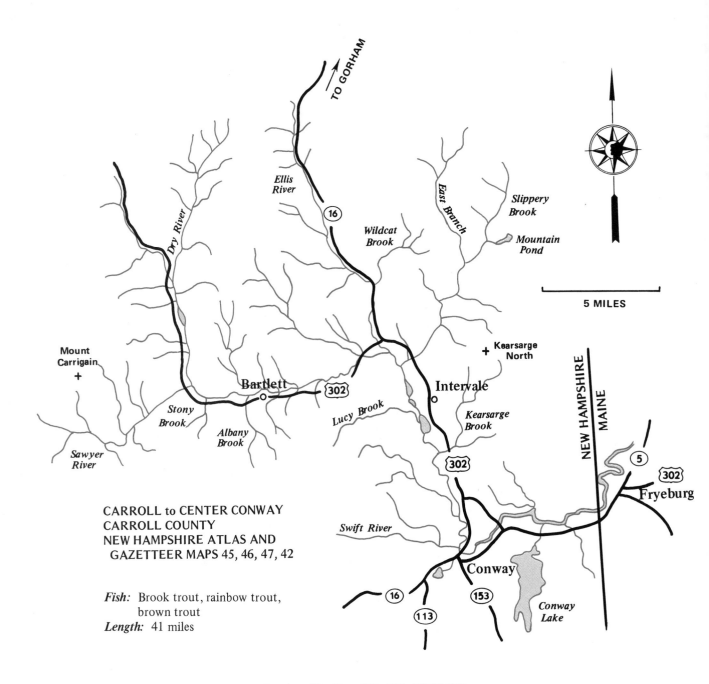

**CARROLL to CENTER CONWAY
CARROLL COUNTY
NEW HAMPSHIRE ATLAS AND
GAZETTEER MAPS 45, 46, 47, 42**

Fish: Brook trout, rainbow trout,
         brown trout
Length: 41 miles

SACO RIVER

The Saco River originates at Saco Lake, a small pond just north of Crawford Notch State Reservation in the town of Carroll. It flows southeast for 41 miles before crossing into Maine near Center Conway. Although the Saco lies in the heart of New Hampshire's vacation region, the river is not heavily fished.

The Saco's upper reaches near Bartlett are filled with small native and stocked trout. The middle section, from Bartlett to Conway, is wider and supports larger fish. It, too, is liberally stocked. The river widens even more as it heads for the Maine border and it holds some exceptionally large brook trout. Anglers who take the time to learn where the big brown trout are in this area may be rewarded with fish that weigh as much as six pounds.

The best time to fish the river is from June 1 to mid-August when the fish feed readily and there is opportunity to catch exceptionally large trophy fish. The river is easily accessible from many state roads. It can be fished and waded over its entire length.

MAP 94

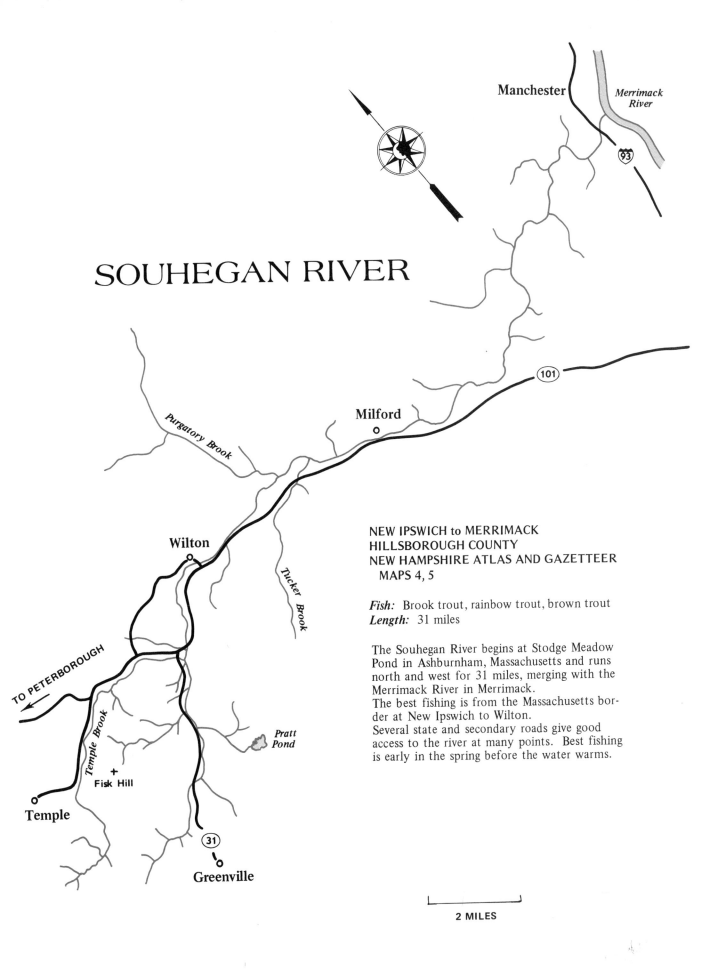

SOUHEGAN RIVER

Manchester

Merrimack River

93

101

Purgatory Brook

Milford
○

Tucker Brook

Wilton
○

TO PETERBOROUGH

Temple Brook

+ Fisk Hill

○ **Temple**

Pratt Pond

31

○ **Greenville**

NEW IPSWICH to MERRIMACK
HILLSBOROUGH COUNTY
NEW HAMPSHIRE ATLAS AND GAZETTEER
MAPS 4, 5

Fish: Brook trout, rainbow trout, brown trout
Length: 31 miles

The Souhegan River begins at Stodge Meadow
Pond in Ashburnham, Massachusetts and runs
north and west for 31 miles, merging with the
Merrimack River in Merrimack.
The best fishing is from the Massachusetts border at New Ipswich to Wilton.
Several state and secondary roads give good
access to the river at many points. Best fishing
is early in the spring before the water warms.

2 MILES

MAP 95

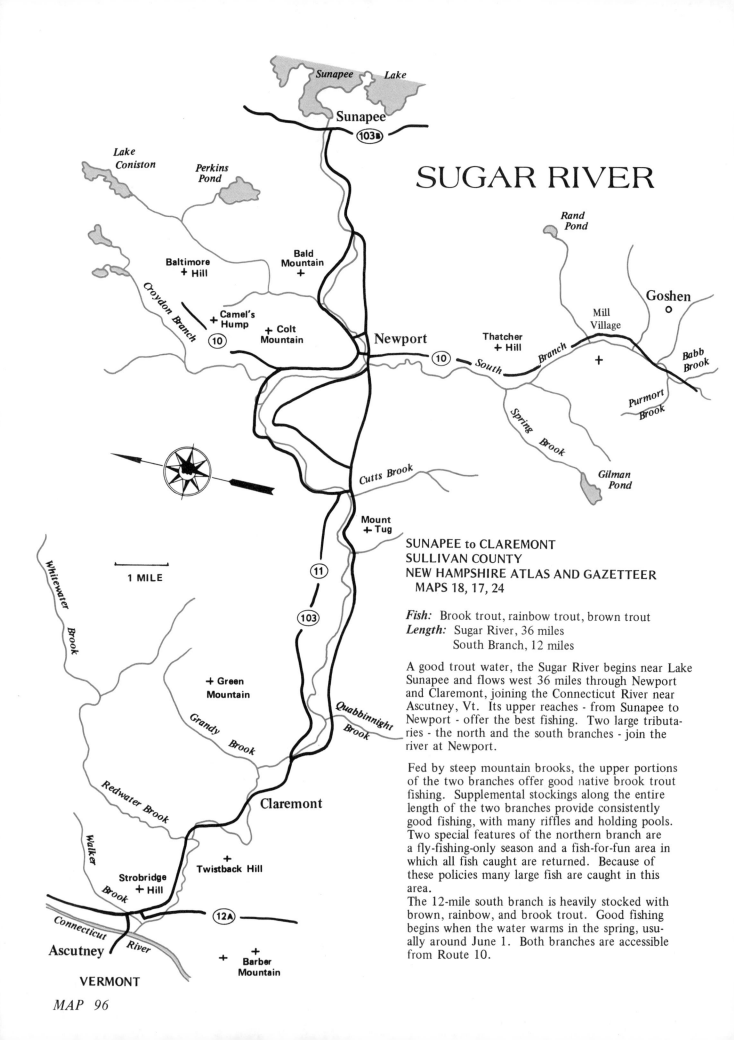

SUGAR RIVER

SUNAPEE to CLAREMONT
SULLIVAN COUNTY
NEW HAMPSHIRE ATLAS AND GAZETTEER
MAPS 18, 17, 24

Fish: Brook trout, rainbow trout, brown trout
Length: Sugar River, 36 miles
South Branch, 12 miles

A good trout water, the Sugar River begins near Lake Sunapee and flows west 36 miles through Newport and Claremont, joining the Connecticut River near Ascutney, Vt. Its upper reaches - from Sunapee to Newport - offer the best fishing. Two large tributaries - the north and the south branches - join the river at Newport.

Fed by steep mountain brooks, the upper portions of the two branches offer good native brook trout fishing. Supplemental stockings along the entire length of the two branches provide consistently good fishing, with many riffles and holding pools. Two special features of the northern branch are a fly-fishing-only season and a fish-for-fun area in which all fish caught are returned. Because of these policies many large fish are caught in this area.

The 12-mile south branch is heavily stocked with brown, rainbow, and brook trout. Good fishing begins when the water warms in the spring, usually around June 1. Both branches are accessible from Route 10.

MAP 96

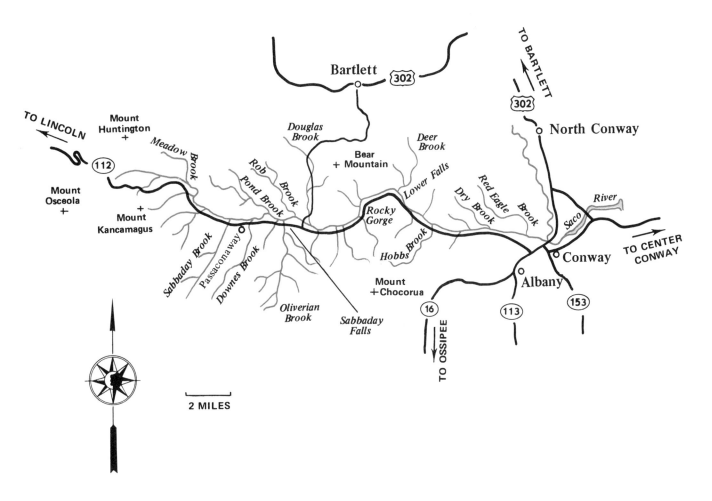

SWIFT RIVER

LIVERMORE to CONWAY
GRAFTON COUNTY, CARROLL COUNTY
NEW HAMPSHIRE ATLAS AND GAZETTEER MAPS 40, 41

Fish: Brook trout, rainbow trout, brown trout
Length: 23 miles

With its mountain scenery, rushing waters, and cool temepratures, the Swift River is a typical mountain stream - a beautiful place to be and fish. Its source is deep in the White Mountain National Forest, near Mount Kangamagus. From there it flows east 24 miles along the Kangamagus Highway (Route 112). It cascades through falls, rapids, riffles and deep pools as it travels to Conway where it merges into the Saco River.

There are plenty of good-sized trout in the Swift River, particularly brook trout. The tributaries of the river are also well-known for fishing; Sabbaday Brook deserves special note. There are several campgrounds along the river. The heaviest fishing pressures are near the campgrounds and close to the Kangamagus Highway. Tourists fish the Swift River heavily, but only from the easy access points. Because the Fish and Game Department stocks the river, there is always a good supply of fish. Fishermen willing to walk to some of the remote fishing areas will be amply rewarded.

The best fishing on the Swift River begins June 1 and continues until August.

MAP 97

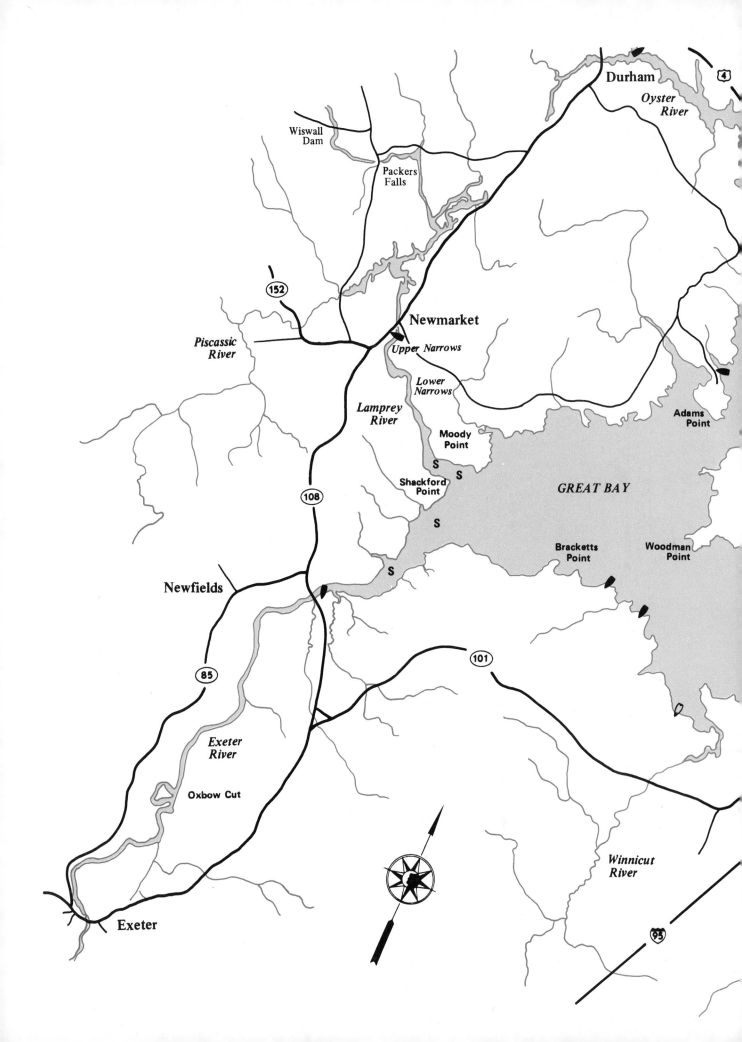

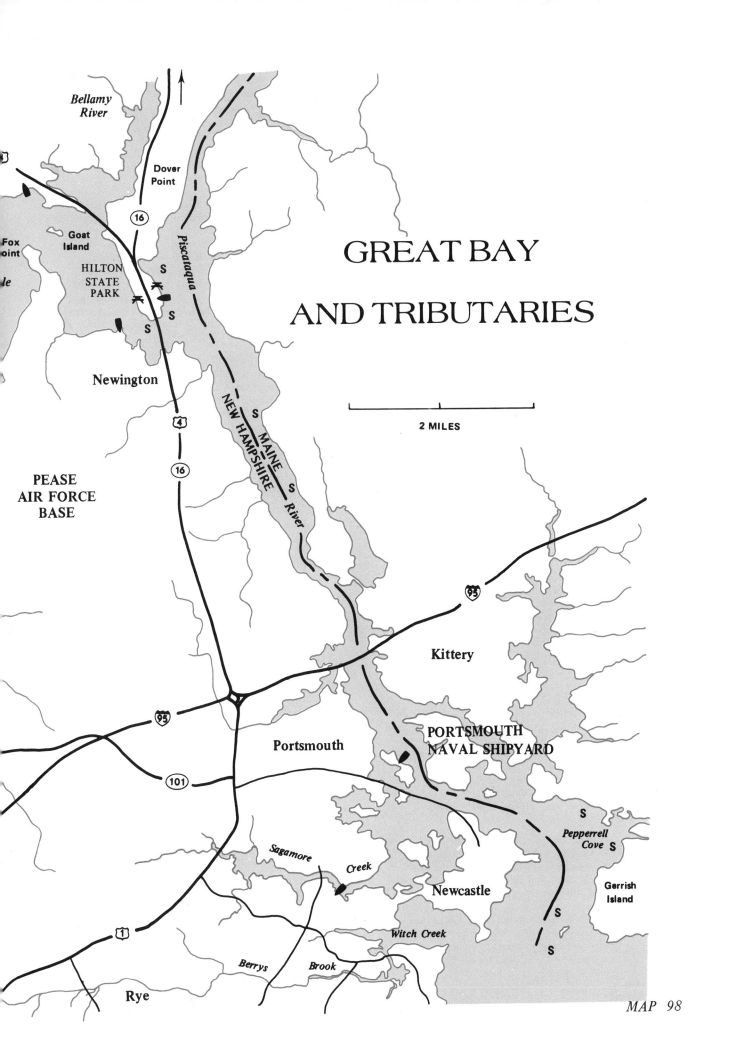

Bellamy
River

Dover
Point

Fox
Point

Goat
Island

HILTON
STATE
PARK

(16)

S
S
S
S
S

Piscataqua

Newington

(4)

(16)

PEASE
AIR FORCE
BASE

MAINE

NEW HAMPSHIRE

S

S

River

GREAT BAY

AND TRIBUTARIES

2 MILES

(95)

Kittery

(95)

Portsmouth

PORTSMOUTH
NAVAL SHIPYARD

(101)

S

Pepperrell
Cove S

Sagamore

Creek

Newcastle

Gerrish
Island

(1)

Witch Creek

S

Berrys   Brook

S

Rye

MAP 98

GREAT BAY AND TRIBUTARIES

SEA-RUN SALMON

The Great Bay and its tributaries offer some tremendous opportunities to catch three species of sea-run salmon. Atlantic, Coho and Chinook salmon live in these waters and can be caught by those holding valid N.H. fishing licenses.

The Atlantic salmon is the first to appear in the spring. Unlike the Coho and Chinook, Atlantic salmon make repeated freshwater spawnings. Coho and Chinook salmon return from the ocean to freshwater, spawn and die.

Fishing for salmon usually begins in early July at the mouth of the Piscataqua River. When the fish are in this area, they may be taken by trolling in the mouth of the river or in the open ocean out in front of the river's mouth. Best success is with brightly colored lures and large bright flies. Lures resembling herring are the best; favored colors are red and white or purple and white. Suggested lures include floating rapalas, numbers 9 and 11; flatfish, sizes X to L; and four-to-five-inch silver spoons. Trolling should be from the surface to about 25 feet in depth with a trolling plane, downriggers or lead core line. One lure should always be trolled in the prop wash within 10 feet of the boat.

The fish soon move into Pepperrell Cove. Here the preferred method of fishing is from an anchored boat in 25 to 60 feet of water. The best bait is either live herring or tommy cod. Also effective is a strip of mackerel belly one-inch wide, one-eighth inch thick and three or four inches long on a No. 2 or No. 4 hook. The bait should be fished between 10 and 20 feet with a light weight allowing the current and the rocking of the boat to provide the necessary action. Fishing is usually best at daybreak and on the outgoing tide.

By mid-August fish begin moving into the vicinity of Dover Point and may be seen breaking water in numbers. Trolling this area with lures and spinfishing from shore are both effective ways of taking fish. Hilton State Park, on both sides of Route 4, provides excellent access. From this time until the time when salmon appear at the mouth of the Lamprey River (usually around early September), trolling between these two locations is effective. Popular spots are Fox Point, Adams Point, the mouth of the Oyster River and the Goat Island area. Fishing usually peaks in the Hilton Park area during the first two weeks of September.

From early September on, salmon begin increasing in numbers at the mouth of the Lamprey and Exeter Rivers. Again, they will be seen breaking water continually. Trolling in this area and up into both rivers is effective through October and beyond if the weather holds. During this time fish are continually moving up these two rivers and concentrating in increasing numbers. Casting to jumping fish from an anchored or drifting boat, especially during low tide, often works as well as trolling. Fluorescent and shiny lures are usually best. Fishing generally peaks around the latter part of October with fish continuing to move upriver until mid-December or until it gets very cold.

Good spots on the Lamprey River are the Upper and Lower Narrows and the pool below Newmarket Dam. While there is a fish ladder in this dam, New Hampshire Fish and Game Department authorities trap all the salmon in order to get an accurate count of migrating fish and to check previously marked fish. Some fish are retained for breeding stock; the rest are put into the fresh water above the dam. From here, the salmon continue to migrate upstream to the last barrier, Wiswall Dam. Salmon may be found in pools and riffles from Wiswall Dam downstream a mile or more, with fish continuing to move up and down the river.

While the salmon are in the fresh water, they do not feed, but strike out of pure meaness. They may be taken on a variety of lures including daredevils, Mepps spinners, Mooselook Warblers and the Otter-Get, and on plugs such as flatfish and tadpolleys. Salmon may also be taken on flies in fresh water. Large, bright streamers and bucktails work well. The blondes, Cardinelle, marabou and various steelhead patterns are good choices. Use hook sizes 2 to 4 on most patterns, 2/0 to 1/0 for the blondes, and choose bright colors such as fluorescent orange or red, green and yellow.

Access to the upper Lamprey is the Packers Falls Road out of Newmarket. Parking is somewhat limited on the upper river, but there are small parking areas at Packers Falls and near the Wiswall Dam. Much property along the upper river is posted and landowners' rights should be respected. Fishermen should refrain from littering or more posting could result.

SEA-RUN BROWN TROUT

Berry Brook, which crosses Brackett Road in Rye, just off Route 1-A, boasts a population of sea-run brown trout. These fish ascend Berry Brook to spawn in September or early October and may be taken until December 1, the end of the special season for this species. The trout tend to run large and can be seen in numbers from the bridge during the spawning run. Extreme care should be exercised when stalking these fish. While they may be taken by any legal means, many anglers prefer flies and patterns resembling the natural food found in tidal estuaries.

Brown trout are wary and difficult to catch under ordinary conditions, but Berry Brook, with its lack of cover, offers a special challenge. However, for the patient angler with a desire to catch a trophy brown trout, a unique opportunity awaits him at Berry Brook.

COOS

GRAFTON

CARROLL

BELKNAP

STRAFFORD

SULLIVAN

MERRIMACK

ROCKINGHAM

CHESHIRE

HILLSBOROUGH

HOW TO USE THE NEW HAMPSHIRE
ATLAS AND GAZETTEER TO LOCATE
THESE LAKES AND PONDS...

SIXTY-SEVEN PAGES OF MAPS DETAILING THE ENTIRE STATE OF NEW HAMPSHIRE

The
New
Hampshire
Atlas

and
Gazetteer

DeLORME
MAPPING COMPANY

TOWN POPULATIONS   CITY STREET MAPS

AFTER THE NAME OF EACH LAKE OR POND
LISTED IN THIS DIRECTORY IS THE NAME
OF THE TOWN WHERE IT IS LOCATED. TO
FIND THE TOWN, LOOK IN THE ATLAS ON
PAGES 2 AND 3 AND TURN TO THE MAP
NUMBER GIVEN FOR THAT LOCALITY.
NOTE: ATLAS MAP NUMBERS ARE GIVEN
FOR EACH FISHING MAP PRINTED IN THIS
BOOK.

**ABBREVIATIONS
OF FISH SPECIES**

A   Alewife

BS	Bass
LB	Largemouth Bass
SB	Smallmouth Bass
BG	Bluegill
HP	Bullhead (Hornpout)
C	Burbot (Cusk)
BC	Black Crappie

WP	White Perch
YP	Yellow Perch
PK	Pickerel
P	Northern Pike
S	Landlocked Salmon
SM	Rainbow Smelt
SP	Splake

BK	Brook Trout
BN	Brown Trout
LT	Lake Trout
RT	Rainbow Trout
G	Sunapee Trout (Golden Trout)
W	Walleye
WF	Whitefish

FISHING DIRECTORY OF NEW HAMPSHIRE LAKES AND PONDS

**BELKNAP
COUNTY**

Adams Pond, Barnstead: SB, PK, HP, WP, YP
Badger Pond, Belmont: HP
Bear Pond, Alton: LB, HP, PK (no motorboats)
Bear Pond, Center Harbor: PK, HP, YP

Belknap Recreation Area Pond, Gilford: BK
Brindle Pond, Barnstead: SB, PK, HP, WP, YP (boating restriction: electric motors only)
Cawley Pond, Sanbornton: PK, HP, YP (no motorboats)
Clough Pond, Belmont: BK
Crystal Lake, Gilmanton: see Map 18
Forest Pond, Meredith, New Hampton: PK, HP, YP
Gilman Pond, Alton: LB, HP, YP (no motorboats)
Halfmoon Pond, Alton, Barnstead: see Map 30
Hawkins Pond, Center Harbor: PK, HP, YP
Hermit Lake (Plummer Pond, Bog Pond), Sanbornton: LB, PK, HP, YP
Hills Pond, Alton: PK, HP, YP
Hunkins Pond, Sanbornton: RT (no motorboats)
Huntress Pond (Pinkham Pond), Barnstead: SB, PK, HP, YP
Jackson Pond, New Hampton: PK, HP, YP
Knights Pond, Alton: LB, HP (no motorboats)
Lily Lake (Horn Pond), Barnstead, Pittsfield: LB, PK, HP, WP, YP
Lily Pond, Gilford: LB, HP, PK, YP
Little Pond (Page Pond), Meredith: PK, HP, YP (no motor-

boats)
Long Pond (Winona Lake), Center Harbor, New Hampton: SB
Loon Pond, Gilmanton: SB, PK, HP, YP
Lougee Pond (Skunk Pond), Barnstead: PK, HP, YP (boating restriction: electric motors only, maximum speed 5 mph)
Manning Lake, Gilmanton: see Map 40
Meetinghouse Pond, Gilmanton: PK, HP, YP (boating restriction: electric motors only)
Mountain Pond, Sanbornton: BK
Otter Pond, Center Harbor: PK, HP, YP
Pemigewasset Pond (Kelly Pond), Meredith, New Hampton: see Map 53
Pickerel Pond, Laconia, Meredith: PK, HP, YP
Pout Pond, Belmont: HP, YP
Randlett Pond (Robinson Pond), Meredith: PK, HP, YP
Rocky Pond, Gilmanton, Canterbury, Loudon: PK, HP, YP
Rollins Pond, Gilmanton: PK, HP, YP (boating restriction: electric motors only)
Round Pond, Gilford: BK, HP

Round Pond, Gilmanton: HP, YP
Saltmarsh Pond, Gilford: BK, RT (no motorboats)
Sargent Reservoir, Belmont: BK, HP
Sawyer Pond (Sawyer Reservoir), Gilmanton: HP, YP
Shellcamp Pond, Gilmanton: PK, HP, YP
Silver Lake, Tilton, Belmont, Northfield: RT, BN, S, SB, BK, HP, YP, SM
Sky Pond, New Hampton: BK
Spectacle Pond, Meredith: PK, HP, YP
Squam Lake, Holderness, Center Harbor, Sandwich, Moultonboro: see Map 61
Suncook Pond, Lower, Barnstead: see Map 67
Suncook Pond, Upper, Barnstead: see Map 68
Sunset Lake (Places Pond), Gilmanton: see Map 69
Waukewan Lake (Measley Pond), Meredith, New Hampton: see Map 74
Wickwas Lake, Meredith: see Map 78
Winnipesaukee Lake, Alton, Center Harbor, Gilford, Laconia, Meredith, Moultonboro, Tuftonboro, Wolfeboro: see Map 81
Winnisquam Lake, Sanbornton, Laconia, Tilton, Meredith, Belmont: see Map 80

CARROLL COUNTY

Archer's Pond, Ossipee: PK, HP, YP
Atwood Pond, Sandwich: BK
Balch Pond, Wakefield: see Map 7
Barville Pond, Sandwich: PK, HP, YP
Batson Pond, Wolfeboro: PK, HP, YP
Bean Pond, Ossipee: BK
Bearcamp Pond, Sandwich: PK, HP, YP
Beech Pond, Lower, Tuftonboro: SB, PK, HP, YP
Beech Pond, Upper, Wolfeboro: SB, PK, YP
Berry Pond, Moultonboro: PK, HP, YP (no motorboats)
Black Mountain Pond, Sandwich: BK
Blue Pond, Madison: BK
Chocorua Lake, Tamworth: see Map 11 (no motorboats)
Church Pond, Livermore, Albany: PK, HP
Conner Pond, Ossipee: BK, G
Conway Lake, Conway, Eaton: see Map 16
Cooks Pond, Brookfield: SB, PK, HP, YP
Cooks Pond, Madison: PK, HP, YP
Copps Pond, Tuftonboro: BK
Crescent Lake, Wolfeboro: SB, PK, HP, YP
Crystal Lake (Robertson Pond), Eaton: RT, LT, SP, PK, HP, YP
Dan Hole Pond, Ossipee, Tuftonboro: see Map 20
Dan Hole Pond, Little, Ossipee: see Map 20
Danforth Pond, Lower (Danforth Bay), Freedom: BK, SB, PK, HP, YP, C
Danforth Pond, Middle (Danforth Bay), Freedom: SB, PK, HP, YP
Danforth Pond, Upper (Goodwin Pond), Freedom: SB, PK, YP
Davis Pond, Madison: PK, HP, YP
Dinsmore Pond, Sandwich: PK, HP, YP
Dollof Pond, Conway: HP, YP
Duck Pond, (Stacy Mt. Trout Pond), Freedom: BK, PK, HP, YP
Duncan Lake, Ossipee: BK, RT
Durgin Pond, Madison: PK, HP, YP
Falls Pond, Albany: BK
Garland Pond (Upper Red Hill Pond), Moultonboro: SB, PK, HP, YP
Garland Pond, Ossipee: PK, HP, YP
Great East Lake, Wakefield: see Map 28
Great Hill Pond, Tamworth: PK, HP, YP
Great Hill School Pond (Hemmingway Pond, Duck Pond), Tamworth: HP
Guinea Pond, Sandwich: BK, SM
Hall Pond, Lower, Sandwich: BK
Hall Pond, Middle, Sandwich: BK
Hall Pond, Upper, Sandwich: BK (no motorboats)
Hatch Pond (Hidden Pond), Eaton: BK
Hutchins Mill Pond (Wilkinson Pond), Effingham: BK
Intervale Pond, Sandwich: SB, PK, HP, YP
Iona Lake, Albany: SB, PK, HP, YP
James Pond, Tamworth: BK
Kanasatka Lake (Long Pond), Moultonboro: SB, PK, HP, WP, YP
Kiah Pond, Sandwich: BK
Kimball Lake, Lower, Chatham: see Map 37
Kimball Lake, Upper (Webb Pond), Chatham: see Map 37
Kingswood Lake, Brookfield: SB, PK, HP
Kusumpe Pond, Sandwich: SB, PK, HP, YP
Labrador Pond, Conway: SB, HP, YP
Ledge Pond, Madison: BK (no motorboats)
Lees Pond, (Lower Red Hill Pond), Moultonboro: SB, PK, HP, YP
Little Pond, Sandwich: BK (no motorboats)
Long Pond, Eaton: BK

Loon Lake, Freedom: BK, RT, SB, PK, HP, YP, SM
Loud Pond, Madison: PK, WP, YP
Lovell Lake, Wakefield: see Map 39
Mack Pond, Madison: PK, HP, YP
Melvin Pond (Pope Pond), Tuftonboro: PK, HP, YP
Mirror Lake, Tuftonboro: see Map 45
Moody Pond, Ossipee: BK, YP
Moores Pond, Tamworth, Madison: BK, BN, PK, HP, YP
Mountain Pond, Chatham: BK
Ossipee Lake, Ossipee, Freedom: see Map 50
Pea Porridge Pond, Madison: BN, PK, HP, YP, SM
Pea Porridge Pond, Middle, Madison: PK, HP, YP
Pequawket Pond, Conway: PK, HP, YP, SM
Pine River Pond, Wakefield: see Map 54
Province Lake, Effingham, Wakefield: see Map 56
Province Pond, Chatham: BK
Pudding Pond, Conway: PK, HP, YP
Purity Lake, Madison, Eaton: PK, HP, YP
Red Hill Pond, Sandwich: PK, HP, YP
Round Pond, Wakefield: SB, PK, HP, YP
Rust Pond, Wolfeboro: see Map 57
Sargent's Pond (Duncan's Pond), Wolfeboro: PK, HP, YP
Shawtown Pond, (Shaw Pond), Freedom: BK
Silver Lake, Madison: see Map 58
Squam Lake, Big, Holderness, Center Harbor, Sandwich, Moultonboro: see Map 61
Trout Pond (Stacy Pond), Freedom: BK
Union Meadows Pond (Cate's Pond), Wakefield: BK, PK, HP, YP
Wakonda Pond (Round Pond), Moultonboro: PK, HP, YP
Wentworth Lake, Wolfeboro: see Map 76
White Lake, Tamworth: BK
White Pond, Ossipee: BK
Whitton Pond, Albany, Madison: SB, YP
Winnipesaukee Lake, Alton, Center Harbor, Gilford, Laconia, Meredith, Moultonboro, Tuftonboro, Wolfeboro: see Map 81

CHESHIRE COUNTY

Abbott Forest Pond (Cold Spring Pond), Stoddard: BK, RT (no motorboats)
Babbidge Reservoir, Roxbury: BK, PK, YP
Baker Pond (Baker-Hubbard Pond), Chesterfield: PK, HP, YP
Barrett Pond, Stoddard: PK, HP, YP
Beaver Pond, Harrisville: PK, HP, YP
Bolster Pond, Sullivan: PK, HP, YP
Bowker Pond, Fitzwilliam: PK, HP
Bullet Pond, Rindge: SB, PK, HP, YP
Caldwell Pond, Alstead: BK
Center Pond, Nelson: RT (no motorboats)
Center Pond, Stoddard: PK, HP, YP
Chapman Pond, Sullivan: BK
Chesham Pond (Symonds Pond), Harrisville: SB, LB, PK, HP, YP
Cheshire Pond, Jaffrey: LB, PK, HP
Childs Bog, Harrisville: LB, PK, HP, YP
Clapp Pond, Marlborough: LB, PK, HP, YP
Contoocook Lake, Jaffrey, Rindge: see Map 15
Corey Pond, Troy: PK, HP
Cranberry Ponds, Alstead: PK, HP, YP
Crane Pond, Alstead: BK, PK, HP, YP
Cummings Meadow Pond, Jaffrey: SB, PK, HP
Dark Pond, Dublin: LB, SB, PK, HP
Depot Pond (Collins Pond), Fitzwilliam: PK, HP, YP
Dinsmore Pond, Harrisville, Peterborough: RT, PK, HP, YP
Divol Pond, Rindge: LB, PK, HP
Dublin Lake (Monadnock Pond), Dublin: see Map 23
Ellis Reservoir, Nelson, Sullivan: PK, HP, YP
Emerson Pond, Rindge: LB, SB, PK, HP, YP
Farrar Pond, Troy: HP, YP
Forest Lake, Winchester: BK, RT, SB, PK, HP, YP
Frost Pond, Dublin, Jaffrey: SB, PK, HP
Fullam Pond, Chesterfield, Winchester: PK, HP, YP
Gilmore Pond, Jaffrey: SB, PK, HP
Goose Pond, Keene: PK, HP, YP
Granite Lake (Munsonville Pond), Nelson, Stoddard: see Map 27
Grassy Pond, Rindge: LB, PK, HP, YP
Gustin Pond, Marlow: BK, PK, HP, YP
Harrisville Pond (Upper Pond, Village Pond), Harrisville: BK, S, SB, PK, HP, YP, SM
Highland Lake (Long Pond), Stoddard, Washington: see Map 31
Howe Reservoir, Dublin, Harrisville: LB, SB, HP, WP, YP
Hubbard Pond, Rindge: SB, PK, HP, YP
Island Pond, Rindge, New Ipswich: PK, HP, WP
Island Pond, Stoddard: LB, SB, PK, HP, YP
Kidder's Pond, Alstead: BK, PK, HP, YP
Kilburn Pond, Hinsdale, Winchester: PK, HP, YP

Laurel Lake, Fitzwilliam: RT, SB, PK, HP
Lily Pond, Chesterfield: PK, HP, YP
Meetinghouse Pond, Marlborough: LB, PK, HP, YP
Monomonac Lake
  Rindge: see Map 46
Mud Pond, Dublin: PK, HP, YP
Mud Pond (Parker Pond), Harrisville: PK, HP, YP
Newell Pond, Alstead: BK
Nubanusit Lake, Hancock, Nelson: see Map 49
Parker Pond, Jaffrey: SB, PK, HP, WP, YP
Pearly Lake (Tarbell Pond), Rindge: LB, SB, PK, HP, WP, YP
Pisgah Reservoir, Winchester: BK, PK, HP, YP
Pool Pond, Rindge: SB, PK, HP
Robbins Pond (Harrington Pond), Rindge: SB, PK, HP, YP
Rockwood Pond, Fitzwilliam: SB, PK, HP, YP
Round Pond, North, Winchester: PK, HP, YP
Russell Reservoir, Harrisville: LB, SB, PK, HP, YP
Sand Pond (Echo Lake), Marlow, Lempster: BK
Sandown Pond, Troy: BK, PK, HP, YP
Sandy Pond, Richmond: BK
Scott Pond (Scott Meadow Pond), Fitzwilliam: LB, PK, HP
Silver Lake, Harrisville, Nelson: see Map 59
Sip Pond, Fitzwilliam: LB, PK, HP, YP
Skatutakee Lake, Harrisville: RT, SB, PK, HP
Spectacle Pond, Marlborough, Roxbury: PK, HP, YP
Spofford Lake, Chesterfield: see Map 60
Spoonwood Lake, Nelson: see Map 49
Spot Meadow Pond (Putnam Pond, West Meadow Brook Pond), Winchester: PK, HP
Stillwater Pond, Lower, Marlow: BK, BN, RT, SB, PK, HP, YP
Stone Pond, Marlborough, Dublin: BK
Stone Pond, Marlow: PK, YP
Swanzey Lake, Swanzey: BK, RT, SM
Taylor Pond, Stoddard: PK, HP, YP
Thorndike Pond, Dublin, Jaffrey: see Map 72
Tolman Pond, Nelson: SB, PK, HP, YP (no motorboats)
Trout Pond, Stoddard: BK, PK, HP, YP
Village Pond, Marlow: SB, PK, HP, YP
Warren Lake, Alstead: LB, SB, PK, HP
Wellman Pond, Alstead: PK, HP, YP
Wheeler Pond (Case's Pond), Richmond: PK, HP, YP
Wight Pond, Dublin: LB, SB, PK, HP, WP, YP
Wilson's Pond, Swanzey: LB, SB, PK, HP, YP
Woodward Pond (City Water Works Pond), Nelson, Roxbury: PK, HP, YP

COOS COUNTY

Abenaki Lake, Dixville: BK
Airport Pond, Whitefield: BK
Akers Pond, Errol: see Map 1
Back Lake, Pittsburg: see Map 6
Back Pond, Stewartstown: RT
Baker Pond, Lancaster: PK, HP, YP
Bear Brook Pond, Errol: BK, HP
Bear Brook Pond, Little, Wentworth's Location: BK
Big Brook Bog, Pittsburg: BK (no motorboats)
Blood Pond, Lancaster: BK, PK, WP
Bog Pond, Little or "Fourteen and a Half," Odell: BK
Burns Pond (Long Pond), Whitefield: BK, LB, SB, PK, HP, YP
Carr Pond, Clarksville: BK
Carter's Ponds, Bean's Purchase: BK
Cedar Pond, Milan: BK, RT, SB, PK, HP, YP, C, SM
Cherry Pond, Jefferson: PK, HP, YP (no motorboats)
Christine Lake (North Pond), Stark: BK, BN, SM
Clarksville Pond, Clarksville: BK, SM
Connecticut Lake, First, Pittsburg: see Map 12
Connecticut Lake, Second, Pittsburg: see Map 13
Connecticut Lake, Third, Pittsburg: see Map 14
Connecticut Lake, Fourth, Pittsburg: BK
Coon Brook Bog, Pittsburg: BK (no motorboats)
Corser Pond, Errol: BK
Devils Washbowl, Odell: BK
Diamond Pond, Big, Stewartstown: see Map 22
Diamond Pond, Little, Stewartstown: see Map 22
Dream Lake, Success: BK
Dummer Pond, Big, Dummer: BK
Dummer Pond, Little, Dummer: BK
Dustin Pond, Wentworth's Location: BK
East Inlet, Pittsburg: BK
Fish Pond, Columbia: BK, RT
Forest Lake (Round Pond), Dalton, Whitefield: LB, SB, PK, HP, WP, YP
Four Mile Pond, Dix's Grant: BK
Francis Lake, Pittsburg: see Map 24
Gentian Pond, Success: BK
Gloriette Lake, Dixville: BK
Greenough Pond, Big, Wentworth's Location: see Map 29

Greenough Pond, Little, Wentworth's Location: see Map 29
Harper's Meadow, Errol: PK
Harris Pond, Pittsburg: BK
Head Pond, Berlin: BK, PK, HP, YP
Hellgate Pond, Second College Grant: BK
Jacquith Pond, Pittsburg: BK
Ladd Pond, Stewartstown: BK
Lime Pond, Columbia: BK, SM
Lombard Pond, Colebrook: BK
Long Pond, Errol: RT
Long Pond, Millsfield: BK
Martin Meadow Pond, Lancaster: RT, LB, SB, PK, HP
Middle Pond, Pittsburg: BK (no motorboats)
Millsfield Pond, Big, Millsfield: BK
Mirror Lake (Blake Pond), Whitefield, Dalton: BK, RT
Moose Pond (Little Millsfield Pond), Millsfield: BK
Moose Pond, Pittsburg: BK (no motorboats)
Mountain Pond (Boundary Pond), Pittsburg: BK (no motorboats)
Mountain Pond, Errol: PK, HP
Mud Pond, Dixville: BK
Mud Pond, Dummer: BK
Munn Pond, Errol: BK
Nash Bog Pond, Odell, Stratford: dam out
Nathan Pond, Dixville: BK
Nay Pond, Milan: BK, SB, PK, HP, YP
Page Pond, Success: BK
Perry Pond, Pittsburg: BK
Phillips Pond, Odell: BK
Pike Pond, Stark: BK
Pond of Safety, Randolph: BK, HP
Pontook Reservoir, Dummer: BK, RT, PK, HP
Rock Pond, Millsfield: BK
Round Pond, Errol: BK
Round Pond, Pittsburg: BK
Saco Pond, Carroll: BK
Scott Bog, Pittsburg: BK (no motorboats)
Sessions Pond (Corner Pond), Dummer: BK
Shean Pond, Clarksville: BK
Signal Pond, Errol: BK
South Pond (Percy Pond), Stark: RT, LT, SB, PK, HP, YP
Stratford Bog Pond, Stratford: BK
Success Pond, Success: see Map 64
Sweat Pond, Errol: BK
Trio Pond No. 1, Odell: BK
Trio Pond No. 2, Odell: BK
Trio Pond No. 3, Odell: BK
Umbagog Lake, Errol, Cambridge: see Map 73
Unknown Pond, Pittsburg: BK
Weed Pond, Whitefield: PK, HP
Whaleback Pond, Errol: PK, YP
Whitcomb Pond, Odell: BK
Wright Pond, Pittsburg: BK

GRAFTON COUNTY

Armington Lake, Piermont: BK, RT, SB, PK, HP, YP
Baker Pond, Lower, Orford, Wentworth: LB, SB, PK, HP
Baker Pond, Upper, Orford: BK, RT, LB, SB, PK, HP, WP, YP
Beaver Lake, Woodstock: BK
Black Pond, Lincoln: BK, HP
Bog Pond, Lincoln: BK
Bryant Pond, Canaan, Dorchester: BK
Campton Bog (Rowbartwood), Campton: BK
Canaan Street Lake (Crystal Lake), Canaan: see Map 9
Carrigain Pond, Lincoln: BK
Church Pond, Big (Big Deer, Sugar Pond), Livermore, Albany: PK, HP
Church Pond, Little (Little Deer, Sugar Pond), Livermore: BK, PK, HP
Clark Pond, Canaan: SB, PK, HP, YP
Cole Pond, Enfield: BK
Cone Mountain Pond, Thornton: PK, HP
Constance Lake, Piermont: BK
Crystal Lake, Enfield: see Map 19
Cummins Pond, Dorchester: PK, HP, YP, SM
Derby Pond, Canaan, Orange: BK
Dick Brown Pond, Bridgewater: PK, HP
Dodge Pond, Lyman: BK, SB, PK, HP, YP
East Pond, Livermore: BK
Echo Lake, Franconia: BK
Elbow Pond, Woodstock: SB, PK, HP, YP
Ellsworth Pond, Ellsworth: PK, HP
Enfield Reservoir, Canaan: HP
Flat Mountain Pond, Waterville: BK
French Pond, Haverhill: SB, PK, HP, YP
Gardner Lake, Bath: SB, PK, HP, YP
George Pond, Enfield: PK, HP, YP
Goose Pond, Canaan: see Map 25
Grafton Pond (Truell Lake), Grafton: see Map 26
Grant's Pond, Grafton, Danbury: BK

Greeley Pond, Lower, Livermore: BK
Greeley Pond, Upper, Livermore: BK
Halfmile Pond, Enfield: BK
Halfmoon Pond, Grafton: PK, HP
Indian Pond, Orford: SB, HP, YP
Joe Coffin Pond, Lisbon: BK, HP
Katherine Lake, Piermont: PK, HP, WP, YP
Kilton Pond, Grafton: BK, PK, HP
Lary Pond, Canaan: PK, HP, WP
Lily Pond, Livermore: BK
Line Pond (Town Line Pond), Wentworth, Dorchester: PK, HP, YP
Long Pond, Benton: BK
Lonesome Lake, Lincoln: BK
Loon Lake, Plymouth, Rumney: BK, SB, PK, HP, WP, YP
Loon Pond, Lincoln: BK, HP
Mascoma Lake, Enfield, Lebanon: see Map 41
Mason Pond, Orford: PK, HP
Mirror Lake, Woodstock: SB, PK, HP, YP (no motorboats)
Mirror Lake (Mud Pond), Canaan: BK, PK, HP
Moosilauke Pond, Campton: BK
Newfound Lake, Bristol, Alexandria, Bridgewater, Hebron: see Map 47
Ogontz Lake, Lyman: BK, SB, PK, HP, YP
Oliverian Pond, Benton: BK
Orange Pond, Orange: BK, RT
Patridge Lake, Littleton, Lyman: BK, BN, SB, PK, HP, YP
Peaked Hill Pond, Thornton: BK
Pearl Lake, Lisbon: BK, SB, PK, HP, YP
Perch Pond, Campton: BK, RT
Perch Pond, Lisbon: RT
Post Pond, Lyme: BK, RT, S, PK, HP, YP, SM
Pout Pond, Lyme: PK, HP, YP
Profile Lake (Ferrins Pond), Franconia: BK
Reservoir Pond, Dorchester, Lyme: PK, HP, YP
Rock Pond, Wentworth: PK, HP
Rocky Pond, Wentworth: BK
Round Pond, Lyman: PK, HP, YP
Russell Pond, Woodstock: BK
Sawyer Pond, Livermore: BK, G, HP
Sawyer Pond, Little, Livermore: BK
Shoal Pond, Lincoln: BK
Smith Pond, Enfield: SB, PK, HP, YP
Spectacle Pond, Enfield, Grafton: SB, PK, HP, WP, YP
Spectacle Pond, Groton, Hebron: BK, RT
Squam Lake, Big, Holderness, Center Harbor, Sandwich, Moultonboro: see Map 61
Squam Lake, Little, Holderness, Ashland: see Map 62
Stinson Lake, Rumney, Ellsworth: see Map 63
Streeter Pond, Lisbon (Sugar Hill): BK, RT
Tarleton Lake, Warren, Piermont: see Map 71
Tewksbury Pond, Grafton: BK, RT, BN, SM
Three Ponds, Lower, Ellsworth, Warren: BK
Three Ponds, Middle, Ellsworth, Warren: BK
Three Ponds, Upper, Ellsworth, Warren: BK
Trout Pond, Lyme: BK
Wachipauka Pond (Meader Pond), Warren: RT
Week's Crossing Pond, Warren: BK
White Oak Pond, Holderness: see Map 77
Willey Pond (Ethan Pond), Bethlehem: BK
Wood Pond, Haverhill: PK, HP
Zealand Pond, Bethlehem: BK

HILLSBOROUGH COUNTY

Ayers Pond, Hudson: PK, HP
Baboosic Lake, Amherst: see Map 5
Badger Pond, Lyndeboro: PK, HP, YP
Bagley Pond, Hillsboro, Windsor: PK, HP, YP
Bailey Pond, New Boston: PK, HP, YP
Black Pond, Windsor: PK, HP, YP
Burton Pond, Lyndeboro: HP
Campbell Pond, Antrim: SB, HP, YP
Cemetery Pond (Walter Loom Pond, Unnamed Pond No. 2), New Ipswich: SB, PK, HP, YP
Contention Pond, Hillsboro: SB, PK, HP, YP
Crystal Lake (Mosquito Pond), Manchester: PK, HP, YP
Cunningham Pond, Peterborough: SB, PK, HP, YP
Darrah Pond, Litchfield: PK, HP, YP
Deering Reservoir, Deering: see Map 21
Dennison Pond, Francestown, New Boston: YP
Dorrs Pond, Manchester: PK, HP, YP
Dudley Pond, Deering: LB, SB, PK, HP (boating restriction: electric motors only)
Ferrin Pond, Weare: BN, HP (no motorboats)
Flints Pond, Hollis: LB, PK, HP, YP
Franklin Pierce Lake (Jackman Reservoir), Antrim, Hillsboro: LB, SB, HP, WP, YP
Glen Lake, Goffstown: PK, HP, YP
Gould Pond (Sunset Pond), Greenfield: LB, SB, PK, HP, YP
Gould Pond, Hillsboro: SB, PK, HP, YP
Green's Pond (Green Beaver Pond), Merrimack: PK, HP, YP

Gregg Lake, Antrim: SB, PK, HP, YP
Gumpas Pond, Pelham: PK, HP, YP
Halfmoon Pond, Hancock: SB, PK, HP, YP
Harris Pond, Pelham: SB, PK, HP, YP
Haunted Lake (Scobie Lake), Francestown: LB, SB, PK, HP, YP
Hogback Pond, Greenfield: PK, HP
Horseshoe Pond, Merrimack: BC, LB, SB, PK, HP, YP
Hunts Pond, Hancock: BK, RT, SB, PK, HP, YP
Island Pond, New Ipswich, Rindge: PK, HP, WP
Island Pond, Pelham: PK, SB, PK, HP, YP
Juggernaut Pond, Hancock: PK, HP, YP
Joe English Pond, Amherst, New Boston: PK, HP, YP
Long Pond, Manchester: PK, HP, YP
Long Pond, Pelham: LB, PK, HP, WP, YP
Loon Pond, Hillsboro: SB, PK, HP, YP
Lovewell Pond (Tolls Pond), Nashua: PK, HP, YP
Maxwell Pond, Manchester: PK, HP, YP
Melendy Pond (Lakin Pond), Brookline: PK, HP, YP
Moody Pond, Weare: BK, RT
Morton Pond, Mont Vernon: PK, HP
Mt. William Pond, Weare: BK, RT (boating restriction: electric motors only)
Naticook Lake (Reed's Pond), Merrimack: LB, SB, PK, HP, YP
Norway Pond, Hancock: SB, PK, HP, WP, YP
Nutt Pond, Manchester: PK, HP, WP, YP
Osgood Pond (Unnamed Pond No. 1), Milford: PK, HP, YP
Otter Lake, Greenfield: LB, SB, PK, HP, WP, YP
Otternick Pond (Tarnic Pond), Hudson: LB, PK, HP, YP
Pennichuck Pond, Hollis, Nashua: SB, PK, HP, YP
Pennichuck Water Works Pond, Nashua, Merrimack: LB, PK, HP, YP
Pierce Lake, Hillsboro: SB, PK, HP
Pleasant Lake, Francestown: SB, PK, HP, YP
Potanipo Pond, Brookline: SB, PK, HP
Pratt Pond, Mason: SB, PK, HP
Pratt Pond, New Ipswich: PK, HP, YP
Robinson Pond, Hudson: LB, PK, HP, YP
Rocky Pond, Hollis: LB, SB, PK, HP, YP
Rye Pond, Antrim, Nelson, Stoddard: PK, HP, YP
Sebbins Pond, Bedford: PK, HP, YP
Shattuck Pond, Francestown: LB, HP
Silver Lake (Long Pond), Hollis: SB, PK, HP, YP
Smith Pond, Windsor: BK
Steels Pond, Antrim: SB, PK, HP, YP
Stevens Pond, Manchester: LB, SB, PK, HP, YP
Weare Reservoir (Horace Lake), Weare: see Map 33
Weston Pond (Little Baboosic Lake), Amherst: PK, HP, YP
White Pond, Windsor, Stoddard: SB, PK, HP, YP
Whittemore Lake, Bennington, Greenfield: BK, RT
Willard Pond, Antrim: trout (boating restriction: electric motors only)
Zephyr Lake, Greenfield: BN, LB, SB, PK, HP, YP

MERRIMACK COUNTY

Adder Pond (Hopkins Pond), Andover: BK, RT (no motorboats)
Ayers Pond, Washington, Bradford: SB, YP
Bagley Pond, Warner: PK, HP, YP
Bear Pond, Warner: SB, PK, HP, YP
Bear Hill Pond, Allenstown: PK, HP, YP
Berry Pond, Pittsfield: LB, SB, PK, HP, YP
Billings Pond, Sutton: SB, PK, HP, YP
Blackwater Reservoir, Webster: BK, RT, BN, SB, PK, HP, YP
Blaisdell Lake, Sutton: SB, PK, HP, WP, YP
Blake Pond, Pittsfield: PK, HP, YP
Bog Pond, Andover: SB, PK, HP, YP
Bog Pond (Danbury Bog), Danbury: PK, HP, WP, YP
Bradley Lake, Andover: SB, PK, HP, WP, YP
Butterfield Pond, Wilmot: BK (no motorboats)
Carr Pond, Henniker, Hopkinton: PK, HP, YP
Catamount Pond (Bear Brook Pond), Allenstown: BK
Chalk Pond, Newbury: PK, HP, YP
Chase Pond, Wilmot: LB, SB, PK, HP, YP
Chestnut Pond, Epsom: LB, PK, HP, YP
Clark Pond, New London: PK, HP, YP
Clay Pond, Hooksett: PK, HP, YP
Clement Pond (Joe Silver Lake), Hopkinton: SB, PK, HP, YP
Clough Pond, Loudon: BK
Cold Pond, Andover: PK, HP, YP
Crane Neck Pond, Canterbury: PK, HP, YP
Craney Pond, Henniker: PK, HP, YP
Crooked Pond, Loudon: SB, PK, HP, PK
Eagle Pond, Wilmot: PK, HP, YP
Eaton Pond, Pittsfield: PK, HP, YP
Elbow Pond, Andover: PK, HP, YP

Forrest Pond, Canterbury: LB, SB, YP
French Pond, Henniker: BK, RT
Gile Pond, Sutton: PK, HP, YP
Giles Pond, Franklin, Sanbornton: PK, HP, YP
Gorham Pond, Dunbarton: LB, SB, PK, HP, YP
Grant's Pond, Grafton, Danbury: BK, HP
Highland Lake, Andover: see Map 32
Horseshoe Pond (Tannery Pond), Concord: PK, HP, YP
Hot Hole Pond, Loudon, Concord: BK, RT
Kezar Lake, Sutton: SB, PK, HP, YP
Kezar Pond, Henniker: PK, HP, YP
Kimball Pond, Dunbarton: PK, HP, YP
Knowles Pond, Northfield: SB, PK, HP, YP
Lakins Pond (Heads Pond), Hooksett: PK, HP, YP
Lilly Lake (Horn Pond), Barnstead, Pittsfield: LB, PK, HP, YP
Little Pond (Couch Pond), Boscawen: PK, HP, YP
Long Pond, Dunbarton: PK, HP, YP
Long Pond, Henniker: PK, HP, YP
Lyford Pond, Canterbury: PK, HP, WP, YP
Lynxfield Pond, Chichester: PK, HP, YP
March Pond, Hill: BK, RT, HP
Massasecum Lake, Bradford: see Map 43
Messer Pond, New London: PK, HP, YP
Morey Pond, Andover: BK, RT
Mud Pond, Henniker: PK, HP, YP
New Pond (Stump Pond), Canterbury: PK, HP, WP, YP (no motorboats)
Odiorne Pond, Epsom: LB, PK, HP
Otter Pond (Gillingham Pond), Newbury: PK, HP, YP
Otter Pond, Sunapee, New London: SB, PK, HP, YP
Ox Pond, Webster: PK, HP, YP
Penacook Lake (Long Pond), Concord: SB, PK, HP, WP, YP, SM (water supply — closed to fishing)
Pinnacle Pond, Hooksett: BK, SB, PK, HP, YP
Piper Pond, Wilmot: PK, HP, YP
Pleasant Lake, New London: see Map 55
Pleasant Pond (Waukenna Pond), Danbury: BK, RT
Pleasant Pond, Henniker: LB, PK, HP
Pleasant Pond, Warner: PK, HP, YP
Poor Farm Hill Pond (Sutton Reservoir), Sutton, Newbury: PK, HP, YP
Poverty Pond, Hill: PK, HP
Purgatory Pond, Dunbarton: PK, HP, YP
Rocky Pond, Canterbury, Loudon, Gilmanton: PK, HP, YP
Rolfe Pond, Hopkinton: PK, HP, YP
Russell Pond, Sutton: PK, HP, YP
Sanborn Pond, Loudon: SB, PK, HP, YP
Sawyer Pond, Hooksett: PK, HP, YP
School Pond, Danbury: PK, HP, YP
Shaker Ponds, Canterbury: PK, HP, YP
Simmons Pond, Warner: BK
Smiths Pond, Allenstown: PK, HP
Snow Pond, Concord: PK, HP, YP
Solitude Lake, Newbury: BK
Sondogardy Pond (Northfield Pond), Northfield: PK, HP, YP
Stark Pond, Dunbarton: PK, HP
Sunapee Lake, Newbury, New London, Sunapee: see Map 65
Sunapee Lake, Little, New London, Springfield: see Map 66
Tannery Pond, Wilmot: PK, HP, YP
Todds Pond, Newbury, Bradford: PK, HP, YP
Tom Pond (Diamond Lake), Warner: PK, HP, YP
Trumbull Pond, Webster: PK, HP, YP
Tucker Pond, Salisbury: SB, PK, HP, YP
Turee Pond (Three Pond), Bow: PK, HP, YP
Turkey Pond, Concord: LB, PK, HP, YP
Turkey Pond, Little, Concord: PK, HP, YP
Turtle Pond (Turtletown Pond), Concord: SB, PK, HP, YP
Upper Pond, Henniker: PK, HP, YP
Walker Pond, Boscawen: PK, HP, YP
Webster Lake, Franklin: see Map 75
White Pond, Wilmot: BK (no motorboats)
White's Pond, Pittsfield: LB, SB, PK, HP, YP
Whittier Pond (Fry Pond), Hopkinton: PK, HP, YP
Wild Goose Pond, Pittsfield, Strafford: LB, PK, HP, YP
Winnepocket Lake, Webster: see Map 79

ROCKINGHAM COUNTY

Angle Pond, Sandown: LB, SB, PK, HP
Arlington Mills Reservoir, Salem: see Map 2
Beaver Lake, Derry: BK, RT, SB, PK, HP, WP, YP
Beaver Pond, Big (Big Shingle Pond), Deerfield: LB, PK, HP, WP, YP

Bow Pond, Little, Northwood: LB, PK, HP, YP
Canobie Lake, Windham, Salem: see Map 10
Captain Pond, Salem: SB, PK, HP, YP
Clark Pond, Auburn: PK, HP, YP
Cobbetts Pond, Windham: RT, SB, PK, HP
Country Pond (Silver Pond), Kingston, Newton: see Map 17
Cub Pond, Big, Sandown, Danville: PK, HP, YP
Demeritt Pond, Nottingham: PK, HP, YP
Durgin Pond, Northwood: PK, HP, YP
Eel Pond, Rye: HP, WP
Exeter Reservoir (Water Works Pond), Exeter: BK, RT
Ezekiel Pond, Derry: PK, HP, YP
Freeses Pond, Deerfield: PK, HP, YP
Golden Pond (Rock Pond, Simpson Pond), Windham: SB, PK, HP, YP (no motorboats)
Governors Pond, Raymond: SB, PK, HP, YP
Great Pond (Kingston Lake), Kingston: see Map 38
Greenwood Pond, Kingston: LB, PK, HP, WP, YP
Halfmoon Pond, Kingston: PK, HP, YP
Harvey Lake, Northwood: SB, PK, HP, WP, YP
Island Pond, Big, Derry, Atkinson, Hampstead: see Map 34
Janvrin Pond, Hampton Falls: BK, LB, PK, HP, YP
Jenness Pond, Northwood, Pittsfield: see Map 36
Kenison Pond, Nottingham: PK, HP, YP
Long Pond, Danville, Kingston: LB, PK, HP, YP
Long Pond, Northwood: SB, PK, HP, YP
Lucas Pond, Northwood: BK, RT, SM, tiger trout (no motorboats)
Massabesic Lake, Auburn, Manchester: see Map 42
Massabesic Lake, Little, Auburn: PK, HP, YP
Millville Lake, Salem: LB, PK, HP, YP
Mitchell Pond, Windham: PK, HP, YP
Mulligan Pond, Big, Nottingham: PK, HP, YP
North Pond, Chester: PK, HP
North River Pond, Nottingham, Barrington, Northwood: SB, PK, HP, WP, YP
Northwood Lake (Suncook Pond), Northwood, Epsom, Deerfield: see Map 48
Norton Pond, Raymond: PK, HP, YP
Onway Lake (Jones Pond), Raymond: LB, SB, PK, HP, YP
Pawtuckaway Lake, Nottingham: see Map 52
Pea Porridge Pond, Nottingham: PK, HP, YP
Peverly Brooks Ponds (Newington Reservoir), Newington: BK, RT
Phillips Pond, Sandown: LB, SB, PK, HP, WP, YP
Pleasant Lake, Deerfield: SB, PK, HP, WP, YP
Powwow River Pond (Powwow Reservoir), Kingston, East Kingston: LB, PK, HP, YP
Quincy Pond, Nottingham: PK, HP, YP
Rainbow Lake (Upper Shields Pond), Derry: PK, YP
Round Pond, Nottingham: BK, RT, PK, HP, YP
Scobie Pond, Londonderry: SB, PK, HP, YP
Shadow Lake (Hity Tity Pond), Windham, Salem: PK, HP, YP, carp
Shingle Pond, Deerfield: LB, PK, HP, YP
Showell Pond, Sandown: YP
Taylor River Refuge Pond, Hampton: LB, PK, HP
Tower Hill Pond, Candia, Auburn: PK, HP, YP
Tuxbury Pond, South Hampton: LB, SB, PK, HP, WP, YP
Wash Pond (Sunset Lake), Hampstead: SB, PK, HP, WP, YP
World End Pond, Salem: LB, PK, HP, YP

SULLIVAN COUNTY

Anderson Pond, Grantham: PK, HP, YP
Ashuelot Pond, Washington: see Map 3
Bacon Pond, Washington: PK, HP, YP
Baptist Pond, Springfield: PK, HP, YP
Barrett Pond, Washington: HP
Bear Pond, Washington: PK, HP, YP
Chapin Pond, Newport, Claremont: BK, RT
Crescent Lake, Acworth, Unity: LB, SB, PK, HP, YP
Dodge Pond, Lempster: PK, HP, YP
Dutchman Pond (Chalk Pond), Springfield: SB, HP
Eastman Pond, Grantham: PK, HP, YP
Fletcher Pond, Washington: PK, HP, YP
Frog Pond, Washington: PK, HP, YP
Gilman Pond, Unity: PK, HP, YP
Governors Pond, Croydon: SB, HP
Halfmoon Pond, Washington: PK, HP, YP
Hall Pond, Charlestown: HP
Hedgehog Pond, Washington: BK
Hurd Pond, Lempster: PK, HP, YP
Island Pond, Washington: see Map 35
Kolelemook Lake, Springfield: LB, SB, PK, HP, YP
Leavitt Pond, Grantham: PK, HP
Ledge Pond, Sunapee: SB, PK, HP, YP
Long Pond, Croydon: BK, RT, SM
Long Pond, Lempster: SB, SP, SM
Marshall Pond, Unity: PK, HP
May Pond, Washington: LB, PK, HP, YP
Mill Pond, Washington: PK, HP, YP
Millen Lake, Washington: RT, SB, PK, HP
Miller Pond, Grantham: PK, HP, YP
Morgan Pond, Springfield: PK, HP, YP
Moses' Pond, Plainfield: PK, HP, YP
Mountain View Pond (Spectacle Pond), Sunapee: SB, PK, HP, YP
North Pond, Washington: PK, HP, YP
Otter Pond, Sunapee: SB, PK, HP, YP
Perkins Pond, Sunapee: SB, PK, HP, YP
Rand Pond, Goshen: BK, RT
Rockybound Pond, Croydon: LB, PK, HP, YP
Sanborn Pond, Springfield: PK, HP, YP
Sand Pond (Echo Lake), Lempster, Marlow: BK
Smith Pond, Washington: BK
Spectacle Pond, Croydon: SB, PK, HP, YP
Star Lake, Springfield: S, BK, RT, SM
Stocker Pond, Grantham: LB, PK, HP, YP
Sucker Pond (Red Leaf Pond), Croydon: SB, PK, HP, YP
Summers Pond, Croydon: SB, PK, HP, YP
Sunapee Lake, Newbury, New London, Sunapee: see Map 65

STRAFFORD COUNTY

Ayers Pond, Barrington: see Map 4
Barbadoes Pond, Madbury: BK
Bow Lake, Strafford, Northwood: see Map 8
Club Pond (Sportsmen's Pond), New Durham: BK, RT
Coldrain Pond, New Durham: BK
Lily Pond (Coles Pond), Somersworth: SB, PK, HP, YP
Long Pond, Barrington: PK, HP, YP
Long Pond, Little, Barrington, Rochester: PK, HP, YP
March's Pond (Chalk Pond), New Durham: SB, PK, HP, WP, YP
Mendum's Pond (Mendham's Pond), Barrington: LB, SB, PK, HP, WP, YP
Merrymeeting Lake, New Durham: see Map 44
Nippo Pond, Barrington: RT, SB, PK, HP
Rochester Reservoir, Lower, Rochester, Barrington: SB, YP
Round Pond (Rochester Reservoir), Barrington: SB, PK, YP
Shaws Pond, New Durham: SB, PK, HP, WP, YP
Stonehouse Pond, Barrington: BK
Sunrise Lake (Dump Reservoir, Reservoir Pond), Middleton: LB, PK, HP, WP
Swain's Pond (Union Pond), Barrington: see Map 70
Three Ponds (Town House Pond, Milton Pond), Milton: BK, BN, SB, PK, HP, WP, YP
Wheelwright Pond, Lee: SB, PK, HP, WP, YP
Wild Goose Pond, Pittsfield, Strafford: LB, PK
Willey Pond, Big, Strafford: LB, SB, PK, HP, YP
Willey Pond, Little, Strafford: LB, PK, HP, YP

NEW HAMPSHIRE TROUT DIRECTORY

TROUT STREAMS

Ammonoosuc River, Carroll to Littleton: see Map 82
Ammonoosuc River, Upper, Stark, Randolph, Berlin: BK
Androscoggin River, Cambridge, Dummer, Errol: see Map 83
Ashuelot River, Marlow, Gilsum, Surry, Lempster, Washington: see Map 84
Ashuelot River, South Branch, Troy, Marlborough: BN
Baboosic Brook, Merrimack: BK, BN
Back Lake Brook, Pittsburg: BK
Bailey Brook, Unity: BK
Baker River, Warren, Wentworth: BK, RT
Baker River, South Branch, Orange, Dorchester, Wentworth: BK
Bear Brook, Allenstown: BK
Bearcamp River, Sandwich, Tamworth: BK, RT
Beards Brook, Hillsboro, Washington: BK, RT
Beaver Brook, Alton, New Durham: BK
Beaver Brook, Derry, Pelham: BK
Beaver (Quominny) Brook, Mont Vernon, Amherst: BK
Beebe River, Campton, Sandwich: BK
Beech River, Ossipee: BK
Beehole Brook, Loudon, Chichester: BK
Berry Brook, Portsmouth, Rye: see Map 99
Big River, Barnstead, Strafford: BK
Bishop Brook, Stewartstown: Bk
Blackwater River, Webster, Wilmot, Andover: RT, BN
Blood Brook, Lebanon, Plainfield: BK
Blood (Gambel) Brook, Wilton, Temple: BK
Blow-Me-Down Brook, Plainfield: BK
Bow Bog Brook, Bow: BK
Branch River, Milton, Wakefield: BK
Brickyard Brook, Litchfield, Londonderry: BK
Camp Junction Brook, Jefferson, Burbank Grant: BK
Carroll Stream, Carroll: BK
Cascade Brook, Wilmot: BK
Cedar Brook, Stewartstown: BK
Center Brook, Cornish: BK
Chase Brook, Litchfield: BK
Chickwolnepy Brook, Success: BK
Chocorua River, Tamworth: BK, RT
Churchill Brook, Brookfield: BK
Clear Stream, Dixville, Errol, Millsfield: BK
Cocheco River, New Durham, Rochester: BK
Cockermouth River, Groton: BK
Coffin Brook, Alton: BK
Cohas Brook, Auburn, Londonderry: BK
Cold River, Lempster to Walpole: BK, RT, BN
Cold River, Sandwich: BK
Connecticut River, Pittsburg to Stratford: see Map 85
Contoocook River (Upper), Jaffrey, Peterborough: RT, BN
County Farm Brook, Wilton, Temple: BK
Dead Diamond River, Dartmouth College: BK
Dodge Brook, Lempster, Croydon, Newport: BK
Dry River, Cutts Grant, Harts Location: BK
Dudley Brook, Brentwood, Exeter: BK
Eastman Brook, Piermont: BK
Farrar Brook, Belmont, Gilmanton: BK
Ferguson Brook, Hancock: BK
Flints Brook, Hollis: BK
Fordway Brook, Raymond: BK
Fowler River, Alexandria: BK
Gale River, Franconia, Bethlehem: see Map 87
Gig Mill Brook, Brentwood, Kingston: BK
Grant's Brook, Lyme: BK
Great Brook, Kensington, Exeter: BK
Great Brook, Langdon, Walpole: BK
Great Brook, Lebanon: BK
Gunnison Brook, Goshen: BK
Gunstock Brook, Gilford: BK, RT
Halfway Brook, Moultonboro: BK
Halls Brook, Groton: BK
Ham Branch, Easton, Franconia: BK
Hancock Branch, Lincoln: BK
Hartford Brook, Deerfield: BK
Hewes Brook, Hanover: BK
Horse Hill Brook, Rochester: BK
Indian River, Canaan: BK
Indian Stream, Pittsburg: BK
Isinglass River, Barrington: see Map 88
Israel River, Jefferson, Lancaster: BK, RT
Johns River, Carroll, Whitefield: RT
Jones Brook, Middleton: BK
Kelly Brook, Plaistow: BK
Kingston Brook, Springfield, Wilmot: BK
Lamprey River, Deerfield, Northwood, Raymond: see Map 89
Lane River, Sutton: BK, RT
Little Cohas Brook, Londonderry: BK
Little Sugar River, Unity: BK, RT, BN
Little River, North Hampton: BK, RT
Little River, Nottingham: BK
Little River, Plaistow: BK
Lovejoy Brook, Enfield: BK
Lovell River, Moultonboro, Ossipee: BK, RT
Mad River, Farmington: BK
Mad River, Waterville, Campton, Thornton: see Map 90
Mallego Brook, Barrington: BK
Martin Brook, Richmond, Swanzey: BK
Mascoma River, Enfield to Lebanon: see Map 91
Melvin River, Tuftonboro: BK

Mill Brook, Orange, Grafton: BK
Mill Brook, Sandwich, Tamworth: BK
Millsfield Pond Brook, Millsfield: BK
Mink Brook, Hanover: BK
Mohawk River, Dixville, Colebrook: BK, RT
Mollidgewock Brook, Errol, Cambridge: BK
Moon Brook, Antrim: BK
Moose Brook, Hancock: BK
Moose Brook, Randolph, Gorham: BK
Mountain Brook, Newbury: BK
Nash Stream, Odell, Stark: BK
Needle Shop Brook, Hill: BK
Newfound River, Bristol: BK, RT
Nighthawk Hollow Brook, Gilmanton: BK
Nissitissit River, Brookline: BK, RT, BN
No Name Brook, Unity: BK
North Branch River, Antrim, Stoddard: BK, RT
North River, Northwood, Nottingham: BK, RT
Nubanusit River, Harrisville: RT
Oliverian Stream, Haverhill, Benton: BK
Osgood Brook, Milford: BK
Otter Brook, Nelson, Sullivan, Roxbury, Keene: BK
Oyster River, Durham, Lee: BK
Partridge Brook, Chesterfield: BK
Paugus River, Albany, Tamworth: BK
Peabody River, Green's Grant to Gorham: BK, RT
Pemigewasset River, Lincoln, Franconia: see Map 93
Pemigewasset River, East Branch, Lincoln: BK
Pemigewasset River, West Branch, Campton, Thornton: BK
Perry Stream, Pittsburg: BK, RT
Pettyboro Brook, Bath, Lyman: BK
Phillips Brook, Dummer, Odell, Stark: BK
Pike Brook, Brookfield: BK
Pine River, Wakefield: BK
Piscassic River, Fremont, Epping, Newfields: BK, RT
Piscataquog River, Goffstown: BK, RT, BN
Piscataquog River, Middle Branch, New Boston: BK, RT, BN
Piscataquog River, South Branch, Goffstown, New Boston: BK, RT, BN
Piscataquog River, West Branch, Weare: BK, RT, BN
Pond Brook, Sandwich: BK
Punch Brook, Salisbury: BK
Redwater Brook, Claremont, Cornish: BK
Riddle Brook, Bedford: BK
Roaring Brook, Richmond: BK
Rum Brook, Canterbury: BK
Saco River, Bartlett to Conway: see Map 94
Saco River, East Branch, Bartlett, Jackson: BK
Saco River, Rocky Branch, Bartlett, Sargent's Purchase: BK
Salmon Brook, Meredith, Sanbornton: BK, RT
Sand Hill Brook, Springfield: BK
Sawyer River, Harts Location, Livermore: BK
Schoodak Brook, Webster: BK
Shannon Brook, Moultonboro: BK
Shedd Brook, Hillsboro, Windsor, Washington: BK
Simms Stream, Columbia: BK
Skinner Brook, Grantham: BK
Smith Brook, Grafton: BK
Smith River, Grafton to Hill: BK, RT
Soucook River, Loudon: BK, RT, BN
Souhegan River, Merrimack, Greenville, Wilton: see Map 95
South Brook, Greenfield: BK, BN
Spaulding Brook, Brookline, Milford: BK
Stanley Brook, Dublin: BK
Stevens Brook, Warner: BK
Stinson Brook, Rumney: BK
Stirrup Iron Brook, Boscawen: BK
Stony Brook, Wilton, Lyndeboro, Greenfield: BK, RT
Sucker Brook, Andover, Franklin: BK
Sugar River, Sunapee: see Map 96
Sugar River, North Branch, Grantham, Croydon: RT, BN
Sugar River, South Branch, Newport to Lempster: BK, RT, BN
Suncook River, Barnstead, Pittsfield, Chichester: RT
Suncook River, Little, Epsom: BK, RT
Swift Diamond River, Dixville, Dartmouth College Grant: BK
Swift River, Albany, Passaconaway: see Map 97
Swift River, Tamworth: BK, RT
Town Line Brook, Peterboro: BK
Tunnel Brook, Benton: BK
Walker Brook, Danbury, Wilmot: BK
Warner River, Warner: BK, RT
Watts Brook, Litchfield, Londonderry: BK
Weed Brook, Sandwich, Moultonboro: BK
West Branch Brook, Bradford: BK
Whiteface River, Sandwich, Waterville: BK
Wild Ammonoosuc River, Landaff, Bath: BK
Wildcat River, Jackson: BK
Wild River, Bean's Purchase: BK, RT
Willey Brook, Wolfeboro: BK
Wilson Brook, Chester, Sandown: BK
Winkley Brook, Hampton Falls, Seabrook: BK, RT
Winnicut River, N. Hampton, Stratham: BK, RT, BN
Winnipesaukee River, Belmont, Tilton: BK, RT
Wonalancet River, Sandwich, Tamworth

LAKE TROUT LAKES

Bow Lake, Strafford, Northwood: see Map 8
Connecticut Lake, Third, Pittsburg: see Map 14
Dan Hole Pond, Ossipee, Tuftonboro: see Map 20
Diamond Pond, Big, Stewartstown: see Map 22
Francis, Lake, Pittsburg, Clarksville: see Map 24
Granite Lake, Nelson, Stoddard: see Map 27
Merrymeeting Lake, New Durham, Strafford: see Map 44
Newfound Lake, Bristol, Hebron, Alexandria: see Map 47
Nubanusit Lake, Hancock, Nelson: see Map 48
Opechee Lake, Laconia: see Map 51
Ossipee Lake, Ossipee, Freedom: see Map 50
Silver Lake, Madison: see Map 58
Squam Lake, Big, Holderness, Moultonboro, Sandwich, Center Harbor: see Map 61
Squam Lake, Little, Holderness, Ashland: see Map 62
Stinson Lake, Rumney: see Map 63
Sunapee Lake, Sunapee, Newbury, New London: see Map 65
Tarleton, Lake, Piermont, Warren: see Map 71
Winnipesaukee Lake, Laconia, Gilford, Alton, Meredith, Center Harbor, Wolfeboro, Tuftonboro, Moultonboro: see Map 80
Winnisquam Lake, Laconia, Meredith, Sanbornton, Tilton, Belmont: see Map 81

TROUT PONDS

Airport Pond, Whitefield
Akers Pond, Errol: see Map 1
Archery Pond, Allenstown
Back Lake, Pittsburg: see Map 6
Barbadoes Pond, Madbury
Basin Pond, Chatham
Batchelder Pond, Hampton
Bean Pond, Ossipee
Bear Brook Pond, Big, Wentworth Location
Bear Brook Pond, Little, Wentworth Location
Beauregard Pond, Alstead
Beaver Lake, Woodstock
Belknap Area Pond, Gilford
Big Brook Pond, Pittsburg (no motorboats)
Black Mountain Pond, Sandwich
Black Pond, Lincoln
Blue Pond, Madison
Bog Pond, Lincoln
Bog Pond, Little, Odell
Boundary Pond, Pittsburg (no motorboats)
Bragg Pond, Millsfield
Bryant Pond, Dorchester
Butterfield Pond, Wilmot (no motorboats)
Caldwell Pond, Alstead
Campton Pond, Campton
Canes Pond No. 1, Seabrook
Canes Pond No. 2, Seabrook
Carr Pond, Clarksville
Carrigan Pond, Lincoln
Carter Pond, Bean's Purchase
Catamount Pond, Allenstown
Center Pond, Nelson (no motorboats)
Chalk Pond, Effingham
Chapin Pond, Newport
Christine Pond, Stark
Clarksville Pond, Clarksville
Clough Pond, Loudon
Club Pond, New Durham
Coldrain Pond, New Durham
Cold Spring Pond, Allenstown
Cole Pond, Enfield
Connor Pond, Ossipee
Conservation Pond, Wentworth
Constance Pond, Piermont
Coon Brook Bog, Pittsburg (no motorboats)
Corser Pond, Errol
County Farm Pond, Brentwood
Cranberry Bog, Columbia
Derby Pond, Canaan, Orange
Devil's Wash Bowl, Odell
Diamond Pond, Little, Stewartstown: see Map 22
Dublin Pond, Dublin: see Map 23
Dummer Pond, Big, Dummer
Dummer Pond, Little, Dummer
Duncan Pond, Ossipee
Dustin Pond, Wentworth Location
Eagle Pond, Pittsburg
East Inlet Pond, Pittsburg
Echo Pond, Franconia
Exeter Reservoir, Exeter
Falls Pond, Albany
Ferrin Pond, Weare (no motorboats)
Fish Pond, Columbia
Flat Mountain Pond, Waterville
Fourmile Pond, Dix Grant
French Pond, Henniker
Gilmore Pond, Jaffrey
Greeley Pond, Livermore
Greenough Pond, Big, Wentworth Location: see Map 29
Greenough Pond, Little, Wentworth Location: see Map 29
Guinea Pond, Sandwich
Halfmile Pond, Enfield
Hall Pond, Lower, Sandwich

Hall Pond, Middle, Sandwich
Hall Pond, Upper, Sandwich (no motorboats)
Harris Pond, Pittsburg
Hatch Pond, Eaton
Hellgate Pond, Dartmouth College Grant
Hildreth Pond, Warren
Hogback Pond, Greenfield
Hopkins (Adder) Pond, Andover (no motorboats)
Hothole Pond, Loudon
Hoyt Pond, Madbury
Hunkins Pond, Sanbornton (no motorboats)
Hunts Pond, Hancock
Jackquith Pond, Pittsburg
Jericho Pond, Landaff
Joe Coffin Pond, Sugar Hill
Jud Pond, Pittsburg
Kiah Pond, Sandwich
Ledge Pond, Madison (no motorboats)
Lily Pond, Alstead
Lily Pond, Livermore
Lime Pond, Columbia
Little Pond, Sandwich
Lonesome Pond, Lincoln
Long Pond, Benton
Long Pond, Croydon
Long Pond, Eaton
Long Pond, Errol
Long Pond, Lempster
Long Pond, Millsfield
Lucas Pond, Northwood (no motorboats)
Meader Pond, Warren
Middle Pond, Pittsburg (no motorboats)
Millen Pond, Washington
Millsfield Pond, Big, Millsfield
Millsfield Pond, Little, Millsfield
Mirror Pond, Whitefield
Moose Falls Flowage, Pittsburg (no motorboats)
Moose Pond, Pittsburg
Morey Pond, Andover

Mount William Pond, Weare (boating restriction: electric motors only)
Mountain Pond, Chatham
Mountain Pond, Lyman
Mud Pond, Canaan
Mud Pond, Dixville
Mud Pond, Dummer
Mud Pond, Easton
Mud Pond, Greenfield
Munn Pond, Errol
Nathan Pond, Dixville
Newell Pond, Alstead
Oliverian Pond, Benton
Orange Pond, Orange
Peaked Hill Pond, Thornton
Perch Pond, Campton
Perch Pond, Lisbon
Perry Pond, Pittsburg
Peverly Ponds, Newington
Phillips Pond, Odell
Pike Pond, Stark
Pleasant Pond, Danbury
Pleasant Pond, New London: see Map 55
Pond of Safety, Randolph
Profile Pond, Franconia
Province Pond, Chatham
Rand Pond, Goshen
Rocky Pond, Wentworth
Round Pond, Eaton
Round Pond, Errol
Round Pond, Pittsburg
Russell Pond, Woodstock
Saco Pond, Carroll
Saltmarsh Pond, Gilford (no motorboats)
Sand Pond, Marlow, Lempster
Sawyer Pond, Livermore
Sawyer Pond, Little, Livermore
Scott Bog, Pittsburg (no motorboats)
Sessions (Corner) Pond, Dummer
Shaw Pond, Franklin

Shawtown Pond, Freedom
Shehan Pond, Clarksville
Shoal Pond, Lincoln
Signal Pond, Errol
Simmons Pond, Warner
Sky Pond, New Hampton
Smith Pond, Washington
Solitude Pond, Newbury
Spaulding Lake, Thompson, Meserve Purchase
Spectacle Pond, Groton, Hebron
Spectacle Pond, Groton, Hebron
Spofford Lake, Chesterfield: see Map 60
Spoonwood Pond, Nelson: see Map 49
Stacy (Trout) Pond, Freedom
Stone Pond, Marlborough
Stonehouse Pond, Barrington
Stratford Bog, Stratford
Streeter Pond, Lisbon
Stub Hill Pond, Pittsburg
Success Pond, Success: see Map 65
Swains Pond, Wentworth: see Map 70
Swanzey Pond, Swanzey
Sweat Pond, Errol
Terrill or West Branch Pond, Pittsburg
Three Ponds, Ellsworth
Trio Pond, 1st, Odell
Trio Pond, 2nd, Odell
Trio Pond, 3rd, Odell
Trout Pond, Lyme
Unknown Pond, Pittsburg
Weeks Crossing Pond, Warren
Whitcomb Pond, Odell
White Pond, Ossipee
White Pond, Wilmot (no motorboats)
Whittemore Pond, Bennington
Willard Pond, Antrim (no motorboats)
Willey Pond, Bethlehem
Wright Pond, Pittsburg
Zealand Pond, Bethlehem

FISH OF NEW HAMPSHIRE
CONTINUED FROM P. V

caught at the surface early in the season using bait or artificial lures, but later when it seeks deep waters it is effectively taken with bait on wire line employing large metal flashing spoons. It is also popularly taken through the ice with hand line baited with cut fish or tip-ups using live smelt or minnows. Its flesh is tasty though not as much so as other species of trout. Lake trout tend to grow large and the average fish weighs between 3 and 6 pounds, with 10-pounders not uncommon. The New Hampshire record is a 28-pound 8-ounce fish measuring 39½ inches, from Newfound Lake in 1958.

RAINBOW TROUT (RT)
(Salmo gairdneri)
The rainbow trout was introduced into New Hampshire in 1878 and has been planted extensively since that time. It thrives best in cold water and can withstand higher temperatures than the brook trout. It is well adapted to either lake or stream life. It eats mainly insects, except in lakes where the diet of larger fish consists mainly of fish. This fish may be taken in a variety of ways and is easily caught on flies. It jumps repeatedly when hooked and puts up a good fight. It has an excellent flavor when taken from wilderness streams, but only fair when not in prime condition, or recently released from the hatchery. Rainbows are popular with fishermen since they are easily taken and fight well. The average size in New Hampshire streams is between 6 and 12 inches and less than ¾ pound. In some lakes they grow larger and fish between 3 and 5 pounds are not unusual. The New Hampshire record is a 14-pound fish caught in the Connecticut River at Monroe in 1978.

SUNAPEE TROUT (G)
(Salvelinus aureolus)
Also known commonly as golden trout, this species was originally recorded from Sunapee Lake and a few other waters, including Big Dan Hole Pond. It was successfully introduced into several other New Hampshire lakes, but subsequent introduction of lake trout caused the disappearance of the Sunapee trout, either through cross-breeding, direct competition or predation. Its disappearance from Sunapee Lake has also occurred, but the species still exists with brook trout in Conner Pond, Ossipee, the only place left in the state where it is known to exist in any abundance. Tewksbury Pond in Grafton was reclaimed and the species stocked, but it failed to thrive, and it is now uncertain whether it exists there. The state record is an 11-pound 8-ounce fish taken from Sunapee Lake in 1954.

TIGER TROUT
(Salvelinus fontinalis × Salmo trutta)
Also called zebra trout, this fish is the result of crossing brook trout with brown trout. While such a cross occurs naturally, it is uncommon and this fish, along with the splake, has been the subject of experimental stocking in the past. It is now found only in Lucas Pond, Northwood.

WALLEYE
(Stizostedion vitreum vitreum)
Also known as walleyed pike, this species was introduced into New Hampshire and is now numerous in the lower Connecticut River, Merrimack and Contoocook rivers. A single specimen was taken in Spofford Lake, Chesterfield in 1970, but it is not known if the species is established there. The walleye prefers clear water with a firm bottom and does not do well in weedy areas. It is nocturnal, feeding on rocky shoals and bars, and spends the daytime hours in deeper water. It may be found at considerable depth during the warm summer months. The main diet of this fish is other fishes, but it also eats insects and crustaceans. The walleye will not break water like bass, nor does it have speed like trout, but it will put up a good fight and is readily taken on almost any artificial lure. It may also be caught by still-fishing with live minnows or by trolling or casting. It is not an easy fish to catch and the most productive times for fishing are evening and early morning. The flesh of the walleye is firm and bone-free; some claim it is the best eating of all freshwater fishes. Usual size of the walleye is from 1 to 5 pounds, although fish weighing up to 10 pounds are not unusual. The New Hampshire record is an 11-pound 8-ounce fish taken from the Connecticut River at Lebanon in 1979.

WHITE PERCH (WP)
(Morone americana)
The white perch originally ranged in salt, brackish and fresh waters and is more closely related to the striped bass *(Morone saxitilis)* than any freshwater species. It has been successfully introduced and has become established in many New Hampshire waters. White perch travel in schools and are found in abundance in brackish bays, mouths of rivers and muddy ponds which are accessible from the sea. In lakes and ponds, it prefers shallow, mud-bottom areas. The fish feeds mainly on small fish and insects. In salt water its diet consists of crabs, shrimp, small squid and fish fry. Feeding takes place primarily in early evening. It is an easy fish to catch and will take nearly any kind of bait. Worms, minnows, flies and spoons are all effective and best results are obtained when fishing is at dusk when schools of feeding fish move into the shallows near shore. The white perch is an excellent fighting fish for its size and is a real treat on light tackle. It is very tasty eating although slightly bony. Seldom exceeding two pounds in weight, the average white perch is 6 to 10 inches and less than ½ pound. The New Hampshire record is a 3-pound, 6-ounce, 19-inch fish caught in Goose Pond, Canaan in 1975.

WHITEFISH (WF)
(Coregonus clupeaformis, Coregonus cylindraceum)
Two species of whitefish occur in New Hampshire — the lake whitefish and the round whitefish. The lake whitefish inhabits deep, clear, cold lakes, while the round whitefish is primarily a river fish, but also does well in deep, cold, clear lakes. They feed on plankton, insect larvae, mollusks and small crustaceans. Most feeding takes place near the bottom, and most feeding probably takes place at night or in the evening. It is a superb table fish and was once one of the most sought game fish in the state. Whitefish may be taken occasionally on the surface with flies soon after ice-out, but the usual method, either through the ice or in open water from a boat, is baiting a location several days prior to fishing with pieces of cut-up fish (chum) and then bobbing a small sinker and hook with small cut-up fish near the bottom. Whitefish provide an important food source for lake trout. The usual lake whitefish runs from 1 to 2 pounds although 5 to 6 pounds is not unusual. The state record is 5 pounds 1 ounce, taken in Winnipesaukee at Alton in 1974. Round whitefish are smaller, running about 12 to 15 inches in length and weighing about ¾ pound. It is capable, however, of attaining 20 inches and 4 or more pounds. Both species are found in Lake Winnipesaukee, while lake whitefish are also found in Squam Lake and Wentworth Lake, and round whitefish in the upper Connecticut River and Newfound Lake.

YELLOW PERCH (YP)
(Perca flavescens)
This fish is common throughout New Hampshire and is found to be an undesirable species for anglers since the fish tends to be small in larger waters and wormy when taken in weedy ponds. It is also heavy competition for trout and salmon. Yellow perch is usually found in weedy lakes and ponds or in the slower moving parts of larger streams. It is not usually found where there is strong current. In larger bodies of water, the bigger fish tend to move out of the weed areas into deeper water, where they congregate around ledges and bars. Perch feed on a variety of insects, crustaceans and small fish. They are easily taken by almost any method and respond well to flies, lures and trolled spoons. Fishing through the ice is very effective using live minnows on handlines or tip-ups when the fish can be caught in numbers. The flesh is firm and delicious and is a favorite for eating. A 12-inch fish weighing a pound or more is considered large. The New Hampshire record is a 2-pound 6-ounce fish measuring 15½ inches taken in Heads Pond, Hooksett in 1969.